The

MODERN BOOK
of the
DEAD

The
MODERN BOOK
of the
DEAD

A Revolutionary Perspective on
Death, the Soul, and What Really Happens
in the Life to Come

PTOLEMY TOMPKINS

ATRIA BOOKS
New York   London   Toronto   Sydney   New Delhi

ATRIA BOOKS

A Division of Simon & Schuster, Inc.
1230 Avenue of the Americas
New York, NY 10020

First Atria Books hardcover edition February 2012

ATRIA BOOKS and colophon are trademarks of Simon & Schuster, Inc.

For information about special discounts for bulk purchases, please contact Simon & Schuster Special Sales at 1-866-506-1949 or business@simonandschuster.com.

The Simon & Schuster Speakers Bureau can bring authors to your live event. For more information or to book an event, contact the Simon & Schuster Speakers Bureau at 1-866-248-3049 or visit our website at www.simonspeakers.com.

Designed by Rhea Braunstein

Manufactured in the United States of America

10   9   8   7   6   5   4   3   2   1

Library of Congress Cataloging-in-Publication Data

Tompkins, Ptolemy.
    Modern book of the dead : a revolutionary new perspective on death, the soul, and what really happens in the life to come / by Ptolemy Tompkins.—1st Atria Books hardcover edition.
        pages cm
1. Future life. I. Title.
    BL535.T64 2012
    202'.3—dc23   2011047954

ISBN 978-1-4516-1652-1
ISBN 978-1-4516-1654-5 (ebook)

For Colleen

Contents

Preface: The Design in the Sand   xiii

1: A Long, Personal, but Necessary Introduction
    Explaining How I Came to Write This Book   1

2: Ancient Egypt, the Origins of the Afterlife, and the
    Birth of the Idea That Each of Us Is a God in Training   52

3: The Egyptian and Tibetan Books of the Dead,
    the Mortal and Immortal Parts of the Soul, and
    the Key Difference Between the Eastern and the
    Western Views of the Afterlife   63

4: The Need for a Single Map, the Imaginary and the
    Imaginal, What the Brain Does (and Doesn't) Do,
    and the Nonlocal Nature of Consciousness   94

5: Different Kinds of Reincarnation, Different Kinds
    of Evolution, Why Flying Saucers Help Us
    Understand the Afterlife, and Why the Romantics
    Are Still Important   114

6: The Transcendentalists, Reincarnation Reenvisioned,
and What the Universe Was Really Created For   133

7: The Age of Science and the Age of Spiritualism,
the Unsung Discoverer of the Human Unconscious,
the French Schoolteacher Who Spoke to the Dead,
and the Botanist Who Mapped the Afterlife   149

8: Death on the Slopes, the Initial Stages of the Afterlife
Journey, the "Silver Cord," "Ghost Clothing," and
What It's Like to Emerge from Physical Space   195

9: The Removal of the Coat of Images, More on Life as a
Movie, and the Real Significance of the Life Review   220

10: A World Much Like This One, the Waning of the Etheric,
the Rise of the Astral, the "Second Death,"
and Connectivity, Spiritual-Style   226

11: Private and Public Postmortem Worlds, the Zone of the
Earthbound Spirits, the Dangers of the Lower Astral,
and the Continuing Power of Thought   232

12: Seven Planes, the Judgment, to Be Reborn or Not
to Be Reborn, Life as a Movie Worth Watching,
and the Concept of the Group Soul   242

13: The Pulse of Life, Keeping Heaven in Your View,
What Lies Beyond the World of Form, and
What Waits Beyond the End of Time   259

Acknowledgments   273

That is at bottom the only courage that is demanded of us: to have courage for the most strange, the most singular and the most inexplicable that we may encounter. That mankind has in this sense been cowardly has done life endless harm; the experiences that are called "visions," the whole so-called "spirit-world," death, all those things that are so closely akin to us, have by daily parrying been so crowded out of life that the senses with which we could have grasped them are atrophied. To say nothing of God.

—RAINER MARIA RILKE

Preface:

The Design in the Sand

I n the South Pacific island nation of Vanuatu, the second-largest island is called Malakula. Thanks to the encroachments of the modern world, the traditional beliefs of the island's native peoples are gradually dying out. But up until the early years of the twentieth century, the Malakulans practiced a richly imaginative tribal religion.

One of the more interesting rules of this religion concerned a series of designs that were memorized so that they could be drawn on command. These designs tended to be repetitive and made up of squarish shapes that looped together like the braids in an intricately woven fishnet. Simple at first glance, these patterns actually demanded skill and memory to reproduce correctly.

Like many primitive—or as they are more often called these days, "primal"—peoples, the Malakulans envisioned death as a journey. Not a vague, metaphorical journey, but a real and rock-solid one, as full of specific details as any taken by a person in the land of the living. For the Malakulans (and again, for countless other primal peoples besides), death was in some respects a trip like any other—only to a place where no one but dead people (and the occasional shaman, traveling there in spirit form) could go.

The Malakulan voyage usually started out with the newly dead soul walking along a beach. Making its way on foot, the soul would, at a certain point, find the path blocked by a terrifying cannibalistic ghost-goddess with the unlikely name of Le-hev-hev.

As the soul approached, Le-hev-hev would draw an intricate design in the sand—the same looping, fishnet-style design that the newly dead individual had (hopefully) learned how to draw correctly while alive.

Just as the newcomer soul arrived before her, the goddess would rub half of the design out. It was then the soul's job to redraw the missing half of the design from memory. If the drawing was good, then Le-hev-hev would stand aside and grant access to the lands beyond, where the souls of the newly dead person's deceased friends and family were waiting.

If not, however, it was a different story.

The afterlife myths of many ancient and primal peoples feature beings like Le-hev-hev: gatekeepers who only let the newly dead soul pass if he or she knows the right password, or has brought the proper gift along. Cerberus, the three-headed dog of Greek mythology, is the one most likely to come to people's minds today, but he's actually an atypical example of this figure because the Greeks, for much of their history, had a quite negative view of the world beyond. Cerberus's chief job, therefore, was to keep dead souls *in* rather than to prevent them from entering. But for most peoples for most of history—and, most likely, for most of humankind's time on earth before recorded history as well—the world beyond was a place one wanted to get *into* more than it was a place one wanted to get out of: a positive destination and a place of new beginnings rather than a dead end or a prison.

It was also, as in the case of the Malakulans, a place one needed to prepare for.

Among the believers in the ancient Greek mystical religion called Orphism, souls departing for the world beyond were given highly specific instructions for what to do once there:

> *You will find to the left of the House of Hades a spring,*
> *And by the side thereof standing a white cypress.*
> *Do not approach this spring.*
> *But you will find another, from the Lake of Memory*
> *Cold water flowing forth, and there are guardians before it.*
> *Say, "I am a child of Earth and starry Heaven;*
> *But my race is of Heaven alone. This you know yourselves.*
> *But I am parched with thirst and I perish. Give me quickly*
> *The cold water flowing forth from the Lake of Memory."*
> *And of themselves they will give you to drink of the holy spring—*
> *And thereafter among the other heroes you shall have lordship.*

Death, for the culture that produced these lines, was clearly not an ending but a journey that one needed to prepare for carefully. Not in the way we prepare for death these days, by making up a will and seeing that our worldly affairs are in order, but in the way that we prepare when we are about to go to some strange new physical place on the face of the earth.

Learning about the afterlife while one was still alive helped the peoples of these cultures feel confident and upbeat about the transition awaiting them. But it also did something else: it helped them live a better life while still here, in *this* life.

How did it do this? By suggesting (to use a familiar but apt image) that life and death are two sides of the same coin. How we think about and deal with life, in this view, will affect how we think about and deal with death, and vice versa. (That's one reason so many afterlife teachings suggest that where we end up in the world beyond has to do with the quality of our behavior while in this one. Our situation there, in that other world, *has* to be a reflection of our behavior while here, for the simple reason that life and death, while different from each other, *aren't really disconnected.* So whoever you are now, while in this life, can't help but have a strong influence on who and where you will be in the next.)

"Our ideas about death," wrote the twentieth-century Swedish diplomat and writer Dag Hammarskjöld, "define how we live our lives." If we think in purely negative terms about death, life becomes a grim, claustrophobic, and essentially pointless affair: a story that starts out sad and just gets sadder as time goes on. If we hate and fear death, which is inevitably what we will do if we know nothing about it except what we see on the surface (the pain and loss it engenders, the havoc it wreaks), we will quite simply be unable to live a life that is happy anywhere but on the surface as well. But if, on the other hand, we succeed in thinking the *right* way about death (and this book suggests that there really is a way of doing just that), life loses that gloom and becomes something entirely different: something larger, stranger, and infinitely more promising and positive than we might ever have imagined. It becomes—to say it straight out—something that we can actually accept rather than struggle at every turn to deny.

The central idea of this book is that we in the modern world have forgotten how to perform this essential activity of "thinking the right things" about death, and that as a result we have found ourselves, collectively, in the position of a Malakulan native who has shown up before Le-hev-hev both empty-headed and empty-handed. When our time comes and the goddess draws half of the map of the underworld in the sand and then wipes half of it away again, we will not be able to redraw it for her for the simple reason that *we have no genuine idea of how it is supposed to look.*

After all, why should we have any really concrete ideas of what the world that awaits us after death looks like when we don't actually believe in it?

That last question isn't quite fair, of course. After all, countless polls and surveys show that most people in the modern world—and very definitely most Americans—*do* believe in an afterlife of some kind or other.

It's that "some kind or other" part that is problematic. For in truth, in comparison to the peoples of times and places past, our beliefs about the world beyond are hopelessly vague. So much so that you might say that the main afterlife adversary that we in the modern world face—the goddess blocking our own particular path to the life beyond—is our very inability to conceive of death as a concrete journey: one every bit as real and specific as a trip to the airport on a Thursday afternoon.

Why are we so timid about conceiving of the afterlife in any but vague and insubstantial (and therefore, when you get down to it, useless) ways? The short answer, of course, is science. We live in a world full of different faiths, all of which seem to look at the spiritual world differently. Which one is correct? In the old days, most people didn't have to ask this question because, being born into a prescientific culture, they were apt to accept their culture's beliefs about the spiritual world without too much argument. We do the same thing today, but the belief system most of us adhere to (including many who, on the surface at least, consider themselves open to "spiritual" ideas) is that of scientific materialism. Science, most of us learned as kids, has shown that the otherworldly landscapes that the peoples who came before us believed in are all, quite simply, imaginary. Nothing exists "beyond" the physical world because the physical is all there is. Science is the one true story that tells us what life and the world are really like, and it has no room in it for gods and goddesses, for heavens and hells and limbos and any of the rest of those sorts of things that people in the old days—in their prescientific ignorance and befuddlement— used to take seriously.

But is this really true?

A very strong argument can be made that it isn't. The fact of the matter is that rather than rendering all beliefs about worlds beyond this one invalid, science has, in the last century or so, slowly but surely been *giving us back* our license to believe in those worlds, and even more important, to think of ourselves as more—*much* more—than the physical bodies we inhabit while alive.

The beginnings of these developments lie back in the mid-to-late nineteenth century, when a small but significant number of scientific minds began to wonder if the general declaration that science had rendered the spiritual world obsolete was really correct. For a few brief decades, those individuals tried to find out if science and spirit might actually not be mutually exclusive terms after all. During these years, a surprisingly significant amount of evidence was accumulated that suggested that human personality might really and truly survive the death of the body.

But for a number of reasons (none of them good ones), the intellectual tides quickly turned. Funding and enthusiasm for these studies dried up, and by the beginning of the twentieth century any scientist who dared suggest that human consciousness could survive the death of the brain was either ignored or subjected to outright ridicule.

For the scientific establishment in its early years, the twentieth century was felt to be the one in which materialistic science would triumph once and for all over all the old, outmoded ideas about soul and spirit that had kept the peoples of previous times so shackled in ignorance. Mind, consciousness . . . For the dominant scientific thinkers of the early twentieth century, these mysterious entities were close to being pushed completely out of the picture. The question *What is consciousness?* was, for these scientists, not really even worth asking, for consciousness was simply an "epiphenomenon," a mere by-product of physical activity (in particular, the electromagnetic activity within the neurons of the brain). It was something that might *seem* real to the naïve and scientifically untrained, but in truth it had no "solid" existence whatsoever.

The century was barely under way, however, before new discoveries in the world of subatomic physics began to place these confident ideas into question. Solid matter itself, it began to appear, was something of an illusion, for at the core of the atom was found not solidity, but patterns of relationship between states of energy.

Matter itself, it turned out, was completely nonmaterial.

Not only was matter found to be much less solid than people first expected, but consciousness, in turn, was found to be much more substantial—much more *real*. Though it took virtually the entire century to happen, eventually enough evidence accumulated to suggest that far from being a mere secondary function of the brain and body, consciousness is actually much more substantive and long-lasting than either of those other entities. Rather than a simple "nothing" that isn't worth including anywhere at all on our maps of reality, consciousness has now—for some scientists at least—established itself as the central fact of the universe: the nonmaterial ground upon which all else is built. Consciousness isn't, in this line of thinking, some secondary quality that our bodies possess for an all-too-brief time before it vanishes once more into the pure nothingness from whence it came, but *the actual thing we are,* both before, during, and after the time that we possess our physical bodies.

But is this consciousness that so completely defines what we are a single, unchanging entity, exactly the same in all of us? Or is consciousness, along with being immortal, also *specific*? To rephrase this enormously important and entirely serious question, is it not just some generic blanket consciousness that is potentially immortal, but *individual personal consciousness,* like the specific consciousness that defines who you are and defines who I am?

If individual personal consciousness (the nonphysical, postmortem you and the nonphysical, postmortem me) survives the death of the physical body, how does it do so? Does it, as so many spiritual traditions over the centuries have suggested, possess a series of superphysical bodies that it continues to inhabit—each for a shorter or longer time—after it leaves the body? If it does, what is the nature of the world or worlds through which these spiritual vehicles of our identity move? Is there (as spiritual traditions beyond counting have suggested) more than one level to the postmortem universe? And if there are, can we really and truly entertain the idea that we just might visit these levels, one after another, when our physical bodies finally give out?

These are questions that, after a long and unfruitful interim when science declared them meaningless at best and idiotic at worst, some scientifically minded people are beginning to ask again. The default materialism that is built so deeply into anyone born, as I was, in the mid-twentieth century now stands a chance of being at least partially reprogrammed. There is, if you look for it, more than enough accumulated wisdom from times and peoples past, and more than enough genuinely compelling evidence from scientific investigation today to make that possible.

But navigating one's way through the different arguments for and against belief in a world beyond the physical is, now perhaps more than ever before, a very confusing business. The topic is so complex, the voices arguing for one opinion and against others are so numerous, so varied, and (sometimes) so unpleasantly strident, that coming away from this material with a single, clear picture in one's head (the kind that the peoples of the past often had such an easier time arriving at) is close to impossible.

That's why, even though we might like to be otherwise, and

even though the facts increasingly suggest we *should* be otherwise, so many of us in the modern world remain materialists at heart. The materialist view of the world is the one that most of us continue to live within because it was put into our heads long before we knew enough to resist it, and even if we may now and then be pulled away from it for a minute or an hour or even a day or a week, sooner or later we find ourselves drifting right back into our old way of looking at the world. We do this because materialism is the reality we were trained, in countless tiny ways every single day of our lives, to inhabit: the view that the world we live in is built on, the details of which were whispered into our ears virtually since our first day on the planet. As such, it can be argued with, complained about, or simply denied, but genuinely eradicating (or even lastingly modifying) this deep program is challenging in the extreme.

As materialists, we believe that we are bodies, not souls, and that our consciousness (that is, the rootless, undefined entity that knows itself and feels, to most of us, like it resides in our heads just behind our eyes) will come to a full stop when our bodies die. Things will go dark, and we will drift away into nothingness.

I speak with authority on this subject because—despite having been interested in spiritual topics since my teenage years and having grown up in a household where spiritual subjects were discussed constantly—I am deeply infected with this default materialist belief structure myself. I know first and foremost from my own experience that to believe, in our current modern world, that we are at heart something other than purely physical beings doomed to die when our bodies give out, is an extraordinarily challenging task.

But it is not an impossible one. We can achieve it not by adopting the colorful but outmoded beliefs of the cultures that came before us, however, but by gaining a deep and daily understanding of the fact that the materialist perspective, besides being depressing and debilitating, is also increasingly showing itself to be simply wrong. The best way to begin to do this is by developing a new map of reality—of life and of death—that is drawn so simply and so boldly that, like a design sketched quickly but decisively in the sand, it can actually stay in our minds even after the tide—or the arm of the goddess—has swept it away.

The spiritual teacher Jiddu Krishnamurti used to say that though life is complex, we need nonetheless to approach it simply. If this is true of life, it is even truer of death. Not because what might await us at death is in any way simple (in fact, if we listen to the most sober, intelligent, and convincing voices on the matter it is complex beyond imagining), but because we need nonetheless to think about it that way if we are to keep our thinking clear and strong and unvague enough to break through the thick walls of unbelief that our culture has, like it or not, built up around us.

That's why, despite the fact that to those with a materialistic bent its subject matter is itself the very definition of nonsense, this aspires to being a very no-nonsense book. It tries, by using both traditional wisdom and the latest insights and discoveries of physicists, psychologists, near-death researchers, and others, to outline a picture of the elements of the afterlife that is clear enough to stay in the mind's eye even after the book has been put down. It tries, in short, to create a kind of "design in the sand" for our own day.

The idea that life continues after the death of the physical body is one that the great majority of peoples who came before us on this planet took very seriously. It was a subject they were not afraid to talk and think about with all the energy, imagination, and intellect they possessed.

That, I believe, is what it should be for us today as well. Not because we owe the peoples of the past anything in terms of what we do or don't believe, but simply because now as then, life and death remain the twin poles of our existence. To fail (out of a mistaken but deep-seated belief that science has proved it to be nonexistent) to learn how to think properly about the life that awaits us in the world beyond this one is to hamper our ability to think about and negotiate the life each one of us is living right here and now. It is, if you really get down to it, to doom ourselves to living only half the life we really could be living.

While I hope this book manages to say at least a few genuinely new things on the subject, its chief aim is to bring to light an extraordinarily empowering new geography of the afterlife that has been laboriously staked out by a number of people, but which remains far too little known. I have tried to give an outline of this geography, to tell the story of where it came from, and to give an account of why we should take it seriously in a sufficiently fast, bold, and *personal* manner (for reasons that will become obvious, I have not been shy about bringing my personal story into the proceedings) that hopefully some of its power will come across to the reader as it has to me. It has been my experience that when this old/new picture of the afterlife is sketched fast and clean and with minimal fuss, the mind's resistance to these truths falls away and something else appears:

recognition. Reading this book will, I hope, make at least some readers feel that strange shock of the familiar that I have sometimes experienced when, reading certain passage from the best, smartest, and most convincing literature on the afterlife, I suddenly realize that, fascinating and profoundly cheering as this material is, it isn't really new to me at all. Some part of me—a part deeper, even, than the layers of assumed materialism created by years of living in a materialistic society—*recognizes* what I am being told, because on a deep level I knew it already.

Plato famously suggested that the truest kind of learning is actually recollection—that is, that the really important stuff that there is to learn isn't new at all, because at a deep level we know it already. If death really and truly is the other half of life, it might just be that that half isn't nearly as alien to us as we so often think it is, but only awaits the right hints and reminders to appear to us once more in its full and proper light.

Few things in our hugely materialistic culture are more challenging to think about seriously than what happens to us at death. But few are more necessary, too. For no matter what kind of a brave face we might try to put on it, a life lived without a coherent, focused, and serious picture of the afterlife is, quite simply, a life without context: a life that will, in the end, always be missing half of itself.

That lost half—that missing piece of the design in the sand—is what this book is about.

The
MODERN BOOK
of the
DEAD

1

A Long, Personal, but Necessary Introduction Explaining How I Came to Write This Book

Few kids like going to bed. But when I was a kid, I *really* didn't like it. That each day should have to come to an end with the closing of the door of my room and the (usually) all too long wait for unconsciousness to arrive seemed not only unfair; it seemed downright absurd. The darkness and separation that night brought with it filled me with a pure childish anxiety that I can still conjure up today.

It was while lying in bed as a young child and waiting for sleep to come that I remember doing my earliest significant thinking about death. One night, at about age five, I awoke in a cold sweat from a dream in which the people I knew had appeared as one-dimensional paper cutouts. My father, my mother, my teachers—everyone was reduced, in the dream, to these simple paper shapes, each wearing a single, static expression, some smiling, some frowning, but all equally shallow, all equally empty of true human presence.

In its simple, straightforward way, this dream summed up all the deepest anxieties I had about life as a kid. The notion that the human world was really just a surface event with nothing real beneath it, that the people I knew and the world I lived in had, in fact, no true or lasting substance . . . Wasn't that what the concept of death—impossibly remote and hard to understand, yet at the same time hugely, intimately close and ever-present—really suggested?

The more I thought about death as a kid, the more strange it seemed to me that most people in the world around me had so little to say about it—or at least, so little of any real usefulness. In 1970, when I was eight, my mother read E. B. White's children's book *Charlotte's Web* aloud to me. At the end of the book, when Charlotte the spider died, I struggled to get my head around the idea that Wilbur the pig could have gotten any happiness or consolation from the fact that Charlotte had left a nest of baby spiders behind to keep him company. Babies or no babies, Charlotte was still gone. Wasn't that what really counted?

That same year, I began suffering a new series of nightmares turning around the theme of being kidnapped. In most of these scenarios, a group of malevolent but otherwise unidentifiable men crept up on me while I was sleeping, stuffed me into a sack, and dragged me away to a cabin in the middle of a dark forest.

In an effort to find out what lay at the root of these fantasies, my father enlisted the help of a Scientologist friend of his named Rebecca. For several months in the spring of that year, I made regular visits to a small office in downtown Washington, DC, where Rebecca hooked me up to an E-meter—a lie-detector-like device that Scientologists use to measure electrical fluctuations at the surface of the skin. Over the course of half a dozen of these visits, Rebecca attempted, through a series of questions and a close study of the E-meter's reactions to my answers, to lead me back to my previous lifetimes on earth. For, my father maintained, it was during one of those lifetimes that the event or events that were secretly causing my kidnapping anxieties had actually occurred.

A writer who specialized in occult and esoteric subjects (1971's *Secrets of the Great Pyramid* and 1973's *The Secret Life of Plants* are, today, his chief enduring claims to fame), my father wasn't a card-carrying Scientologist. But he *was* a great believer in the idea—common to Scientology, Theosophy, Anthroposophy, and many of the other new or semi-new spiritual movements that seized so many people's attention in the sixties and seventies—that the human soul preexisted the body, and will outlive it as well. My father revered the great early architects of new age thought. People like Helena Blavatsky (the controversial Russian mystic and founder of Theosophy), Rudolf Steiner (the Austrian philosopher and educator and founder of Anthroposophy), Edgar Cayce (the American clairvoyant famous for predictions he made while in a state of trance), and Scientology's founder, L. Ron Hubbard, came up on a daily basis in our household. Different though the teachings of these thinkers were in certain of their specifics, my father believed that they had all made important contributions to a new way of looking at human beings and their place in the universe: a way that was, he felt, going to have a growing influence on the hopelessly confining antispiritual view of the world that more and more people in the West had been abiding by ever since the scientific revolution had occurred three hundred years earlier.

Like many early enthusiasts of what was just then starting to be called new age thought, my father was strongly suspicious of conventional science, believing that most scientists spent most of their time covering up the real truth about the world rather than revealing it. He distrusted the proponents of traditional religious faith—most especially Christianity—even more, and never missed an opportunity to warn me against believing what the more conventional voices of wisdom in the world I lived in (teachers, school friends' parents, people on TV) had to say about the way things really worked. To my father's way of thinking, conventional science and conventional faith were both roadblocks to experiencing who and what each of us really is: a free spirit living in a cosmos that is not purely material, but material *and* spiritual: a cosmos that humankind was on the verge of seeing and experiencing in a new and infinitely larger way.

At the center of this new picture of the universe was a vision of the human being as an essentially spiritual entity: a being that had taken on a physical body as part of a process of growth, or evolution, that had begun far in the past and would continue far into the future. That humans were more than their present physical bodies wasn't simply interesting news to my father, it was revolutionary news. For when one took this view, human life was transformed in a moment from the painful, puzzling, and generally pointless exercise it so often seemed to be into a *story that is going somewhere.* When you held to the kind of worldview that my father and his new age friends did, at no single moment, no matter how futile and pointless life might seem, was it ever really so. Even on the bleakest days and in the lowest of circumstances, one need never feel totally lost or totally without hope. Instead, even at those points when life seemed to make least sense, one was simply like a football player so disoriented in the confusion of a scrimmage that he has momentarily lost sight of the end zone.

"We're not bodies," my father liked to say, summing up this entire new view of life and the human place within it: "we *have* bodies."

My father (correctly, I would later discover) pointed out that the basic notion of reincarnation—that is, that we are souls, not bodies, and that as such we have each inhabited more than one of the latter over the course of time—had been the norm rather than the exception for most of human history. It was still an accepted reality for the cultures of the Far East, and even the more mystical elements of Judaism and Islam continued to make room for it as well. When you got down to it, it was really only Christianity—that most ideologically thorny of all the world religions—that had said a definite "no" to the possibility that we are born more than once upon the earth.

And yet it was possible—indeed, said my father, even probable—that in their earliest days even Christians had embraced this doctrine as well. Jesus himself, said my father, knew that we move from body to body, taking birth time and again. But for various reasons, the early Church fathers had proclaimed the doctrine of rebirth a heresy, thus removing from Christianity one of the most genuinely useful tools to help us earthbound humans make sense of how and why we had ended up getting (momentarily) trapped in the web of material existence to begin with. Instead of spiritual evolution, instead of a cosmos where people dropped into and came out of earthly incarnation like a line of butterfly-stroking swimmers gracefully plunging into and surging out of the water as they moved down the length of an Olympic-size swimming pool, Christians believed that each of us had come to birth once and only once, created out of nothing at conception and consigned, after a single, short, and (usually) all too painful and confusing life, either to a choking, smoke-filled hell, or to an almost equally undesirable heaven full of clouds, halos, and not much else; a heaven where bad people weren't allowed and where good people went for all eternity—to do what, exactly, it was hard to say.

I had actually been named for one of those early, reincarnation-espousing Christians. Though people tend to assume that my namesake is the ancient Greco-Roman astronomer famous for proclaiming earth the center of the universe, my father always gave a mildly derisive laugh when people suggested this. In fact, I got my name from Ptolemy the Gnostic, an obscure metaphysical philosopher whom my father happened to have been lying in bed reading about when my mother went into labor next to him in early May 1962. "Here comes Ptolemy!" my father had said cheerfully and decisively, shutting the book and reaching for his car keys.

Not that my father thought my mother was necessarily giving birth to that one and the same Ptolemy he was reading about in his book. But my father would have been the first to point out that she certainly *might* have been. For like many advocates of the theory of reincarnation, he believed that we choose our parents each time we leave the light-shot realms of spirit behind and sink back to earth for another go-round. So whoever this new player entering the game board of his personal life was—whichever particular soul had tired of the freedoms of the spirit world and opted for another temporary dive back down into the bracing murk of physical existence— he knew it was someone who, for better or worse, had made the conscious choice to do so as his son.

One might think that having a father with such a positive spiritual philosophy would have prevented me from suffering the kind of anxieties about death and darkness that plagued me so consistently through my childhood. But rather than curing me of my fears about death, my father's philosophy actually put them into sharper focus. For the fact was that though my father talked a good game in the spiritual department, the actual details of his life often fell far short of the ideals he painted so glowingly in his conversation. He and my mother fought a good deal, and the fights did not lessen in number when, in that same year of 1970, my father brought his new mistress, a woman named Betty, to live in our house along with my mother and father and me. The social and sexual experimentation that the late sixties and early seventies are remembered for today took an especially heavy toll on our household, and while peace and love and harmony were the ostensible goals of that experimentation, in our house they tended to produce very different results.

Why bother going into all this personal stuff in a book that's supposed to be on the afterlife, not my personal life? The short and simple answer is that I believe the details of my upbringing are strangely well suited as a vehicle for introducing certain key questions about the afterlife and how we go about understanding it today. One of the main reasons I'm interested in the afterlife—and it has been my central interest for all of my adult life—is that the world I grew up in *taught* me to be interested in it.

When I say "the world," what I am really saying, I suppose, is: my father. Whether he meant to or not, my father doomed me, in a way, to be taken up with the subject of where we were before we were born and what becomes of us afterward, and the details of my life with him provide a kind of synopsis of how our culture got to where it is in terms of its relationship to the world that might or might not lie in wait beyond the body.

My father loved movies, and taking me to them was his primary means of educating me. Whatever film we ended up seeing—usually at one of the Washington, DC, theaters across the river from our (at that time still quite rural) Northern Virginia house—he almost always had something significant to say about it on the drive home: something that put whatever action we had seen on the screen within a larger—usually cosmically large—context.

Many of the movies we went to see together were fairly adult in nature. In 1972, when I was ten, my father took me to a British film called *Tales from the Crypt*. Based on the '50s EC comic book of the same name, it was, like the comic, broken up into several segments, each one featuring a story based on a tale originally published in the magazine.

The film begins with the protagonists of the different episodes all gathering together, apparently by happenstance, in an underground crypt. A groundskeeper singles out each character and tells their story—seemingly as if it hasn't happened yet.

At the end of the film, it is revealed that the characters are in fact all already dead, and that the crypt they have found themselves in is the first section of the underworld, where each has been sent as payment for the bad—the *very* bad—actions they committed while alive.

In the first story segment, Joan Collins plays a woman at home with her husband and daughter, a girl of about eight, on Christmas Eve. While the daughter lies in bed upstairs awaiting Santa, Joan sneaks up on her husband from behind and bashes him in the head with a poker from the fireplace. She then cleans up the mess and stows the body in the basement. As she is finishing up with this, the Christmas carols on the radio are interrupted by an announcement that a homicidal maniac has escaped from a nearby asylum. Everyone in the area, the radio says, should be on the alert for a six-foot-three man with dark eyes, weighing 210 pounds.

Joan locks the door and gets back to what she was doing. Moments later, a very sinister outside shot shows a giant Santa walking through the snow up to the door, a little Christmas bell in hand. He bangs on the door and then peers through the window—eyes bugging, Santa hat askew. Joan hides on the floor just under the window. Does he see her? It's uncertain, but somehow we sense that Santa knows Joan is in there: that he has, in fact, come precisely for her.

Will Santa get Joan before she can clean up the evidence of the murder and call the police? More perplexingly, do we even care if he does? For perhaps, given how awful a person she clearly is, we might actually *want* Joan to get a comeuppance of some kind. Perhaps even one as bad as perishing at the hands of the psychotic Santa.

These questions play in the viewer's head as Joan continues to get rid of the last of the evidence. Just as we think Joan might have things completely under control, her daughter—who by this time we had assumed was asleep—calls out from the living room.

"Mummy, Mummy! It's Santa! I let him in."

A gust of wind—evidence that the elements are now free to enter the house—parts the curtains in front of the door. Then a man's hand pokes through, ringing a little Christmas bell. With a cruel, lustful, slightly animalistic grunt, Santa rushes into the house, pushes Joan to the ground, and strangles her.

The rest of the film follows the fates of the other members of the group in the crypt, detailing the gruesome end each had come to as the result of some bad action committed. But that initial Santa segment was the one that lingered in both my father's and my mind on the drive home.

"Did you notice," he asked me, "that the shot of the Santa Claus character killing that woman was photographed from inside the fireplace?"

Now that he mentioned it, I recalled that the final image of Joan, with Santa strangling her, had indeed been shot from behind the fireplace's burning logs, so that the two figures appeared to be playing out their life-and-death drama within a bed of flames.

"That was a very artful shot," my father said. "And it shows how that film was largely about karma—about why the things that happen to us happen at all, and why they happen to us in the specific way they do."

"It was?" I asked.

"Absolutely," said my father. "All of those people, supposedly,

ended up in that crypt—had gone down to hell, essentially—
for the bad things they'd done, right?"

"Right."

"Well, maybe they did. But a hell you go to for eternity just
for something you did wrong in this one, single life is really an
outmoded Christian idea. In fact, from a more sophisticated
perspective, it's actually *this* world, right here, that's the real hell.
I mean, look around you! People killing and eating other creatures to stay alive, people fighting and torturing each other
constantly, suffering from jealousy and anger and all the other
feelings that make them do all the terrible things they do . . .
It's unspeakable. But of course, that's only half the story."

"What's the other half?"

"The one that appears when we realize there's a way out of
the horror—that we're not stuck in it forever. That film didn't
explain why the man in the Santa suit murdered that woman,
but she may very well have murdered *him* in a previous life. Or
they could have been husband and wife, or parent and child.
That's the way the game goes—on and on, life after life, with
one person doing something to another person, only to have
the roles switched the next time around. But it's all really just
a play, a movie . . . In the final analysis, it isn't real. When a
scene in a movie is over, the director shouts 'cut!' As soon as
he does, the actors stop what they're doing, dust themselves
off, and that's the end of it—at least until he shouts 'action'
and the cameras start to roll again. The mark of a good actor
is his ability to actually *believe* he's the character he's playing.
When he takes on a role, he feels the emotions—the loves and
fears and rages and joys—that his character feels. But at the
same time, there's always a part of him that stays apart from it

all—that doesn't forget that it's really just a role he's playing. A good actor has a bit of all of the characters he's ever played in him. He's all of them, but at the same time he's none of them. Some of his roles were more memorable, some less. But they all mattered while he was playing them. That's what makes him a good actor in the first place. He can completely immerse himself in a character for a while, then, when the movie's over, he can go back to being the person he was beforehand. But that's also the key to living life successfully. All of us are really just actors. When you understand that none of the things that happen to you down here can touch the being you truly are behind the momentary identity you've assumed in your current body, life loses all its terror. And once you become free of the fear that comes along with believing you're just your body and nothing more, you can start to really learn the lessons that you incarnated to learn to begin with—you can start to see what the movie script of your life is really all about."

"How come more people don't know that then?"

"We all *do* know it," said my father. "It's just that we forget it when we come down here. The Greek mystery traditions say that each time we come back to earth we take a drink from a river called Lethe. That water gives you amnesia—it makes you forget where you came from. Then, when we die and leave this world again, we take a drink from another river called Mnemosyne. The waters of that river are the waters of memory—of *anamnesis,* a Greek word that means the opposite of amnesia. The first swallow we take brings us back around, snaps us out of it, and we suddenly remember who we are. *Good God,* we say to ourselves each time, *how could I have forgotten?* But even though that larger sense of who we are is given back to us each time we leave an incarnation behind, we forget it all over again next time around, just like we did the last time, and the time before that. Sometimes, when you're watching a really good film, you can forget where you are for a moment, forget that you're even sitting in a theater, because you're so tied up in what's happening on-screen. You *become* whatever's happening up there. That's what each of our individual incarnations is like. We plunge so deep into whatever life we've ended up in that we forget all about where we originally came from. Plato once said that ordinary people—people who don't understand this—are like a bunch of cave dwellers, watching shadows on the wall. There's a whole world of blazing sunlight right outside the cave, but instead of going out there, they fix their attention on those dim, flickering shadows, mistaking them for reality. Well . . . that's precisely the position most people today are in. They have no idea of where they came from, where they're going, or how many times they've been through this business already."

"So is there really a river called Lethe in the afterlife?"

"I doubt it. Those are just images—a poetic way of talking. The people in those days weren't stupid in the least—despite what I'm sure your history and science teachers have to say on the matter. They knew that there was much more to the world than the material level we see around us. They were also aware that there was more to each of *us* as well—that at heart we're not at all the limited, powerless little beings we feel like most of the time. You can see that old knowledge everywhere in our language. Do you know where the word *person* comes from? The Latin *persona*—'mask.' That's another hint that the ancients knew full well that we're all just playing roles down here, and whether the roles are good or bad or horrible or wonderful, eventually the movie will end and we'll remember who and what we truly are. But if you're smart, you'll come around to all of this *before* you die. Discover—or rather, remember—who and what you really are right now, while you're still down here in this life, and nothing—absolutely *nothing*—can ever get the better of you."

Needless to say, this conversation didn't unfold exactly as I've typed it out. I'm doing my best to re-create it from memories that are now more than thirty years old. But in its essence it is accurate, and the points it describes my father making are points he made numberless times to me over the years. This view of the universe as a kind of grand schoolhouse is, of course, the basic vision of new age thought, and its appeal was immediately apparent to me.

But over time, so were its shortcomings as well.

The results of my E-meter sessions with Rebecca the Scientologist were inconclusive. Though I enjoyed the ritual of coming to the downtown office where the readings were made, allowing her to attach, doctor-like, the two small clamps to my fingers, and letting my mind rove around in answer to her questions ("Do you see yourself wearing any special kind of clothes?" "Do you see yourself living by the ocean or water of any kind?"), at no point during these visits did I ever feel like the answers I was giving were coming from anyplace other than my present, child's imagination, with all its familiar quirks and limitations. My kidnapping fantasies and nightmares continued, and when they finally faded away a year or so later, they were supplanted by other terrors and anxieties, and then by others after that.

But some elements of my situation did change. As the years went on and I moved from childhood to adolescence and then on to my teenage years, I began to get a suspicion as to why my father's cheerful, no-need-to-fear philosophy had so failed to allay my anxieties about life:

My father didn't really believe it.

Or at least, he didn't believe it completely. Sure, it was something he *wanted* to believe in, and it was certainly something he was good at talking about. But anyone who lived in such close proximity to my father day after day could see that he didn't really see earthly life as a play or a movie—as something that couldn't touch the deeper being that he truly was—at all. Try telling him that each year in early April, for example, as tax time approached; or, for that matter, try telling him any number of times in the course of just about any day at all, in one of those many moments when things weren't going exactly his way.

It wasn't just that my father forgot about this larger philosophy of his when he lost his temper, however. It was also that at other moments he had a habit of using it in questionable ways. In 1980, the year I graduated from high school, my father had a brief affair with a woman whom he had ostensibly met up with to discuss a new book project. When my stepmother took him to task for this (my mother, by this point, having long since retreated—literally—from the central action of my father's life by moving to a small house out behind our main one in Virginia), he responded with his usual indignation that he had no choice but to get sexually involved with this woman.

"She believes," my father told my stepmother, "that we knew each other in Elizabethan England. She suspects you were involved with us as well, and that the only way you're going to get past the emotional blocks you built up in that life is by overcoming your jealous impulses in this one."

One day that same year of 1980, my father lost his balance at the top of a steep staircase at the rear of our house and fell down its full length. He fractured his spine and was laid up for several weeks. When he could finally walk again, it was only very slowly and with the aid of a brace.

All that stationary time put him in danger of getting a blood clot. One day that summer I was in my room reading when my father called out from the other end of the house. I dropped my book and ran to see what was up. He was standing in the doorway of his study in his bathrobe, his face pale.

"Get me to the hospital," he said. "My leg hurts terribly. I think I've got a clot." I helped him to the car and we took off.

It soon became apparent that it was not going to be one of those drives where my father felt like talking. His hand clutching the afflicted leg, his face set in a half-angry, half-frightened scowl, he stared ahead of him and kept his counsel, breaking the silence only now and then to tell me to drive faster.

"It's amazing, isn't it?" I said after a while, when we were about halfway to the hospital.

"What is?"

"That here we are in this car, driving along, and you're right here, completely alive, completely present, and in the next second you could be . . . gone. Off somewhere else—or maybe nowhere at all. Who knows? It's all just kind of incredible when you think about it."

It was, of course, a highly inappropriate remark. But looking back, I can see exactly why I made it. Though I don't think

I fully realized it at the time, I was taking advantage of this unusual situation to give my father a test of sorts. Did he really believe that there was more to the world than most of the people I knew thought there was? Did he really see material life, as he sometimes liked to describe it, as a shoal between two seas? A shoal that each of us finds our way to and stands up on for a moment, our legs wobbly and our balance off, and then leaves behind again when we plunge back into the waters of the life beyond this one?

"No," he said after a moment. Just that one, single word. Then he went back to staring straight ahead, out the windshield and down the road toward the hospital.

When we finally got there, a doctor examined my father and told him that he was going to be fine. There was no clot—just a cramped muscle—and no danger to his heart. The incident passed and was forgotten about—at least by him.

It was during those same years of my late teens, as my father's philosophy came to seem ever more hollow and suspect to me, that I got another source of outside help in figuring out what life might or might not be all about. My stepmother Betty's son, Nicky, seven years older than me, became interested in Buddhism, and before too long I was reading books on the subject that he recommended to me. Nicky soon got very serious about his Buddhism—sufficiently so that, in 1986, he took the full vows of monkhood. Virtually from the beginning, Nicky had singled out Tibetan Buddhism as the variety he was especially interested in, and it didn't take me long to realize that its literature had a rigor and solidity to it that put the vague ramblings of the average new ager to shame. If there were any genuine answers to the question of what life and death were really all about, it seemed to me that Nicky might have been correct in seeking them there.

I hadn't read around too long in Buddhist literature, however, before I found myself troubled with some of the answers it gave. Tibetan Buddhism in particular may have been a lot more serious than the *one-big-happy-adventure* spiritual philosophy espoused by my father and his new age friends, but as far as I could see, it was also substantially bleaker. At its heart, Buddhism preached a doctrine of the unreality of life, the unreality of human personality, and the unreality of human relationship that chilled me to the bone. Personality, it said, was an illusion. The people we become in life, and the people we grow to know and love, are also illusory. The world Buddhism told me I currently lived in wasn't so different from that world of paper cutouts that had so terrified me in my dream as a child. If it was Nicky, and not my father, who was really right about what life was all about, this wasn't, it seemed to me, such entirely good news.

When I got a little older and started to write, I soon discovered that the conflicting viewpoints represented by Nicky's and my father's worldviews, and the tension between them, tended to force their way into whatever I wrote about. Is there a world beyond the limited and often quite terrible one that we encounter in this life? If there is, is it a world of personality and individuality and warmth, or of emptiness and impersonality and abstraction? In my thirties, I ended up writing two books that, though ostensibly memoirs, were really both explorations of this subject: the first focused on my childhood with my father and new age thought generally, and the second on the influence that Nicky and Eastern religions had had on me during my teenage years. Both books laid out all the questions I had about each of these perspectives, but neither book tried, except in the most tentative way, to answer them.

In the summer of 1999, when I was thirty-seven and living in New York City, I applied for a position at a magazine I'd never heard of before, called *Guideposts.* Started in 1949 by *The Power of Positive Thinking* author Norman Vincent Peale, *Guideposts* was, it turned out, one of the most popular magazines in the country. It got that way by using a simple, tried-and-true recipe: it told stories by ordinary people—and the occasional celebrity—who used Christian faith and positive thinking to overcome life's various challenges.

Christian faith and positive thinking were both exceptionally alien concepts to me at the time. Save for my sister Robin's wedding, I'd never been to a church service in my life, and I knew more about New Guinea headhunters than I did mainstream American Christians. But the offices, and the people in them, looked normal enough when I visited, and I was cheered by the fact that though it was billed as editorial, the position would mostly entail writing. How bad could that be?

My first morning there, my supervisor, Rick, handed me a story told in the words of a California shrimp fisherman named Gene Pritchard. Gene's boat had gone down off the coast of Santa Barbara when its cables got snagged on the ocean floor, and he and his first mate, named Mark, spent a frigid night in a leaky rubber raft before finally coming ashore on San Miguel Island, some four miles from where their boat had sunk.

With night falling, icy waves slopping over the edge of the raft, and Mark rapidly slipping into hypothermia, Gene found himself in what, I would soon discover, was the classic situation of the *Guideposts* protagonist: crying out to a God who, up to that moment, he thought he had stopped believing in.

Gene's prayers were interrupted by an unlikely sound: the puffing of a California gray whale. Rolling about just yards from their craft, the whale kept the two men company all night and into the early morning hours, at certain points even nudging their raft toward land. When Gene finally staggered out of the breakers on the northwest shore of San Miguel Island, he was a different man from the one who'd gone into the water the day before: a man who knew that even in those moments when he least seemed to be, God was watching out for him every step of the way.

"What am I supposed to do with this?" I asked Rick after reading the story.

"Tighten it up," he said. "Really put us out there on the water with the narrator, and bring out the faith element so that we know that it was God who got him through."

Fair enough. But could one really surmise that God (the God, that is, of traditional Christian faith) *had* gotten Gene and Mark out of their mess? Had he really and truly sent the whale along to a) help nudge Gene and Mark's boat toward shore and b) show that they weren't alone out there on the waves? The answer to this question, for *Guideposts'* millions of readers, was apparently so clearly yes that I didn't even need to waste paper arguing the point. All I had to do was lay the story out in such a way that it was sufficiently rich in detail and drama to provide them with an entertaining reading experience. The story in itself didn't tell them anything they didn't already fully know.

New editors at the magazine were often unofficially assigned the "action-adventure" beat, as action-adventure stories were the ones with the clearest plotlines. Whether the protagonist was a snowmobile rider trapped at the bottom of an icy crevasse, a carjacked soccer mom, or a pilot at the helm of a malfunctioning helicopter, the underlying message of the stories I worked on was always the same: have faith, keep your chin up, and never forget that however little he may seem to be, God is looking out for you.

Strangely, I liked the work. Though the unchanging structure of the *Guideposts* stories could get a little wearing, the basic task of fishing around in the messy stew of life for chunks of apparent meaning—of finding the hidden narrative arc in the seemingly pointless flux of human experience—was one that came fairly naturally to me.

Nonetheless, the whole premise of the magazine continued to puzzle me. How was it, I wondered, that its readers were so happy to read what was essentially the *same* story, for issue after issue and year after year?

"All *Guideposts* stories," an editor who'd been there much longer than I had told me one day, "are about making sense of life. That's why they're all told in the first person. The *Guideposts* reader is a person who wants to feel like his or her life is going somewhere, that there's a point to it. *There's a reason you're alive.* That's really all each of the stories in the magazine says. And that's why people never get tired of reading them."

After a year or so at the magazine, I was assigned my first action-adventure story with a near-death component to it. In this kind of story, which I started to bump into more and more often, God was sufficiently delayed in showing up to save the day that the story's protagonist actually died for a time before being brought back to life by the inevitable emergency medics.

I'd read a fair bit about near-death experiences by that point. Modern NDEs, I knew, had first become widely known in the mid-seventies, after the psychologist Raymond Moody had brought the subject to national attention by telling the story of how, while still a student at the University of Virginia, he had met a man named George Ritchie. Ritchie had told him a story about something that happened to him while he was a soldier, after being admitted to an army hospital with pneumonia. While at the hospital, Ritchie underwent a nine-minute near-death experience containing most of what would later become known as the "classic" NDE features: travel down a long tunnel, a visit to a heavenly (and in Ritchie's case, also a hellish) region, sensations of overwhelming peace and well-being, a meeting with a being of light (whom Ritchie identified as Jesus), and an unshakable conviction, once it was over, that what had happened was not a dream but, if anything, *more real* than ordinary life.

His curiosity awakened by Ritchie's account, Moody began interviewing nurses, doctors, and other actual survivors of close calls with death. He came across story after story, most of which followed a fairly set pattern. Further standard NDE features emerged. They included seeing one's dead body "from outside," usually surrounded by mourning friends and family who, mysteriously, don't see the "dead" person and ignore him or her when he or she tries to speak to them; a review of one's experiences in the life just (apparently) ended; a reunion with deceased family members; a glimpse of landscapes of overwhelming beauty; and, last but not least, the discovery that one's time is not up and that one has to return to earth and—most disagreeably—to the body that one had, for a few moments, been triumphantly free of.

People by the hundreds and perhaps the thousands had, it appeared, been having these experiences for years, but they'd by and large kept them to themselves because they were simply too far outside ordinary experience, too strange and unbelievable, for those people to feel comfortable sharing. They were also, it appeared, happening in ever-increasing numbers these days, as doctors became ever more skilled at pulling people back from the edge of death through sophisticated resuscitation techniques.

I'd known about and been interested in this material in a general way for years, but with the exception of a professional scuba diver I'd met in my twenties while working in the Bahamas on a psychic treasure-hunting vessel run by a friend of my father's, I'd never known someone who'd actually had one of these experiences. Now, at *Guideposts,* I found myself talking to one after another.

"The pieces just fell together," one man told me of the night he'd run into his burning house to rescue his children and passed out from the smoke. "It was like I was looking down from up above, and everything just suddenly slid into place. I saw that my entire life, every last part of it, had meaning—even the stuff that before had seemed most pointless or unpleasant."

Another man, whose car had gone off a bridge in the San Francisco Bay area, told me that when he hit the water he lost consciousness for several minutes. His life, too, had passed before him.

"I saw everything that ever happened to me," he said, "like I was watching this superlong movie that somehow just took a second to unfold. After I saw it, I just totally knew that whatever happened to me next would be okay. Even dying and not coming back would have been okay. In fact, now that I'd gotten a glimpse of what really happens to you, not having to come back to earth would have been the *most* okay thing of all."

"Dying," another narrator told me, "is the best thing that could ever happen. You get bigger, and you get smarter . . . You're yourself—*really* yourself—for the first time. It's like you suddenly remember: Oh yeah, this is me—this is who I really am. When you come back down to ordinary life again, it's more than a disappointment. It's heartbreaking. You don't really want to be back here again. It's so much better up where you are when you're out of your body. And yet at the same time, you also realize that, as crazy as it seems, you belong down here. When you get up there you see that there's a reason we're all born into this life. But because you can only really see that larger picture when you're out of your body, you have to work really hard to keep it in your head when you get back down here. *This isn't all there is.* It's so hard to remember that once you're back, but in reality it's the one thing you have to hang on to, whatever else happens."

Most of the *Guideposts* stories I worked on were about 1,200 words, or five double-space typewritten pages, long. The trick of writing them was to squeeze all the pertinent information from what were often very long phone interviews into those few pages, in such a way that the reader got a vivid, scene-laden story that sounded comfortingly similar to the countless other such stories he or she had read in the past, but at the same time new and different as well. The process from start to finish took four or five days. You started out with a rough idea of what you wanted to do to make the story work, but for most of the time you were working on it, it was largely just a mess. Day two and day three were the worst. On those days, you typically didn't know what you were doing with the story, why you were bothering to write it, or where it was going to go.

But . . . if you kept at it, there would inevitably come a point when things started to fall together, when the extraneous details fell away almost by themselves and the story took on an obviousness that—now that you saw it—had been right there from day one.

All of that usually happened, however, only on day five.

That day five feeling seemed to me to be what NDE subjects felt about their own lives when they were out of their bodies. Seen from outside, one's life took on a narrative coherence that was woefully absent when one was actually inside and living it. And remembering that "from outside" perspective became a crucial key to most of these people's remaining happy and content with life once their other-world experience was over and they were back down here in their physical bodies.

It was all so different from the master picture of what life was about and how to be happy in it that my father had presented to me so many times when I was a kid. Yet at the same time it was all *not* very different. Sometimes, as I listened to my (largely Christian) *Guideposts* interviewees, they would drop a sentence that would bring me back to my new age childhood. Stuff like "Each one of us is special," or "Everything that happens has significance," or "The universe has a purpose for all of us . . ." And, perhaps most familiar of all: "We're here to learn." These kinds of statements had often irritated me when I was younger, because it was usually so apparent that the people saying them didn't really believe what they were saying at all. But somehow, when a person who'd been clinically dead for five full minutes reeled off one of these clichés to me, I found myself less resistant to the truth that might just possibly lie behind it.

Of course, I was still perfectly aware that the fact a person believes in something doesn't mean that it's necessarily true. But it began to occur to me that NDE survivors, as a group, seemed often to have a particular outside perspective that really and truly allowed them to navigate their lives in a more successful fashion than many people did these days. I began to suspect that in these people I had stumbled upon a group for whom my father's adage that we're all much more than we normally think we are was not simply a pleasant fancy but a living, breathing truth—and that this discovery had genuinely changed the way they lived their lives.

After a year or so at *Guideposts* I started traveling around the country more, meeting my interviewees in person rather than just talking to them on the phone. It was especially important to do this if you were interviewing someone famous, my boss told me, because celebrities met so many people in the course of their days that if you just talked to them on the phone they'd inevitably forget about you by the time the story was done and you needed to get them to sign off on it.

Studying up for an interview with George Foreman at his church in Houston, I discovered that he, of all people, had had a near-death experience himself—or (if one was being technical) at the very least an OBE or "out-of-body" experience, which in terms of psychological results could sometimes amount to almost the same thing.

It had happened back in the seventies, down in San Juan, Puerto Rico, after a fight in the wake of Foreman's disastrous loss to Muhammad Ali in the "Rumble in the Jungle" in Zaire. Foreman had lost consciousness while getting a rubdown in the stifling hot dressing room following the San Juan fight, and he suddenly found himself, literally, in another world. It was a landscape he could only describe with extreme negatives. Horror, emptiness, pure and total meaninglessness . . . Foreman hadn't been afraid of too much in his life up to that point, but the experience so terrified him that he found himself crying out to God to save him. The instant he did, he was lifted out of that hellish realm and into another one of equally overwhelming beauty and goodness.

The story was full of great details. Coming to on the rubdown table, Foreman leapt off and began hugging Don King and the rest of the boxing bigwigs in the dressing room and telling them that he loved them. Sure that the champ was suffering some kind of momentary dementia due to exhaustion or dehydration, they pushed him underneath a cold shower. But the freezing water only increased Foreman's excitement. "Jesus," he cried out to the men beyond the curtain, "is coming alive in me!"

As it happened, Foreman never "recovered" from his experience, and it became the catalyst for his 180-degree change from the mean-spirited bully people had loved to hate to the perennially cheerful Christian minister and product pitchman that people know him as today.

Foreman was the most flamboyant example I'd met of a person who'd had the entire course of his life changed by an event that seemed to have happened genuinely *outside* of that life. If life, his story suggested, was to be an event that made sense, it could only do so when it was seen (at least for a moment) from a perspective beyond the one we have when we're actually living it.

Another interviewee of mine in those early years at *Guideposts* was a painter and art teacher named Howard Storm. Storm's book, *My Descent into Death,* told the story of an experience he'd undergone in Paris after suffering a near-fatal attack of peritonitis while on a holiday with his wife. Like countless NDE subjects before him, Storm had made the surprising discovery that the physical body we normally inhabit is not the only body we have. After lying in agony in his hospital bed for hours, Storm found himself getting up, turning around, and marveling at the sight of his wasted physical body lying there, without him in it. Suddenly not only pain-free but profoundly refreshed and energized, he wandered out of his room and down the hall of the hospital, ever more perplexed at how alert and alive he felt. "All my senses," Storm wrote, using the kind of outlandish yet strangely believable details that fill his book, "were extremely acute. Everything felt tingly and alive. The floor was cool and my bare feet felt moist and clammy. This had to be real. I squeezed my fists and was amazed at how much I was feeling in my hands just by making a fist."

Storm then heard voices calling to him from farther down the hallway. He asked who they were, and the voices responded that they were there to take care of him. But the more questions Storm asked, the more evasive the answers became, and though he perceived dim figures, Storm couldn't make out much more than that. The voices continued to insist that he keep making his way down the hall.

As Storm proceeded, the voices took on a mocking tone.

Storm looked back and—with the weird dreamlike omniscience typical of near-death experiences—saw his body still lying on the hospital bed, even though he was far away from it now. Drifting back and forth from first to third person, at one moment seeing things from inside and at the next from a position outside himself, Storm began to make out the shapes of the people walking with him down the hallway more sharply.

As he did so, their voices got meaner.

"The more questioning and suspicious I was," wrote Storm, "the more antagonistic and rude and authoritarian they became. They began to make jokes about my bare rear end . . . and about how pathetic I was."

The number of people grew, and they began to push and shove at Storm. "They were playing with me just as a cat plays with a mouse. Every new assault brought howls of cacophony. Then at some point, they began to tear off pieces of my flesh. To my horror I realized I was being taken apart and eaten alive, slowly, so that their entertainment would last as long as possible."

Unpleasant as it was, this section of Storm's narrative had a strangely tonic ring for me. In a genre where the words *love* and *light* are used so relentlessly that they soon get drained of all effect, Storm's words underlined the idea that in genuine near-death narratives, what is being talked about is a *genuine place*, where genuine beings move and act, and genuine events occur: both positive ones *and* negative ones.

I also liked the way Storm's descriptions so clearly painted the chaotic nature of the hellish region he'd found himself in. If heaven is a place where things make sense, then hell, his narrative suggested, is a place where things *don't* make sense, and that lack of order is as painful and horrific to experience as all the other things that go on there.

Terrified and demoralized and completely out of ideas of how to help himself, Storm, like Foreman, finally got the notion to cry out to God. Also like Foreman, he was instantly pulled up from the hellish region and into a heavenly one. And, once again like Foreman, upon recovering from his ordeal he completely changed his ways, even going so far as to become, just as Foreman had, a Christian minister. Storm's change of personality was so extreme that his wife initially thought he had simply lost his mind. The first thing Storm did upon the couple's return to America was to find a church. Upon entering, Storm burst into tears and had to be dragged out until he'd pulled himself together.

Another key interview in my growing series of personal encounters with modern believers in the world beyond the body was Janis Amatuzio, a forensic pathologist whose (for her profession highly uncharacteristic) belief in the soul's survival of death had led to her nickname, "the Compassionate Coroner." On the morning I arrived in her basement offices in a suburb of Minneapolis, she'd already performed three autopsies before changing out of her scrubs and into a cheerful magenta suit for our interview. Conducting an autopsy, Janis told me, was like going through someone's wallet.

"There isn't," she said, "a more personal possession in the world than your body. But in the end, that's still all it is."

Hearing those words once again took me straight back to those drives home from the movies with my father as a kid: talks in which it was first suggested to me that the body I currently inhabited was but the momentary habitation of a larger, more multifaceted, more mysterious entity: the real and true "me" that overflowed the boundaries of the single life I was currently living, stretching far into the past and equally far into the future. The secret stranger whom I both knew and didn't know: my larger—my *true* self. What people like Janis Amatuzio, George Foreman, and Howard Storm were giving me, in different language and from highly different perspectives, was yet another version of that same essential narrative.

On my office door at *Guideposts* since the day I'd arrived (and on a number of other places in the offices as well) there was a small, slightly age-yellowed, magnetic sticker with a quotation from a back issue of the magazine written on it: "We should consider ourselves as spirits having a human experience, rather than humans having an occasional spiritual experience." No one seemed to know who, exactly, was responsible for the quote, but one person told me it had originally come from Pierre Teilhard de Chardin, the Jesuit priest and philosopher famous for his controversial attempts to meld the teachings of Catholic Christianity with the theory of evolution. Beneath its friendly, generic-sounding surface, this passage was a fairly controversial adage to have found its way into the *Guideposts* offices. After all, if a spirit was having a human experience, didn't that suggest that this spirit preexisted its current human/earthly state? The doctrine of reincarnation was anathema at *Guideposts.* Just saying the word in the pages of the magazine would have brought forth a sackful of outraged letters within a few days. What, given the strongly anti-reincarnation stance of the magazine's mainstream Christian readership, was a sentiment like this doing stuck to doors and filing cabinets throughout the office?

Sociologists and historians of religion sometimes use the term "transcendent narrative" to describe the story a culture tells itself about what life, and death, are at bottom all about. A genuine transcendent narrative needs to be one thing above all else: it has to be understood as *true* by the people who tell it. If it isn't true, it might still remain an interesting story, but it won't be useful: not *really* useful, the way the stories that actually help people to successfully navigate their lives need to be. Transcendent narratives are not just stories among other stories; they are *the* story, the one that, once heard and absorbed and believed down to one's bones, allows one to genuinely navigate the seas of life rather than simply drown in them.

My culture's current doubts about its own transcendent narrative (or more accurately, its *lack* of one) were well-known. The standard argument went like this. Christianity was a transcendent narrative that had served Western civilization handily until about three hundred years ago, when, with the rise of modern science, it had died a swift and ugly death. The transcendent narrative of the moment was supplied by science, which, while it had made quick work of the old beliefs about the universe being a meaningful place and human beings having an equally meaningful part to play in it, hadn't yet replaced them with any new ones. The problem with the scientific view as it stood so far was that it really wasn't very much of a narrative at all. Life was random, had started by accident, and would eventually disappear again. Not much of a story.

Of course, not everybody had thrown the old religious narratives out in favor of the new scientific one. The *Guideposts* readers whom I had met (and who so many of my jaded, depressed, postreligious New York friends couldn't resist making fun of) still in large part believed that God had created the world, that Adam had fallen from grace in Eden, that Christ had redeemed that fall, and that all people (or at least the redeemed among them) would one day be with Christ again, in a thoroughly renewed cosmos from which every last taint of sin and corruption had fallen away. But the fact remained that materialism—the idea that physical atoms bouncing around in three-dimensional space is the only reality there is, and that human consciousness is an ephemeral, insubstantial by-product of electrochemical activity in the brain that will cease completely when the brain dies—is the default setting for most of Western culture today. The suspicion that we are really nothing more than mortal material bodies eats away, beneath the surface, at the beliefs of even the most adamantly and self-consciously "spiritual" people, plenty of believing Christians included.

In fact, and despite all his protestations to the contrary, it was what I suspect my father believed deep down as well, and its presence at the very core of his psyche was what had made him respond the way he did to my comment in the car that day back in my late teens when we were rushing to the hospital.

It's the story that we, as citizens of the modern world, are all but doomed to believe in whether we want to or not.

It seemed clear to me that to truly defeat this materialistic perspective, to put an end to the inertia and despair that it produces among so many people today, we need to do more than read the occasional spiritual book or have the occasional spiritual thought. We need to find a new master narrative that we can genuinely grasp and absorb and completely believe in, in the way that the people I met at *Guideposts* who had undergone those transformative near-death experiences had.

But where, in our day and age, are we to find this single story? How are we to come up with a new transcendent narrative capable of embracing the faiths of both East and West, of tradition and of modern science? What is the clear, simple, single story—the "day five" story, as I started to think of it—that could tell us who we are and what we're doing here on earth in such a way that it does not fatally contradict one or another or yet another of the countless philosophical and spiritual perspectives in our deeply pluralistic modern world?

Maybe, I began to suspect, the key to finding this story lay in realizing that a working transcendent narrative did not, in fact, need to provide *all* the answers to what life is about (a fairly tall order, after all), but only a few key ones. What those answers were exactly I didn't know, but I was beginning to have a strong suspicion that they had something to do with what the near-death survivors I'd met at *Guideposts* had told me of what they'd seen in those short but life-changing moments when they'd left their physical bodies behind. And, curiously enough, they also had something to do with the way those stories so cleanly overlapped with certain things my father had told me on all those evening drives we'd taken home from the movies so long ago.

I hadn't, by this time, been speaking to my father for several years. Not too long after I'd settled into my job at *Guideposts,* he had gotten into a dispute with an old friend of his who was living for a time in a trailer on a section of his rambling West Virginia property. Throughout my childhood my father had moved from one large, ill-kept property to another, populating them with friends or random acquaintances and inevitably getting into arguments over some picayune issue that ended up poisoning all the good-vibe, one-big-family intentions these arrangements had started out with. I tended to side somewhat automatically with my father in these disputes, but this time around the individual whom my father was bickering with was someone who had been around a lot when I was a child. Somewhat testily, I'd suggested to my father that it was really he who was at fault.

Click.

I'd seen my father hang up on countless people over the years. Friends, enemies, book editors . . . Hanging up on people was one of the things he did most naturally. But until now he'd never hung up on me.

I didn't call back, and neither did he. At a certain point, word got back to me that my father had moved semipermanently to Italy and married an Italian woman, some fifty years his junior, whom I'd met a few times during the last months before we'd stopped talking and to whom I'd taken an instant dislike. What was happening to the West Virginia property? How was he surviving?

In the summer of 2006, my nephew Oliver called and told me he was going down to West Virginia. My father, now in his late eighties, had just returned there and was regrouping after having fallen out with his Italian bride.

"He can't stand being by himself," I said. "If that Italian woman isn't there, he must have someone else looking after him."

"He does," my nephew said. "A woman named Rebecca. She knew you when you were a kid."

Rebecca? It could only be the same Rebecca who had investigated my past lives by E-meter back in 1970. Like it or not, my

father had always told me, the people we find ourselves interacting with in a given life are there for a reason. The people we
like, the people we don't like . . . even the people we're totally
indifferent to: all of them are there not by happenstance but
because we, or rather, the higher being we were before coming
down here to incarnate, wants and needs them to be there.

"How's he looking?" I asked my nephew by email once he
was down on my father's property.

"Good, pretty much," my nephew wrote back. "But he's
definitely getting older. He told me he wishes you guys could
forget about the fight."

I sent my father an email, and he wrote back. Email had still
been something of a novelty when we'd broken off contact, and
I discovered that in the interim he had developed a style of address on the medium that mirrored the way he interacted with
people in real life. Short on appropriate capitalizations, loaded
with misspellings, the messages that started popping into my
inbox at work had the quality of last-minute telegrams sent
from behind enemy lines.

There was a great deal of talk in these emails about reincarnation. This was no real surprise, of course, as the topic had
never been far from his mind. But he now seemed especially
taken up with an aspect of the subject that had received little
attention back in the days of his lectures to me in my youth:
the phase that the discarnate soul spends *between* earthly incarnations.

Most of what I knew of the so-called between-life or (in
Tibetan) *bardo* state had come from what I'd read and learned
from Nicky about Buddhism. The Buddhist view of the time
between incarnations is that it is short (forty-nine days is the

usual number given) and (if we have not lived lives of exceptional virtue) disorienting and often quite painful. Buddhist teaching suggests that because most of us spend most of our lives acting like we are more important than other people (not to mention other sentient beings like animals), once we are dead and in the spirit world, where this illusory separation no longer holds sway, we spend much of our time there both witnessing and actually experiencing the damage that we did to others while down in the world.

My father seemed to be taking great solace from the fact that according to the authors he was now reading, all this press about the between-life state being a time of fearful reckoning was overblown. Like the excessively moralistic Catholic view he'd been subjected to as a child in boarding school, the Buddhist view was, my father was starting to suspect, just another judgmental projection on the part of a humanity dead set on making the cosmos a grim, bleak place when it was actually a glorious and altogether good one.

"'All man's experiences,'" wrote my father in an email, quoting a book by Walter Russell called *The Secret of Light,* "'are part of his unfolding. Each experience is part of his journey from the dark to the Light. There is no evil. There is naught but LIFE. There is no death.'"

Typical new age goop, I thought to myself. This was precisely the kind of callow, one-dimensional, we're-all-beings-of-light-and-everything's-wonderful attitude that I had often found so irritating when my father and his new age friends would lay it out to me when I was a kid.

At the same time, though, I couldn't blame my father for being attracted to it—especially now. Given a choice between the *bardo* hells of Buddhism and the eternal fires of the Catholic afterlife, it only made sense that at his now very advanced age my father would be more attracted than ever to the more syrupy zones of new age afterlife speculation. Given the missteps he'd taken in the course of his life, how could he fail to be seduced by a philosophy that told him he wouldn't have to pay for those actions once he was dead?

All through the summer my father gave me more email details on his new thinking on the afterlife, while I promised vaguely that I would come down and visit him in West Virginia when time permitted.

Actually, such a visit would not have been very difficult to pull off. All I'd have needed to do was walk down to my parking lot some Friday after work, get in my car, and make a dull but easy four-and-a-half-hour drive.

But week after week I didn't do so—for the simple reason that I really didn't want to. Thanks to the prophylactic qualities of computer communication, I had, so far, succeeded in reentering my father's life while at the same time *not* reentering it. All that would change, I knew, the minute I actually got out of my car down there and stepped physically back into his world.

Back in the early nineties, my father had learned that he had prostate cancer. For a few months it had seemed like his life was in imminent danger, but after surgery at a West Virginia hospital the problem seemed to disappear. The doctor who performed the surgery cautioned my father that there was a strong likelihood the cancer would show up elsewhere, but my father waved him off. He contacted an alternative cancer doctor whom he knew named Gaston Naessens, set himself up with a course of Naessens's prescribed treatments of daily injections of a specially formulated substance called (somewhat comically to my mind) 714-X, and went back to his life.

But that fall, during a checkup, my father learned that his 714-X-fueled idyll of cancer-free living was at its end.

"Looks like I'm riddled with it," he told me matter-of-factly on the phone. "I've told Gaston and he's sending down a new course of 714. He says there's every possibility I can turn the whole thing around."

Typically this would have been the point where I'd have offered a tepid word of assent to humor my father in whatever far-fetched nonsense he was attempting to put across. But no words came to me. In some deep part of myself I knew that my father's long dance with the hard facts of reality was at an end.

The following weekend, I drove down to West Virginia. The door to the front house where my father had been living ever since finances had forced him out of the larger house at the rear of the property was unlocked, and the steps leading onto the porch let out a series of creaks that hadn't changed a note since I'd last walked up them, ten years before. My father's study looked onto the porch, and through the big picture window I saw him laid up in his daybed, an assortment of books, TV remotes, crumpled Kleenex, and other half-useful detritus spread around him. I pushed open the unlocked door, walked through the kitchen, down a hall lined with hammered-together bookshelves loaded with a motley collection of titles that I recognized from years before, and into my father's study.

My nephew (who along with Rebecca was still staying down in West Virginia, keeping my father daily company in a way I couldn't help but feel guilty about failing to in contrast) was right. He was visibly older. His eyebrows, white and bushy for as long as I could remember, seemed to have been reset from the all-knowing scowl they always used to be in, so that now they registered an attitude of weary sadness. He was skinny, too—*very* skinny—and that in combination with the strange new vulnerability of his expression gave me the general impression of a bird out of its nest with no one around to pick it up and put it back. Looking at this new and disconcertingly different version of my father, I thought of a remark he'd made to me some years back, when he was in his seventies. "You know, I forget, until I look into a mirror, how ancient I am. Inside, I feel the same as I did when I was twelve."

My father half-smiled, held out his hand, and pressed mine. Then he gave a kind of shrug, as if to say: *You see how it is.*

Twenty minutes later, he was embarked on a lengthy, and familiarly urgent, description of Pope Pius IX's responsibility for the rise of the Nazis and the role of the CIA in covering up the evidence of greenhouse gas buildup. Despite his loss of weight, despite the new and distinctly uncharacteristic atmosphere of weakness he had about him, he was, underneath it all, still himself: so much so that it felt to me like it had been less like a decade and more like a week that we'd been out of touch.

Throughout that fall, I made a point of calling my father every few days to check up on his mood and his physical condition. On a Friday in mid-December, I told him after a short chat that I'd be down again soon for another visit.

"If I'm still around," my father said.

"What do you mean?" I asked.

"Don't worry," he said. "I'm just joking. I'm fine."

The following night, Saturday, I went to bed early. I took the phone off the hook just in case somebody might call late. It was past eleven the next morning before I remembered that the phone was still off the hook from the night before. I placed the receiver back in the cradle and checked my cell phone. There was a message on it from Rebecca.

"Ptolly, if you get this, please give me a call. If you want to see your dad again, I think you better get down here as soon as possible."

I called my father's number. Rebecca answered and told me he'd taken a bad turn in the course of the previous evening. My wife was away till late that evening so I got a neighbor to look after our dogs, packed a small bag, and headed down to the parking lot. It was a chilly, overcast day, and as I drove the weather got worse. By the time I hit the Pennsylvania border it was getting dark and starting to snow. I called my father's number, and this time my sister Robin answered. She'd been out of contact with my father for a lot longer than me, and had always had a considerably harder a time getting along with him than I had. But in the wake of his diagnosis she'd taken a stab at patching things up with him as well, and had just arrived from the airport a few hours earlier.

"He's alive," she said, shocking me with the implied suggestion that he might already not be. When I finally pulled in around 7:00 PM, Robin and Rebecca were seated by my father's bed. His eyes were closed, and Robin was holding his hand.

The cancer had spread to my father's liver, and his liver was now failing. Later that evening, his doctor told us that his condition was now terminal. "All you can really do," he said, "is make him as comfortable as possible with medication."

Someone needed to be sitting by my father's bedside at all times. Feeling that I had been of little use elsewhere up to this point, I elected to take the night shift. Over the following two days my father never completely regained consciousness, but instead alternated between a dead slumber in which the intervals between his breaths stretched out to an almost impossible degree, and a strange twilight state in which he appeared to be traveling through some country located between sleeping and waking consciousness. Beneath his closed lids his eyes moved back and forth as if taking in some alien landscape, and his mouth moved as he uttered words to persons or entities unseen by me.

Every now and then when he was in this latter state his eyes would, out of the blue, pop open. He would look blankly into space for a moment, then focus on me, sitting in my chair in front of him. Sometimes, taking me in, he would look completely shocked, as if to say: "What on earth are *you* doing here?" At other times, however, he seemed to take my presence completely for granted.

Sometimes, in these latter moments, he would say things to me: things that, because of his extreme weakness, I could rarely make out. But I knew my father, and I knew his attitudes. And there was no mistaking what he was attempting to do now.

He was trying to tell me something.

A few times I made out a bit of what that something was. Once, opening his eyes and seeing me, he smiled a (for him) curiously benign smile and said, "I'm just trying to see if I can walk on the bottom of it."

Walk on the bottom of what? I had, of course, no idea. But there was no getting around the feeling that my father was speaking to me in a voice that, in different circumstances, had been his all of his life: that of an explorer. Another time, opening his eyes and seeing me, he again smiled that strangely uncharacteristic smile and said, "I'm trying to understand it."

"Trying to understand what?" I asked.

"What you and the sunlight bring me," he answered, cheerfully and almost matter-of-factly.

My father, while a great talker on the subject of the importance of happiness over the years, had never, to my view, really been all that happy. That, I'd determined in the end, was why he had needed such an endless succession of women, why he'd wanted attention all the time—why he always insisted on making such a grand, sloppy, colossal mess of his life. In his last days, the sadness of that knowledge had been written clearly on his face. But now, lying there in bed, thinner than I'd ever seen him, unable for the most part to talk or even keep his eyes focused, my father would occasionally open his eyes and look directly at me with an expression that communicated, simply and almost shockingly, an unmistakable emotion:

Happiness.

So it went. Sitting there in my father's office-lair, surrounded by row upon row of books on the occult and esoteric subjects he'd spent his life studying, I found myself trying to put together a rough picture of what might be happening to him. Not from my outside, third-person perspective, but from the inner, *first-person* perspective he was seeing things from: the perspective that, as my bosses were always reminding me at *Guideposts,* was the one that really counted.

From Edgar Cayce to Rudolf Steiner to the Theosophists and the Rosicrucians and all the way down to the cheerful new age afterlife commentators my father had recently discovered, there was, I knew, a general consensus about the basics of what happened to a person at death. As the physical body waned, the nonphysical body loosened itself until it floated invisibly just above the physical body, attached to it by a slender cord like a boat at anchor in a shallow sea. Over the course of several days immediately after death, this spiritual body was supposed to gradually disintegrate into the ether of the spirit world, like an Alka-Seltzer dropped in water. During that time, I also knew, my father would presumably go through the initial postmortem experiences familiar to me from my near-death reading. He would, at a certain point, find himself outside his body and able to move around the room. With a slight chill, I realized that in fact, according to the literature, he could already be out of his body and standing right next to me now, seeing me clear as day but unable to communicate with me. At some point after that he would slowly but inexorably be pulled into the beyond, where he would encounter . . . what? A being of light radiating love and compassion? A review of his life including all the good, not so good, and downright awful things he'd done in it? A crowd of demonic beings who would mock him and pull at him and perhaps even try to devour him as they had Howard Storm?

From new age wonders to Buddhist terrors, all these sundry spiritual concepts swam around in my head, competing for my attention. Yet out of this vast jumble of ideas and images, there was no *single picture* that rose above the others. Just as my father had been present when I entered the world, giving me the unlikely name that would travel along with me through my life, I was now going to be present when he made his departure from it. But the details of this departure, as I tried to envision it, were maddeningly vague and unfocused. I knew, it occurred to me, too much about the afterlife, and at the same time entirely too little. What I wanted, at this enormously important moment, was a clear and simple picture in my head. A picture that might not have been correct down to the very last detail, but that was at least sufficiently right, sufficiently clear and believable, that I would be able to hold on to it and use it to orient myself.

By Tuesday afternoon, the occasional brief moments of lucidity passed altogether, and my father slipped into a state of unconsciousness from which he would not again waken. Later that day, and much to my irritation, his estranged wife arrived from Italy. I was still so set against her that I didn't want to let her into the house, but my sister insisted, saying that it was no time for indulging negative feelings whether justified or not. That night, after everyone else fell asleep (including the estranged wife, who soon succumbed to jet lag), I drank my usual two cans of Red Bull and sat by my father's side, listening to my iPod and feeling—as I had the previous two nights—strangely serene.

At a few minutes after six the following morning, just as the other members of the house were awakening and I was preparing to head off to the couch in the kitchen to get some sleep, my father died. In the end, his breaths were coming so slow, and the intervals between them were stretched out so impossibly, that it took me a full minute or so to understand that he had, really and truly, at last left his body behind.

I was still getting used to that idea when, a few weeks later and back in New York, I walked over to Nicky's apartment, just a few blocks away from mine. Nicky did a lot of work for the Dalai Lama, much of it in Dharamsala, in northern India, the Dalai Lama's headquarters-in-exile in the wake of the Chinese invasion. Though Nicky had suffered considerably at my father's hands over the years, and though it was no doubt the last thing in the world they'd wanted to do, he and his brother Alexander had paid my father a visit in West Virginia the previous fall and made their peace with him as well. Sitting on one of the maroon futon pillows that were pretty much the only furniture in his apartment, Nicky listened without comment as I laid out all the details of my visit, and of my father's death.

When I was done, I couldn't resist asking a question.

"So where," I said, "do you think he is right now?"

Nicky looked away, taking the question seriously and seemingly really thinking his answer over. For a moment there was only the muted sound of Greenwich Village traffic coming up from outside his closed windows.

"I don't know," he said finally, and not without what struck me as a real tone of compassion, and even pain, in his voice. "Some hell, I imagine."

Another person who had not been present at my father's death was my brother Timothy, or TC, as he liked to be called. Fifteen years older than me, and just nine months younger than Robin, TC had long since absented himself from my father's world, and had resolutely refused to enter back into it during those last months of his life the way Robin and Nicky both had. In May of that same year when my father died, shortly after leaving my job at *Guideposts* to work full time on a book about the spiritual life of animals, I traveled down to Memphis for a few days for a wedding. TC lived in Atlanta, and walking around downtown Memphis, I got the idea to give him a call and tell him where I was. TC had been having a lot of difficulties lately, and I couldn't help but suspect that a big reason for them was his refusal to talk to my father before he died. He usually didn't pick up the phone when I called, and I was planning on just leaving a message. But this time he picked up on the first ring.

My father didn't come up in the conversation at all. Like me, my brother had had some serious struggles with alcohol and drugs over the years, and in recent months he had been sliding back into all of that. In fact, the main reason I didn't call him much anymore was because even on those occasions when he did answer, he was rarely in much shape to talk.

Today, however, his voice was strangely and surprisingly clear. For ten or fifteen minutes, as I meandered around the streets of downtown Memphis, we had one of the more interesting conversations we'd had in years. It was, when I thought back on it later, weirdly philosophical in its tone. In particular, TC seemed to be concerned that I myself not be drawn back into drinking and drugs . . . all the kind of stuff that had been plaguing him in recent months. Normally I'd have been offended at the arrogance of him doing so. After all, who was he, given his recent troubles, to worry about *me*? Yet there was something in the earnestness of his voice that kept me from getting my nose out of joint at what he was saying. Finally I wished him luck, we hung up, and I went into a few tourist shops to buy some souvenirs for my friends back north.

A few hours later, during dinner at a crowded restaurant, my cell phone rang. The caller ID told me it was TC.

"What's up?" I said into the receiver, wondering why he would be calling me again so soon. It took a moment, straining to hear over all the noise in the restaurant, to realize that it wasn't TC on the phone at all, but his son, Henry. Just a few hours earlier, Henry told me, and no more than an hour or so after our conversation, TC had gone into the bathroom of his house, wrapped a towel around his head, placed the barrel of a .32 revolver beneath his chin, and pulled the trigger.

TC's suicide was the catalyst for a difficult summer. By the end of July my wife and I had split up and I was staying in Nicky's West Village apartment while he was away, once again, in India. One day during my stay there, I walked over to Twelfth Street Books, the last of what had once been Greenwich Village's many used bookstores, and discovered that it was moving to Brooklyn. All the stock was now discounted, and picking around the stacks of books I came across a Library of America paperback edition of Walt Whitman's collected writings. The last thing I needed, at that point in my extremely disjointed life, was another book. But I liked the way it looked, with the familiar floppy-hatted sepia shot of Whitman from his later years on the cover. So I bought it, took it back to Nicky's, and put it on one of the several stacks of books I'd carried over from my wife's place.

Nicky's apartment was small and, to say the least, sparsely furnished. In fact, it was less someone's apartment than a Buddhist shrine. Scrolls of various Buddhas and bodhisattvas lined the walls, and prayer bowls and incense trays took up shelves that in another apartment might have held photographs or knickknacks. Over the next few days, writing my animal book in this tranquil but strangely intense environment, I found myself repeatedly picking up that Whitman volume and leafing around in it. Whitman had seen a lot of death close up in his life, especially during his days as a nurse for the Civil War wounded, and much of what he'd had to say about the subject had appealed to me when I'd stumbled across one passage or another over the years. While putting together a piece on Emerson and Transcendentalism at *Guideposts* a few years back, I'd been particularly interested to discover that Emerson, Thoreau, and Whitman had all been believers in reincarnation—though it appeared they had envisioned it in a somewhat different manner than the Eastern religions they'd picked up the idea from.

Now, as I stumbled from one intriguingly suggestive line of Whitman about the soul's destiny to another, an idea began to form in my head. Though I didn't know a huge amount about his life, I did know that Whitman had been born into a significant time in America's spiritual history. In the mid and later years of the nineteenth century, the first English translations of Far Eastern spiritual ideas had made their way to America's shores, and Whitman, Emerson, and Thoreau had been among the first Americans to read them seriously. When Whitman had written of himself as "I, Walt Whitman, a cosmos," and had sung of the countless lives that lay behind and ahead of him, he had had not just Buddhism but, most important, the Hindu doctrine of atman, or soul, at the front of his thoughts.

During those same years of the nineteenth century, the first occult and esoteric ideas that would one day meld with Eastern thinking to produce that loose body of ideas known as "new age" were making their way to America as well. Whitman had done his best to take in this new mix of ideas and forge them into a vision of the soul and its destiny that was genuinely capacious enough for the unique time he found himself living in. It was a vision that, in Whitman's characteristically all-inclusive fashion, had room for Christianity, for the mystics of the East, for spiritualism and the occult—and last but not least for science as well, for Whitman saw science not as an enemy of the spiritual perspective but potentially the source of its full and final validation.

Whitman had sought a picture of the soul and its destiny that would honor all these different perspectives, but at the heart of his vision was an insistence that death was something not to be feared, but celebrated.

Joy, shipmate, Joy!
(Pleas'd to my soul at death I cry,)
Our life is closed, our life begins,
The long, long anchorage we leave,
The ship is clear at last, she leaps!
She swiftly courses from the shore,
Joy, shipmate, joy.

The world, my father had told me many a time, was, from a certain perspective at least, a kind of hell: a place where, whether we wanted to or not, we just about always ended up doing damage to others, and to ourselves as well. But if we could learn to see this life within the context of a larger life that lay beyond it, all of that would change. All of life's pain would still be there, but by changing one's perspective one could transform the way that one experienced that pain. While things might still hurt, they would not hurt in the so often supremely horrible way they hurt for people who had no larger picture—no story-above-the-story—within which to see their lives.

Leafing through my copy of Whitman's writings, and with all those Buddhas and bodhisattvas of Nicky's staring down at me, it occurred to me that I had been born into a time when the beginnings of a genuinely new vision of that narrative, of the story-above-the-story that every culture needs if it is to make any kind of deep and lasting sense of life, was coming into being. This story had started to fall together a while back—at least as far back as Whitman's day—and the new age narratives my father had raised me on, narratives of the soul's journey through a cosmos that exists not to punish or torment the soul but to season and educate it, were versions of it as well. They were imperfect versions to be sure. But they also held— beneath their inconsistency, outlandishness, and, occasionally, their outright silliness—an allure that I simply couldn't deny.

It also occurred to me that my encounters with traditional religious/spiritual perspectives—from Nicky's Buddhism to the Christian readers of *Guideposts*—had in the end only made me more curious to understand that emerging story and to find the ways in which (in its smartest and best versions) it contradicted, and the ways in which it agreed with, those traditional visions. How, in its best and deepest form, did this emerging narrative of the soul and its destiny, this new master narrative of life and afterlife, really run?

What follows is my own best attempt to sketch it.

2

Ancient Egypt, the Origins of the Afterlife, and the Birth of the Idea That Each of Us Is a God in Training

There is only a single supreme idea on earth: the concept of the immortality of the human soul; all other profound ideas by which men live are only an extension of it.

—FYODOR DOSTOYEVSKY

Sometimes I go about pitying myself, and all the time I am being carried on great winds across the sky.

—OJIBWA DREAM SONG

O ther than "Is there a God?" the question "What happens when we die?" is arguably the single most important one that human beings have ever asked. The question's only other real competition—"What kind of universe do we live in, a good one or a bad one?"—is really just another way of asking the same thing, for a universe that does nothing with its creations but throw them away when it is done with them is, by definition, not a very good universe but a bad or, at best, an indifferent one.

A shorter way of asking "What happens when we die?" is simply to ask "Who are we?" because, as most of the world's primal and ancient peoples knew, you can't find out who you really are until you find out about *all* of yourself. Today that tends to mean finding out about the parts of us that are buried away in our unconscious: the parts that we are only in touch with in stray, unguarded moments while awake, and more completely, if more cryptically, in dreams. In times past, though, it could mean more than that. It could mean, to be precise, the part of you that preceded the "you" of here on earth right now and that would outlast it as well.

In primal societies, initiation ceremonies (coming-of-age events in which boys became men and girls became women) inevitably centered on the twin mysteries of birth and death: the moment when we come into this world, and the moment when we leave it behind. For young men and sometimes for young women as well these ceremonies often involved a symbolic death and resurrection in which the young men were dragged away from their village, attacked and "killed" by the gods of the universe, taught the mysteries of what lies beyond the boundaries of death, and then resuscitated and returned to their village as full human beings.

In much ancient and traditional thought, to become a genuine human being entailed consciously knowing three things:

1. That each of us comes, originally, from beyond the physical world,

2. That we will eventually return to that place beyond, and
3. That there is a part of us that, even right here and now, is *still* "out there," in that spiritual world, because it never came completely to birth with us to begin with.

In spiritual traditions the world over, awareness of the hidden part of ourselves—the part that was not born when we were born, and so will not die when we die, either—is what gives each of us our power in this world: the power to know (as my father liked to point out so much) that whatever happens down here on earth, there is a part of us that can't be touched by any of it and that will prevail no matter how many challenges we have to face while alive, and how well or badly we do in facing them.

In addition to being the most important question human beings have ever asked, "What happens when we die?" is also probably one of the very *first* questions human beings ever asked, for asking it is proof in itself that we have placed ourselves outside ourselves to a degree, and hence stopped being animals pure and simple and entered the domain of abstraction: that form of thinking for which we humans, of all the earth's creatures, seem to have the most talent. To think abstractly is to go up and above the world even while remaining within it: to see the situation from beyond one's skin, even while still stuck inside one's skin. As such, and though rarely described this way, it is a kind of ecstasy, just as the departure of a shaman's spirit from his body is—a way of dying before we actually die.

To such a degree is "What happens when I die?" *the* human question that we humans were most likely starting to ask it long before we were even fully human. The Neanderthals that inhabited the earth for millennia before true *homo sapiens* came along sometimes buried their loved ones in a fetal position and placed flowers, stone tools, and other (presumably) valued objects in their graves along with them. Whatever else these gestures signified, they tell us one thing quite clearly: our earliest forebears believed that, when one of their number died, he or she *went somewhere.* Death was the end of one chapter of existence, but it was also the beginning of another chapter.

This isn't to say that from the beginning of time death has been a positive event. Anthropologists and archaeologists tell us that early peoples were often so horrified by the fact of death that they refused even to bury their loved ones and instead left them where they fell, never returning to that spot again. Yet even in these negative, terror-filled reactions to the fact of death, we see a respect for its simple hugeness, for its absolute centrality in human life. In this respect such peoples have gone further than so many of us in the modern world who, for as long as we can, pretend that death simply doesn't exist.

When people think about the idea of death in the ancient world, they tend to think of Egypt—and with good reason. Along with being the most stable and unchanging civilization the world has ever known, ancient Egypt was also the civilization that thought more about death than any other. The Egyptians revered above all things the idea of *ma'at*—a term that can be translated as "order," "truth," or "justice." All *ma'at,* the Egyptians believed, came from the spiritual world, which in their view lay both beneath the ground they walked on, and up in the sky above them, where the sun god Re glided in measured splendor from east to west each day. All their thinking about death was in one way or another tied up with this idea of order: with the idea that there is a deep and abiding *sense* to the cosmos and the way that it is made up, and that the job of humans is to comprehend that order and fit themselves properly into it.

Like so many of the primal peoples who had come before them, the Egyptians believed that when a person died he or she left the middle realm of physical existence to join the company of the dead in the lands of spirit that stretched out invisibly beneath them and in the sky above. Egyptian civilization lasted at least three thousand years, so there is understandably some variation in how they envisioned the journey of the dead, but essentially they saw it as a drama in two acts. In the first, the underworld act, the newly dead soul plunged down into the terrifying darkness and obscurity of the Duat—the Egyptian name for the underworld. Like the underworld regions of later cultures (the Greek Hades, the Christian Hell), the Duat was in large part a scary place. Going down into it was frightening and disorienting, like jumping into a body of murky water where one has never swum before and where one can't see an inch once one has placed one's head beneath the surface.

Confusing as it was to one first entering into it, the Duat was, like everything else in the ancient Egyptian universe, actually a highly structured place. Like the prototype of a modern video game, it was made up of multiple levels—worlds, almost—each one overseen by a specific god. Like the Malaku-lans' Le-hev-hev, these gods would present the newly dead soul with a series of challenges in the form of questions, physical contests, and general tests of character, which the soul needed to bear up under successfully. If it succeeded in this, the trials would eventually come to an end, and the soul would leave the underworld behind, rising up triumphantly to join Re each morning in his journey across the daytime skies, and the swirling stars that moved across it at night. Each star, according to later Egyptian belief, was the soul of a person who had died and successfully navigated the terrors of the Duat in times past.

Like most ancient and primal peoples, the Egyptians saw humans as possessing not one but several souls or spiritual bodies. The most important of these was the *ba,* or free soul, which escaped from the physical body at death and traveled down to the underworld. Meanwhile, another soul, the *ka,* stayed behind along with the deceased's mummified body, waiting till the free soul was done with its ordeals, at which point the souls would reunite in a new entity combining all the attributes of those former bodies, called the *ach.* The mummy, which seems like such a bizarre invention to us, was to the Egyptian mind a kind of cocoon that housed and incubated one part of the postmortem soul while another part of it traveled through the lands below the earth. Perhaps the best way to envision the *ba* or free soul and the *ka* or stationary soul is by comparing them to the parts of one of those toy helicopters that fly at the end of a tether. At the base of the tether is the battery that powers the helicopter. In a similar way, the mummy, and the *ka* soul that stayed with it, served as the controls and the battery power for the *ba* or free soul as it moved from station to station across the lands beneath.

Complicated as all this sounds, at the base of all the more important Egyptian concepts of the afterlife was one absolutely central one:

Immortality.

For the ancient Egyptians, *all* of life was a preparation for death, because to them nothing was more desirable than the condition of immortality. While in Egypt's early days only the pharaoh himself was thought to be truly immortal, over the course of centuries this honor was extended to more and more of the Egyptian populace, starting with nobles and royalty but reaching eventually to every member of the Egyptian population.

For a high-ranking member of Egyptian civilization to be able to meet death in the right way, a long list of preparations had to be made. One needed to be buried properly, in a suitable tomb with suitable hieroglyphic inscriptions upon the walls and on the sarcophagus itself; one needed to have one's body mummified, and one's internal organs preserved in special "canopic" jars (named for Canopus, a town in ancient Egypt), each capped with the head of one of four major Egyptian divinities, and which were buried in the tomb alongside the coffin. One also needed to have one's tomb supplied with the objects one might need in the other world, from foodstuffs all the way down to small wooden figurines of servants that, with the proper magic spells, would come to life and serve one when needed in the lands beyond.

But because the Egyptians were above all a people who venerated the ideal of *ma'at,* one also needed to possess something else if one expected to fare well in the world beyond, something that, unlike elaborate coffins or carved wooden servants, could not be procured, before one died, with money or standing or even with magic spells.

One needed to have been a person of *ma'at.*

Stated more simply, one needed to have been a good person. The final test of the Egyptian underworld journey was the so-called weighing of the heart. In this procedure, the jackal-headed god Anubis balanced the newly dead soul's heart on one side of a scale, with the "Feather of Truth" on the other side. If the life of the person in question had been a good and decent one, his or her heart would weigh the same as the feather, and the gates of the underworld would open for him or her onto the heavenly lands above, where Re and the circling star ancestors were waiting. If the deceased's heart weighed more than the feather, on the other hand, he or she was handed over to Ammut—a crocodile-headed god with the body of a hippopotamus and lion—and (no real surprise here) devoured.

Once again there was, over all those centuries of Egyptian civilization, some variation in the details of this part of the scenario as well. In some versions of the Egyptian afterlife journey the soul's final goal was not the sky but the "Field of Reeds"—a kind of improved, superterrestrial version of earth where the dead soul would reunite with friends and loved ones and consort with the gods who ran the universe (this later developed into the Greek notion of the Elysian Fields).

Different gods also became either more or less important to the afterlife drama in different periods of Egyptian history. While for some periods Re was the main model for the dead soul to follow, at other times it was the "dying god" Osiris. A vegetation god whose death, burial, and resurrection were patterned on the seasonal disappearance and return of the crops, Osiris was a god who, like Christ (whose story he strongly prefigures), didn't just survive death through life in the spirit, but actually *returned to physical life,* thus uniting the world of matter and the world of spirit.

The Egyptians, like the Jews and the Christians and the Muslims of later centuries, believed in physical resurrection. What this means, basically, is that they envisioned a time far in the future when the physical world and the spiritual world, which now are separate, would once again become *one* world. Despite their enormous preoccupation with what happens after it is all over, the Egyptians actually appear to have had a very deep love for life and all it contained. When they turned their thoughts to how the universe might end, therefore, they inevitably imagined a kind of marriage between the physical world and the larger world of spirit from which it drew all its energy, beauty, and purpose.

It was the Egyptians' unwavering faith in the reality of the spiritual world that, ironically, ended up making Egyptian culture such a durable one from the *material* point of view. All the sturdy and long-lasting creations we know them best for today—from tombs to pyramids to mummies—were inspired by their love and respect for the spiritual side of the universe. The Egyptians worked hard to make the objects of their culture last forever, but at bottom they did so because they believed that the human soul would last forever as well.

The Egyptians' passionate interest in and optimism about the immortality—and perhaps even divinity—of the human soul becomes even more dramatic if we compare it with the spiritual outlook of some of the other cultures of the ancient world. Over in the lands of the Fertile Crescent that eventually produced the religions of Judaism and Christianity, for example, the ancient Mesopotamians speculated about the activities of the gods in heaven every bit as much as the Egyptians did, but the answers they came up with were starkly different. For the Mesopotamians, all human cities were built on the model of heaven itself, just as their kings and queens modeled their actions on those of the gods who ruled the heavens. (The name for Babylon, for example, the Mesopotamian capital city on the banks of the Euphrates River, derives from *Bab-il-ani,* or "gate of the gods.") But unlike the Egyptians, who saw the gods as being more than ready to take human beings into their company, the Mesopotamians saw heaven as a place to which human beings were definitely *not* invited. The Mesopotamian afterworld was a very grim and gray place, where humans survived, if they survived at all, as mere shade-like traces of what they had been in life.

And yet, as the Mesopotamian hero Gilgamesh demonstrated when he journeyed to the lands beyond in an unsuccessful attempt to secure the secret of immortality for humans, the Mesopotamians were haunted by the idea of human divinity every bit as much as the Egyptians were. In fact, one seeks in vain for an ancient civilization that did *not* give thought to the question of human divinity, whichever way they chose to answer it. The hope that humans are potentially gods—or anger and frustration at the possibility that they aren't—is one of the most consistent of all human ideas.

Countless ancient peoples had interesting and, to us, often quite outlandish and romantic, things to say about death. The Egyptians had more of these than just about any other ancient people, and their most interesting was this: that the human being is, in essence, a god in training. All of the things that to us are most characteristically Egyptian—their complex and intricate techniques of mummification, their vast tombs and sprawling necropolises or cities of the dead—were rooted in a single idea: that the living person as he or she existed on earth was not yet a finished product, but the seed form of something else; a being that would emerge fully into the light only after the earthly chapter of life had ended. A being that, at least in later times, the Egyptians were not afraid to suggest was itself divine.

Likewise, if there is a single insight that Egyptian civilization has bequeathed to the world that is more valuable than all the others, it is its unrelenting, centuries-long focus on this idea that each of us is a potentially divine being: that we have, as the Egyptians liked to put it, "a royal destiny."

3

The Egyptian and Tibetan Books of the Dead, the Mortal and Immortal Parts of the Soul, and the Key Difference Between the Eastern and the Western Views of the Afterlife

Rudolf Steiner, the philosopher and founder of the Waldorf schools whom my father admired so much, once said that the single greatest shock most of us will ever experience in our lives is actually the moment immediately *after* the earthly portion of our life is over. This is the moment when, to our astonishment, we will discover that we are not only still *here,* but still *the same person we were before we died.*

But if we remain "ourselves" in the moments immediately after death, the question then arises of how long we will stay this way. Howard Storm's narrative of his encounter with that dim crowd of mean-spirited people who started out by insulting him but then moved on to biting and tearing at him has many counterparts in the afterlife myths and legends of the world. In fact, when negative aspects of the afterlife are being discussed, the chief terror of the afterlife according to most peoples around the world and over history is that it will tear us apart.

And not just physically, either. Psychic dissolution—the danger of losing the sense of secure and single identity that we take so for granted while alive and in the body—is the real threat presented by all the various monsters and devouring creatures that show up in the course of the Egyptian afterlife journey and its equivalents in other ancient cultures. While the idea of being physically devoured is certainly terrifying, being *psychically* devoured (losing one's inner identity through fragmentation and disintegration, going crazy, in other words) is even more so.

This connects to the idea, expressed by the mystical litera-ture of many spiritual traditions, that our essential goodness comes not from following external rules, but from going within and finding a mysterious inner center: a core that comprises our true and lasting identity and defines who we are "at heart." It was this inner core that Jesus, in the gospels, described as being more precious than all the riches in the world. If we look at this idea within the context of Egyptian religion, we can see the Christian idea as a development of the original Egyp-tian one that each of us possesses a kind of heavenly identity: a supremely central part of ourselves that is our birthright as humans created in the image of the divine. This is the part of us that remains after all the outer stuff is cooked or frozen or blasted away: the part that needs to ask no questions at all about what heaven is like or how to get there, and isn't even concerned about whether it will make it all the way to heaven, because it is, by its very nature, *a part of heaven already*. It's the belief in that heavenly identity that made the Egyptians suggest that once one is dead one must struggle at all times to "remember one's name"—to keep in touch with that essential core where all a person's real goodness, all that makes that person who he or she is and no other, is stored.

This isn't to suggest that Christianity got its ideas directly from Egypt, but it *is* to suggest that Christianity grew up out of a world where people had been thinking hard and deeply about the soul and its fate for a long, long time.

We know what the Egyptians thought about the afterlife largely because of their hieroglyphic writings. These were first inscribed in stone on the tomb walls of their kings and queens, but were later written on papyrus, where they became much more accessible to the public at large, who as the centuries went by were granted more and more access to the secrets of the soul's destiny that were at first reserved to royalty alone.

The information contained in the Egyptian hieroglyphic afterlife writings was supposed, as much as possible, to be absorbed by a person while he or she was alive so that it would be safely tucked away in memory when the time came for that individual to leave the earth behind. Then, as now, however, there are limits to what a person taken up with the business of daily life can be expected to memorize. Therefore, at a certain point the Egyptians began outfitting their dead with papyrus "books" (scrolls, actually) that outlined the journey through the afterlife realms in detail. Since the Egyptians felt that any physical object packed in a tomb with a dead person could take on a spiritual existence and be used by them when they entered the afterlife, these books functioned, in the eyes of the Egyptians, as actual guidebooks that could be consulted by the dead as they navigated the challenges of the underworld landscape on their way to the world of light above.

Papyrus, in the ultradry Egyptian climate, lasts a very long time, and these afterlife texts were still sitting by the mummified bodies of their owners when those tombs began to be opened in large numbers in the eighteenth and nineteenth centuries. The tombs' raiders, logically enough, started calling these scrolls Kitab al-Mayyitun—"dead people's books"—and the name stuck. In 1842, the German scholar Richard Lepsius borrowed the term when he published the first translation of this material (which in the original Egyptian was called *Pert em hru,* or "The Book of Coming Forth by Day") in a single volume called *Das Todtenbuch der Aegypter:* The Egyptian Book of the Dead. Translated into English, it very quickly became popular with general readers, and in one edition or another has stayed in print ever since.

Though perfectly comprehensible to a literate member of ancient Egyptian culture, who would have lived with and thought about the gods and supernatural situations described in its pages every day of his or her life, from our modern perspective *The Egyptian Book of the Dead* is an extremely strange and challenging piece of work to read through, much less understand. It is not easy. It is not familiar. It's not even particularly friendly. Yet none of this has gotten in the way of its popularity, especially in the sixties when it was embraced by Timothy Leary and the drug culture, and then in the seventies when it was taken up by the burgeoning new age movement. For however bizarre its ideas and images may be, *The Egyptian Book of the Dead* takes seriously the idea that there is a genuine landscape lying beyond the gates of death. And that seriousness strikes a cord in a culture like ours, where more often than not the details of the afterlife are either extremely vague or simply nonexistent.

Even more popular with readers today is that other most intricate and sophisticated how-to manual of life after death bequeathed to us from former times: *The Tibetan Book of the Dead.* Traditionally believed to have been composed in the eighth century by the monk Padmasambhava (who brought Buddhism to Tibet from India and is one of the founders of the school of Mahayana Buddhism, of which Tibetan Buddhism is a branch), *The Tibetan Book of the Dead* is actually a combination of two texts: *The Supplication of the Bardo of Dharmata* and *The Supplication Pointing Out the Bardo of Existence.* Otherwise known as *The Great Liberation Through Hearing,* these two texts were designed to prevent the newly deceased person from being overwhelmed by what the Tibetans, like the Egyptians before them, believed were the very considerable terrors, attractions, and confusions that awaited the soul when the body was left behind.

Buddhism got much of its view of the afterlife from the much older religion of Hinduism, altering those views in sometimes subtle and sometimes radical ways. Like their Hindu predecessors, the Buddhists saw the world as a place of cyclic reincarnation. Beings were born and born again, moving through a multiplicity of bodies, until they obtained what Hinduism called *moksha,* or liberation, finally breaking free of the cause-and-effect chains of karma and attaining the condition of nirvana—a Sanskrit term that means extinguishment, like that of a candle being blown out.

In the view of the ancient Tibetans, knowledge of what to do in the world beyond the body could not be packaged and brought along with quite the ease that the Egyptians thought it could. (You couldn't bring, that is, an actual spirit version of the *Great Liberation* with you into death, just as you couldn't bring along spirit versions of little wooden slaves to do your work for you.) Individuals were therefore encouraged to memorize passages of *The Tibetan Book of the Dead* while still alive, so that its wisdom would stay lodged in the psyche even after the soul had cast off from the physical body.

But for the Tibetans as for the Egyptians, memory had its limits. So when a person died, they were helped in their navigation of the worlds beyond by monks back in the land of the living, who read passages of *The Tibetan Book of the Dead* to the deceased for the entire forty-nine days that they believed it took before a newly discarnate soul would find incarnation in its next body. Like a kind of otherworldly book-on-tape, these directions would sound in the consciousness of the postmortem spirit as it struggled to find its bearings amid the flashing lights and looming terrors of the discarnate world.

> **When the consciousness-principle gets outside the body, it says to itself "Am I dead or am I not dead?" It cannot determine. It sees its relatives and connections as it had been used to seeing them before. It even hears their wailings.**
>
> —*The Tibetan Book of the Dead*
> (Walter Evans-Wentz translation, slightly modernized)

The chief terror that hearing *The Tibetan Book of the Dead* was designed to help the disembodied listener cope with was the same for the Tibetans as it had been for the Egyptians: psychic dissolution. Or again to use more simple terms: *falling apart in the mind*. Buddhism teaches that while we are alive the physical body acts as a kind of buffer, shielding us from the blinding intensity of spiritual-psychic realities that flood in immediately upon us when we die and break free of the dense corporeal shell that we had gotten so used to inhabiting while we were alive. For the Tibetan as for the Egyptian book of the dead, one must cling above all, once in the lands beyond the shores of physical life, to two key pieces of knowledge: *where* one is, and *who* one is. (The same idea exists in Hinduism, where the most important thing for an individual to remember in life *or* in death is his or her unity, beneath all the illusory surface separateness, with Brahman or God.)

The answers to the questions *Who am I?* and *Where am I?* that *The Tibetan Book of the Dead* gives are, however, quite different from those of its Egyptian cousin. Like the Egyptians (and again like the Hindus, from whom they took so many of their basic ideas about the universe), the Tibetans believed in a world of gods above and people below. They believed as well that a human being could one day join the company of those gods if he or she did the right things in this world and kept the right thoughts and intentions in his or her heart.

But in the Tibetan view the fact that a human being might one day become a god was not nearly as noteworthy or exciting an idea as it had been for the Egyptians or the Hindus. The simple reason for this was that the gods were, like everything else in the Buddhist universe, impermanent. Gods aplenty inhabit the crowded spiritual universe of Tibetan Buddhism, but in the end they are no better off than the various devils and other hell-beings that inhabit the eighteen Tibetan under-worlds. To the Buddhists who studied (and, as my stepbrother demonstrated to me, continue to study) the truths laid out in *The Tibetan Book of the Dead,* the only lasting thing in the universe was not a "thing" at all, but a nirvana-like condition called *sunyata.*

Sunyata comes from the Sanskrit word *sunya,* meaning "zero" or "nothing," and is often translated as "emptiness." That's somewhat misleading, though, since *empty* is a word born from the realm of manifestation, and the really important thing about *sunyata* is precisely that it exists beyond all such conditioned states. One could, in fact, just as well characterize *sunyata* as overwhelming fullness, for neither *full* nor *empty* do proper justice to its transconceptual nature. (As the Chinese Buddhist sage Hui-neng put it, "When you hear me talk about the void [*sunyata*], do not fall into the idea of vacuity.")

Sunyata has nothing to do with the life we are currently living, and yet at the same time it has everything to do with it, for personally realizing the truth of *sunyata* is the only true key to happiness in the universe. (Unlike nirvana, *sunyata* is also not to be confused with ideas of God or a divinity of any kind, since Buddhism, virtually alone among the world religions, doesn't believe in God.)

So it is that while the quintessential Egyptian artwork is the pyramid or the sarcophagus, the quintessential Tibetan art-work is probably the sand mandala: a large and extremely in-tricate symmetrical design created by monks who, in a state of meditation, first sketch the general shape of the mandala, then fill it in using powders made of finely crushed colored stone. Sand mandalas take days of careful labor to put together, and once finished are promptly swept away with a broom: a vivid illustration of the primary insight of Tibetan Buddhism that nothing—either in this world or in the many worlds that lie beyond it—lasts forever.

The Tibetans didn't, and don't, believe that the human personality survives death, because for them the human personality is in reality not an actual entity in itself but an assemblage of parts: parts that seem for a time like they amount to something genuinely real and lasting, but that in truth are no more durable than the colorful and alluring shapes in one of their beautiful but short-lived sand paintings.

For years I've had a recurring (and not particularly original) dream in which I'm back in high school, sitting down for a test that I suddenly realize I've forgotten to study for. This dream is always full of perfectly sensible details. In fact, as far as dreams go, it's kind of aggressively boring and ordinary. The desks in class are laid out in an orderly fashion. The classroom, the students in it, and sometimes even a detail or two from the test itself on the desk in front of me (it's usually either on math or biology, both tiresome subjects for me back then) all appear with considerable clarity. It even makes sense, as the dream is happening, that I'm anxious about taking the test. After all, why shouldn't I be?

And yet, of course, at the same time and in the midst of all this sensibleness, there's the decidedly nonsensical fact that I left high school a little over thirty years ago. Yet while I'm having the dream, this crucial piece of information is completely unavailable to me. While part of me is reacting to the situation just as I would in real life, I'm also ignoring a preposterously huge piece of knowledge that changes the entire picture of what's going on. I'm blind, in short, to the fact that I am not experiencing full, but rather only partial, consciousness of who and where I really am.

That's the maddening thing about dreams, of course: the way they mix knowledge together with ignorance. But according to Buddhism, that's how *all* of life is. Whether we are currently in a physical body (be it human or animal or supernatural) or in the forty-nine-day period that separates one incarnation from the next, all of us suffer from having forgotten one absolutely crucial piece of information: neither we, nor anyone else, nor any single thing or quality or situation in the entire universe, has any underlying *separate* existence whatsoever. Ignorant of *sunyata,* we are doomed to a restless wandering from one incarnation to the next until we finally wake up. When we do, the situation will be much like what happens when, in a dream, we suddenly realize that we're dreaming. That flash of awareness brings the dream to an end, our eyes blink open, and we are able to see the whole dream scenario, which just seconds ago we were completely embroiled in and convinced by, for the flat-out illusion that it was.

Illusion and reality, then, are the twin concepts that drive Buddhist thought, just as Egyptian culture was driven by the twin concepts of order and disorder. Different as these two systems of thought are, though, the central mystery each focuses on is the same:

What is the ultimate fate of human beings?

The short answer given by the Egyptians is that human beings survive death, but in a changed form. The short answer given by the Tibetans is that human beings don't survive death, because they never existed to begin with.

Two very different cultures; two very different books of the dead. Yet in each we find the two basic answers that *any* religious system can give to the question of our fate at death. Though we could talk about countless other faiths and the nuances that distinguish them, Egypt and Tibet give us the two basic responses to the question of what does, or doesn't, happen to the individual after he or she leaves this world behind.

In Tibetan Buddhism as in so many ancient views of the human being, humans have two parts. The part of our mind that is doomed to fall apart at or soon after death the Tibetans called *sem*. Everything that we normally identify ourselves with—everything in our ordinary, everyday consciousness that feels most familiar and close, from our liking for orange marmalade, to our inability to laugh at puns even when other people think they're funny, to our tendency to become depressed on Sundays, to our tendency, when we were fourteen, to like Elton John songs even when it was perceived by our classmates as tremendously uncool to do so—is *sem*. All of this stuff, attached to it and identified with it though we might be, is doomed to disperse with the death of the body or soon thereafter. People believe, says Buddhism, that their likes and dislikes are important, because if we are not our likes and dislikes, our passions and our attachments, then we must be simple blank books, identical with every other book in the great library of sentient beings that populate the universe. But, says Buddhism, blank volumes are in fact just what we are—and it is our desire to deny this fact that is the true source of all our suffering. As Sogyal Rinpoche, author of *The Tibetan Book of Living and Dying*, writes, Buddhism believes that "when we die, whatever memories we have gathered in this life die utterly, and that when we are reborn, we develop a fresh memory." According to the fourteenth Dalai Lama, meanwhile, the self or soul is "a cluster of mutually dependent qualities—a complex flow of mental and physical events, clustered in clearly identifiable patterns." And that cluster is destined to fall apart eventually. For life after life, reincarnation after reincarnation, the slate of individual consciousness gets wiped absolutely clean.

But if this is the case, then what is the "we" that reincarnates, the thing that, for life after life after life, *does* last? For—paradoxically or not—Buddhism does indeed posit that, unimportant as our personal thoughts and experiences are to who we really deeply are, there is nonetheless some part of us that *does* move from one incarnation to the next, surviving through countless deaths and births.

This part of us Tibetan Buddhism calls *rigpa,* which can be translated as "core consciousness." *Rigpa* is the Tibetan equivalent of that center of centers, that heart of hearts, that the Egyptians envisioned as being weighed, at the climax of the Egyptian afterlife journey, against the Feather of Truth. *The Tibetan Book of the Dead* even has its own equivalent of this procedure. Just prior to rebirth, it says, Yama Raja, the Lord of the Dead, weighs a person's bad actions in their previous life (which take the form of black pebbles) against their good actions (which take the form of white ones). The whole goal of existence, and of the countless lives that, in the reincarnation-centered worldview of Buddhism, each of us lives, is to recover our direct knowledge of this core essence. For *rigpa* is, in the deepest sense imaginable, *what we really are.* As such, it is identical with *sunyata,* for at heart that is what the universe itself is.

In suggesting that the individual personality has no inherent underlying existence, Buddhism disagrees with Judaism, Christianity, Islam, and to a degree Hinduism as well. But the fact remains that for Buddhism as for these other faiths, it's the central part of a person that really counts. This central self is the germ in the grain that, in the New Testament, the wheat is winnowed to uncover. It's the part of the soul that Plato likened to a chariot driver who (hopefully) steers the "horses" of his lower passions rather than being led around by them. In Hindu philosophy this central self is the atman, the center of centers that survives countless incarnations and returns, in the end, to Brahman or the Godhead, with which it has always, in truth, been identical. It's also the part of us that the early Hindu religious texts called the Upanishads are talking about when they describe the human soul as being composed of two parts that are like two birds sitting on a tree: one that eats, flaps its wings, and makes noise and one that sits silently, looking on, taking the actions of the other bird in with total dispassion. It's the part of us that does not engage in action, that does not do the things we do, but that hangs back and stays apart, watching with approval if we do what is right, and with keen but calm disapproval if we do what is wrong (for though unconcerned with action, this center of centers *is,* odd as it may seem, nonetheless concerned with right and wrong).

This central part of us is what both Hindu and Sufi philosophy sometimes call the "Witness." It's also the part of us that the modern Spanish poet Juan Ramón Jiménez was talking about in his famous poem "I Am Not I."

I am not I.

   I am this one
  Walking beside me whom I do not see,
 Whom at times I manage to visit,
 And at other times I forget.
 The one who remains silent when I talk,
 The one who forgives, sweet, when I hate,
 The one who takes a walk when I am indoors,
 The one who will remain standing when I die.

(ROBERT BLY TRANSLATION)

This witness or secret stranger is the person we most want to be, for the simple reason that we are it already, and have just lost touch with this knowledge due to our being enmeshed in the confusions and temptations and disorientations of incarnate existence. The Tibetans suggest that this secret self is perfectly empty, devoid of all taint of quality: that it is, in other words, not really a "self" at all. Yet at the same time, the Tibetans also tell us that the impossibility of attaching adjectives to it of any kind should not prevent us from understanding that this part of us is (again, paradoxical as this may seem) *good*. Good behavior—in particular, compassion for our fellow beings—will get us closer to this part of ourselves, while bad behavior will alienate us from it.

So though it remains the case that *sunyata* possesses not the vaguest taint of personality, and that if we are to rejoin ourselves with it we must divest ourselves of all the individual, personal qualities that seem to make us most ourselves while we are alive on earth here and now, this qualityless thing that we must once again become can nonetheless be described as good and not as bad. A paradox? Maybe. But a paradox that is, for the Tibetans, the key to extricating oneself from the mire of cyclic existence. And that, above all else in this view, is what a person needs to do if he or she desires to be happy.

For the Hindus, and even more for the Buddhists, ordinary earthly life was nothing to be desired. Whether for humans or for animals, the endlessly circular character of existence (moving from the death realms back to life, then back to the death realms, then back to life again, ad nauseam) made life at best a disappointing affair and at worst a downright horrific one. The universe was, in the minds of the great thinkers of these two traditions, analogous to a vast wheel: an ever-spinning yet never-changing round of fear, ignorance, and desire that turned and turned and turned without ever actually moving forward. Upon this wheel the souls of men, women, and all other incarnate beings were trapped like bugs on flypaper. The "wheel of karma" (as both Buddhism and Hinduism call the mechanism of cause and effect that keeps the soul returning to body after body) was in the majority of schools of Hinduism and all schools of Buddhism a creaking, crushing, stone-hard contraption: one to which the reincarnating soul was tethered like a blinkered donkey in a medieval grain mill. Round and round the donkey-soul went—getting nowhere, gaining nothing, driven ever onward by the implacable and merciless forces of fear, ignorance, and desire. Do something in this life, pay for it in the next . . . on and on and on, with no rest or respite in sight.

For the Buddha, as well as for the Hindu authors of the Vedas and the Upanishads, it would have been an altogether better thing if the whole business of incarnate life had never gotten started to begin with. The point was, for them, precisely *not* to stay on the great and ever-turning wheel of birth, death, and rebirth, but to get free of it, once and for all, through union with the absolute, and escape from the world of relativity, the world of fears and lusts, of desires and dislikes—in short, the marmalade world.

If it sounds paradoxical and even nightmarish that when we die we lose all of the most identifiable characteristics of the person we had been but continue (in our next incarnation, and the one after that, and the one after that) to suffer the consequences of having been that person anyway, Buddhism answers that this is only because we have succumbed to the mistaken idea that there is anything genuinely desirable about personal individuality to begin with. While for the Egyptians the goal of the afterlife journey was a divine or semidivine state in the skies above or the Field of Reeds lying far to the west, and while for the Hindus (especially in their earlier texts) heaven was a fairly worldly and concrete place where humans became larger and more powerful and godlike but remained, in essence, who they had been on earth, for the Tibetans true immortality was impersonal and general, not personal and specific, and to get there you needed to toss off as superficial impediments all those qualities and predilections that you had, during life, mistakenly identified yourself with. Though a person could, in the Buddhist view, definitely reincarnate as a god in one of those heavens, coming to existence there was essentially no better than coming into existence as an animal or insect on earth, or as a devil or hungry ghost in one of the hell regions that Tibetan Buddhism believes lie beneath the earth. This was so because godhood, fun as it might be while it was going on, would eventually come to an end. It had to, because gods, like humans, were individuals, and the individual self wasn't really real. To be a god or goddess might be extremely pleasant (and in terms of pleasures the gods of Buddhist belief have as good a time as any), but those good times counted for nothing in the end precisely because they were *destined to end.* You couldn't be a god forever, because in Buddhism you couldn't be *anything* forever. The only thing that really and truly counted—the "great treasure," as *The Tibetan Book of the Dead* calls it—was full and conscious reawakening to the fact of one's primordial identity with *sunyata.*

Life, in the Tibetan Buddhist view, is divided into a series of parts or chapters, all called *bardos.* (The word doesn't just designate the afterlife, but rather the different segments that go to make up the whole spectrum of existence, the afterlife portion of that existence being one of these individual segments.) *Bardo* is a Tibetan word meaning "gap" or "interval," and each of these intervals presents us with various challenges and opportunities for extricating ourselves, once and for all, from the circular nightmare of incarnate existence through recovery of the knowledge of our timeless identity with *sunyata.* As with the Egyptians, the Tibetan afterlife is structured as a series of zones that the soul must pass through one after another, with the key difference that the ultimate goal is not to join the gods in heaven but to escape the whole merry-go-round of existence once and for all.

This series begins with the Chikhai Bardo, or the Bardo of the Moment of Death. As the physical body dies, *The Tibetan Book of the Dead* explains, sensation gradually decreases, retreating first from the limbs and finally leaving the dying person without any bodily sensation at all and struggling simply to maintain consciousness and ward off increasing feelings of confusion and disorientation.

Once sensation in the physical body is entirely gone, the dying person seeks consolation in the fact that they can still think and make sense of things—can still remember their name, know where they are, and basically remain rooted in their current identity ("I'm John Smith, dying of cancer at Sloan-Kettering Memorial Hospital," etc.). But as death advances, keeping hold of this individual identity—of _sem_— becomes harder to do. Finally one's memory of who and where one is slips away entirely, and the only thing the dying individual has left to cling to is emotions: vague feelings of love or hate left over from their life in the physical body.

Finally, these emotions too give way, and the psyche of the individual—who can no longer remember who or where it is, or what it thinks or doesn't think about anything or anybody in the life just lived—begins to fall to pieces in earnest.

Nothing is more elementally frightening than disintegration—the feeling of losing one's center. Now, as the dying individual, no longer conscious of who they were during life but conscious nonetheless that they were _someone,_ feels a terror more intense than any they ever experienced in life. But at the same time as this terror threatens to overwhelm them, in the midst of this moment of supreme fear and disorientation a fantastic opportunity is said to arise. If all our lives we have identified with _sem_—that superficial part of ourselves that likes this and doesn't like that and basically doesn't last because it isn't really real—we now have the opportunity to make a last-minute team switch and identify ourselves instead with the part of us that *does* last, and that *is* real: with *rigpa*. Like the protagonist in a car chase who has to jump from one speeding vehicle to another before it crashes, our consciousness has the chance to avoid falling apart along with the *sem* part of itself by realizing that it is not, in reality, that part anyhow, but has instead always been *rigpa*.

Consciousness researcher and student of comparative after-life mythologies Stanislav Grof describes this moment, as Tibetan Buddhism lays it out. "At the actual moment of death," he writes, "one has an overwhelming vision of Dharmakaya, or the Primary Clear Light of Pure Reality. [*Dharmakaya* is yet another word, in the nomenclature-heavy world of Eastern religion, for the ultimate reality of *sunyata*.] It is as if the whole of existence suddenly appeared in its absolute totality and in an entirely abstract form. In this experience, all dualities are transcended. Agony and ecstasy, good and evil, beauty and ugliness, burning heat and freezing cold, all coexist in one undifferentiated whole. Ultimate enlightenment and total insanity seem to be equally plausible interpretations of this experience."

Quite a situation. But—and this of course is, for Buddhism, the all-important point: "In the last analysis, the *Dharmakaya* is identical with the experiencer's own consciousness, which has no birth and no death, and is by its very nature the Immutable Light. If one recognizes this truth and has been prepared by systematic practice for the immensity of this experience, the vision of the *Dharmakaya* offers a unique opportunity for instant spiritual liberation. Those who let themselves be deterred, and shy away from the *Dharmakaya,* will have another chance immediately after death when the Secondary Clear Light dawns upon them. If they miss this opportunity as well, they will be involved in a complicated sequence of spiritual adventures with an entire pantheon of blissful and wrathful deities, during which their consciousness becomes progressively more estranged from the liberating truth as they are approaching another rebirth."

It's like being in a very complicated dream, at the very beginning of which we have a brief, glancing moment of waking up. Something—a sound in the kitchen or the singing of a bird outside—almost stirs us out of sleep. But instead, for most of us, the moment passes. We roll over and plunge back down into a deep, dream-filled slumber. In each new stage of the adventure after missing that first opportunity for liberation, the soul will experience yet another moment when it will be possible to waken from its sleep, when it will be given a glimpse of the higher realms of spirit that can, at least potentially, jolt it back into remembrance of its core identity with *sunyata*. But for most people these chances will again be missed, and the dreams—along with all the assorted wonders and terrors they contain—will continue.

> The real me was up there; not this here [pointing to her physical body].
>
> —near-death subject, quoted in
> Kenneth Ring's *Life at Death*

Though it is as packed with events and as crowded with flamboyant gods and goddesses as its Egyptian counterpart, the Tibetan afterlife journey is, in the end, an adventure that is important not because of the things that go on during it and the beings that one meets, but for those occasional opportunities for escape it offers: opportunities when the reincarnating soul entity can see past all the nonsense of life *and* death, catch a glimpse of the clear light of *sunyata,* and find its way back to conscious identity with it once and for all. If one grabs this chance (and Tibetan spiritual practitioners train for lifetimes in order to do so), one vanishes into the clear light, leaving the chains of cyclic existence behind forever. If not (as is much more likely), the newly dead person will be sucked into the remaining stages of the afterlife process, the next step of which is entrance into the Chonyid Bardo, or the Bardo of the Luminosity of the True Nature. In this *bardo,* the newly dead soul is confronted with a succession of alternately terrifying and alluring spiritual beings. These rise up before it much like the supernatural beings of Egyptian afterlife belief arose before the Egyptian soul in his or her journey through its own afterlife realm.

But in the Tibetan version of the game, the way to win against each new adversary is always the same: one must recognize it as a being that only appears to be real, but in truth is nonexistent, a mirage, basically. If, by the end of this long series of confrontations with imaginary beings, the postmortem soul has failed to understand that each deity of lust or fear or anger that has arisen before it was really just a projection of its own mind, the game continues in a new zone called the Bardo of Becoming.

Here conditions change a bit—and largely for the better. As Sogyal Rinpoche says in an essay in Gary Doore's anthology *Who Survives?,* the soul "now possesses a 'mental body' that has a number of characteristics: it is very light and lucid, the consciousness is nine times clearer than in earthly life, and it possesses clairvoyance and other miraculous powers. This body is similar to the body of the previous existence, but perfectly complete and in the prime of life. It can move unobstructed almost anywhere and can travel just by thinking, although its only light is a dim glow that illuminates the space directly in front of it."

If these new powers and characteristics of the soul sound familiar, this is because they are the ones that countless subjects of modern near-death experiences have described having during the time when they were out of their physical bodies. Nor are these the only similarities between this portion of the Tibetan afterlife journey and a classic NDE. In the Bardo of Becoming, says Sogyal Rinpoche, the deceased also undergoes a life review, "repeating all the experiences that it had in life; returning to places where it even spat just once [that is, places where it committed even the most minor of karmic infractions]; suffering all kind of terrors; and having precognitive visions of where it is to be reborn. At first, not realizing that it is dead, the consciousness of the deceased tries to converse with its family, only to be tremendously distressed when it receives no response. Finally, however, when it sees its relatives weeping, disposing of its possessions, and not laying its place at the table, it realizes that it is dead. Moreover, it finds that it can see and converse with the many other travelers it meets in the bardo world."

> **Why did you bring me back?**
>> —first words of resuscitated heart attack victim to
>> his doctor following a near-death experience

Though Raymond Moody was the first person to bring the modern NDE to mass attention, he was not the only or even the first person to have become aware of the phenomenon—that is, of the fact that people who undergo brushes with death have often had inexplicably vivid experiences of leaving their body and traveling, with their personalities entirely intact, to worlds beyond the physical. At the time Moody was writing his book, in Sweden a Lutheran minister named Johann Christoph Hampe was working on one of his own, called *Sterben ist doch ganz anders.* Translated into English in 1979 as *To Die Is Gain,* it was seen by considerably fewer readers than the 14 million who have read Moody's to date. But Hampe's is just as important a book, for it focuses even more than Moody's on the intensely personal and individual quality that NDEs tend to have. Hampe's work shows, even more clearly than Moody's, that while NDEs may differ in their minor details, if there is one thing that near-death experiences are *not,* it's impersonal.

In the initial phases of the near-death experience, Hampe writes, "the dying person finds that he is growing beyond the organic and mental categories, in which our individuality expresses itself, into a higher form; and yet he remains conscious of still surviving as a person—the person belonging to the soul which bears his name." The dying individual "lets go without himself being let go of; he achieves surrender without being lost; he is resolved but not dissolved; he thinks that he belongs to a greater whole without thereby being himself any less."

This is a little on the abstract side, but what it points out is the key difference between ancient Eastern and modern Western ideas about and experiences of what happens when we die. According to the near-death experience as outlined by

Hampe, when we leave the physical body behind, we become *more,* not less, personal; more of the person who we had been on earth, not less. Not only does the individual personality not pop into complete and total nonexistence (as the materialists would have it), and not only do we not relinquish the intricate and fathomless personal attributes that made us who we truly were during our physical life (as traditional Eastern faiths and especially Buddhism believe), but we instead recover our best and deepest selves in the most personal and individual sense imaginable. Far from evaporating, the "me" part of us assumes its true size and stature for the first time ever. (In the words of one of the NDE subjects I spoke to at *Guideposts,* "When you die, you get bigger.") In this view, it turns out that we were never able to be our full selves while on earth because (and this idea should now sound familiar) we never completely went down to begin with. What we go through at death, then, is the equivalent of a triumphant and completely surprising recovery of a larger, smarter, better self that we had forgotten about in the course of descending into our physical body and making our way through the terrible amnesia-and-obstacle course of incarnate life.

"Widely though these accounts differ," writes Hampe of the stories he uncovered, "they unite in saying one thing: the consciousness of the dying person by no means becomes feebler and feebler, like a dying candle. . . . On the contrary, it undergoes an unheard-of intensification, such as it had hardly ever experienced in life." When we die, according to this view, we become what we never had a chance to become in life, for the simple reason that life never gave us the room to be able to completely do so. "This new 'I,'" says NDE subject Stefan von

Jankovich in Hampe's book, "was not the I that I knew, but rather a distilled essence of it, yet something vaguely familiar, something I had always known buried under a superstructure of personal fears, hopes, wants and needs. This 'I' was final, unchangeable, indivisible, indestructible pure spirit. While unique and individual as a fingerprint, 'I' was, at the same time, part of some infinite, harmonious and ordered whole. I had been there before."

This vision of death completely reverses the scheme of the Tibetan model, where the emphasis is always on the impermanence of our personal selves and their eventual dissolution as we struggle to return to the all-encompassing void of *sunyata*. "The initial stage of dying seems," says Hampe of the people who underwent near-death experiences that he interviewed, "like an awakening. They find that their consciousness is intensified. It is drawn together, perhaps in the head, or at a particular point in the head. The authors of the reports maintain that they were calm, collected, and lucid, when they suddenly saw themselves confronted with the conviction of being outside their bodies."

The initial phase of what Hampe calls the "exit of the self" involves that self "staying near the body, but elevated above it. The self observes its own body and its nearby surroundings from the outside, without interest and without regret. Then the self retreats from its body, attempts to leave it, reaches the open. . . . The self tries to find another reality or soon finds itself in one. . . . A strange, new bodily state was experienced, weightless and full of light. . . . The exit of the self is only the first step which the dying person takes and is the pre-condition for everything else that he experiences afterwards."

Again, while this is similar to the descriptions of what happens at death in *The Tibetan Book of the Dead,* at the same time it's *not* similar. This notion that our personal individualities—the *sem* part of us—isn't transitory and illusory but real and lasting, and is in fact so huge that we can *only* come into full contact with it when we leave this world behind, is a hallmark not just of Hampe's book but the great majority of near-death experiences. In a nutshell, what contemporary NDEs tell us is that when we die we rejoin a larger part of the universe, one that in life was largely hidden from us, and that in doing so, *we don't have to leave behind the person we had been on earth.* In fact, in many of these narratives the individual consciousness expands so much that you could say that *it is only in death that we know the true dimensions of our individuality to begin with.*

So which, if either, of these views is correct? Must we, if we are interested in finding a map of the beyond that we can genuinely believe in and draw inspiration from, choose between the death experience as it is outlined in *The Tibetan Book of the Dead* or as it is described in contemporary near-death literature? Instead of simply jettisoning one or the other perspective, might there be a way of marrying these two views so that *neither* is denied and both are, in their different ways, affirmed?

To find out, we need to go back to the *Chonyid Bardo,* and that stretch of *The Tibetan Book of the Dead* that sounds so similar, in the experiences it describes, to modern NDEs. If we really listen to what is going on there, without getting distracted by what the rest of the book says about the unimportance of the individual personality, we discover that *The Tibetan Book of the Dead* agrees with the view of modern NDE subjects that after death not only do we retain our earthly individuality, but (during this period at least) our personality actually *expands,* becoming truly godlike. We can, while in this zone of the Tibetan afterlife trajectory, move wherever we want, either on the earth or in the worlds above. We can know the thoughts of others and recall our past lives. Our power to act and our ability to think, in other words, has ballooned out, so that the consciousness we possessed on earth suddenly seems, by comparison, hopelessly cramped and limited.

Sure, it all passes. But at least for a moment *The Tibetan Book of the Dead* seems to grant us everything that, in life, we've ever dreamed of wanting. For the fact of the matter is that Buddhism is as ready as any other of the world's religions to acknowledge that in life, what we really want is to become gods. We want to attain to those elusive yet persistent intimations of being *more* than we are right now that haunt us through all our lives: possibilities that are gone practically the same moment they appear, but that have made human beings, for all of history and no doubt long before it, feel like it is our secret destiny, and perhaps even our inbuilt right as products of the universe that has brought us forth, to become beings who are much more than the ones we are right now.

One of the elements most often remarked upon in modern near-death experiences is the "white light" that the newly dead soul often glimpses at the very beginning of the afterlife journey. The theoretician of consciousness Ken Wilber identifies this white light with the *Dharmakaya,* the subtle light of pure reality, which, as we described, the newly dead person also glimpses briefly at the beginning of the Tibetan version of the afterlife journey (and which it usually doesn't recognize).

"The experience of the subtle-level light," Wilber writes, "is very pleasant—in fact, amazingly blissful. Indeed, people who have had NDEs report that they have never experienced any-thing as peaceful, as profound, as blissful. But we need to keep in mind that all of the experiences up to this point are molded by the 'lifetime indestructible drop.'"

The "lifetime indestructible drop" is the part of the soul that, in Tibetan Buddhism, is identified with *sem* and is to be distinguished from the "eternally indestructible drop" that is identified with *rigpa*. "Drop" is really an unfortunate term for this entity, it seems to me, since for most of us in the West the term doesn't conjure up anything that we would ordinarily identify with our deepest inner selves. Defining what the "eter-nally indestructible drop" actually means has proved a brutally daunting task for even the most accomplished interpreters of Buddhism to Western readers. The Buddhist scholar Robert Thurman, for example, takes the following heroic shot at the task.

This entity, says Thurman (clearly not exaggerating), is "very hard to describe or understand." It is also, he says, "not to be misconstrued as a rigid, fixed identity." It is "beyond body-mind duality" and "consists of the finest, most sensitive, alive, and intelligent energy in the universe. It is a being's deepest state of pure soul, where the being is intelligent light, alive and singular, continuous yet changing, aware of its infinite inter-connection with everything."

Not long after the soul has caught a glimpse of this pure white light, the lesser "drop" (that is, the "lifetime indestruc-tible drop") is shed. And along with it, writes Wilber, goes "all the personal memories and impressions and specifics of this particular life." With all this personal stuff left behind, the

eternally indestructible drop then moves into the *bardo* state
lying fully beyond the physical body. "And thereupon," continues Wilber, "commences the bardo ordeal—a real nightmare
unless one is familiar with these states through meditation."

What Wilber is here suggesting is that the warm, cozy, and
above all *personal* qualities of the near-death experience as we
tend to hear about it these days (the stuff, that is, that my father
in his last days was so anxious to hear about) are but the first,
friendly parts of a journey that, in its later chapters, is not nearly
so friendly, and not in the least bit personal. Like an automo-
bile on a reverse assembly line, the soul, in the Tibetan version
of the afterlife journey, gets slowly disassembled, the stages of
this disassembly being alternately agonizing or blissful. When
this savagely intense process is at last finished, it then reverses
and the impersonal soul essence, provided that it has missed all
the various chances offered to it along the way to extricate itself
from the process of birth and rebirth, sinks back down to the
realm of earth (or wherever in the Tibetan Buddhist universe
it is slated to reincarnate) for another go-around. If it's another
human incarnation that's in order, the descending soul essence
at a certain point sees a bluish light emanating from the earthly
realm, and then glimpses its future parents having sex. The
sight fills the ready-to-be-reborn soul with feelings of lust and
jealousy, and—depending on which partner it feels the lust for,
and which the jealousy—it reenters the stream of physical life
in either a male or female body.

There is little disputing that *The Tibetan Book of the Dead*
represents an extraordinary high point in the world's spiritual
literature on the afterlife state, or that Buddhism in general
has, through centuries-long cultivation of advanced meditative

states, uncovered truths about the nature of consciousness that the modern world ignores to its detriment. If we want to learn about what happens after death, and if we want to consult the wisdom of former cultures on the matter, it is to it that we must first turn.

But at the same time, it may be that though we should have the highest respect for its descriptions of the nature of consciousness and of reality at large, it may be a mistake to take *The Tibetan Book of the Dead*'s images completely at their word. The worlds of experience lying beyond bodily life are, by definition, *beyond* what we can fully envision while down here in the physical world. It therefore makes sense to see each vision of the life beyond offered by the world's different spiritual traditions as precisely that: images that are particular to each culture that has developed them, and that cannot be imported into another culture without modification. If we are spiritually and psychologically different people than the dynastic Egyptians or Tibetan monks who created the most sophisticated and elaborate afterlife maps of the past, then our map of the afterlife must differ to the degree that our psychological realities differ from theirs.

This doesn't mean the older views were entirely wrong. But it *does* mean that when we attempt the very challenging task of formulating in language the realities of life beyond the body, we must use our *own* language and the cultural understandings that come along with it. For just as a drawing of a sheep or a house or a flower made by an artist in the twelfth century CE or the third millennium BCE differs from a drawing of one of those subjects done in the twentieth century (even while the subject of each picture will still most likely remain recognizable as what it is), so it might be that both the Egyptian and Tibetan books of the dead are describing the same *realities,* but in a different way. While these are realities that all of us will encounter after the death of our bodies, whether we like it or not, the details with which they are described by those traditions are not *our* details. And when you get down to it, consulting the works of completely foreign cultures on so intimate a matter as the fate of the individual person at death is a little bit like sending away to Egypt for a street map of New Jersey. On one level, from century to century the human condition doesn't change. But on another level it very much *does* change, and if we are to obey our inner urgings and take the idea of postmortem survival seriously, we need a description of what that life may be like that speaks in modern, not ancient, language and that takes the very particular realities and discoveries of our modern world completely into account.

So how do we do this?

By adding, we'll suggest in the next chapter, a single word to our vocabulary.

4

The Need for a Single Map, the Imaginary and the Imaginal, What the Brain Does (and Doesn't) Do, and the Nonlocal Nature of Consciousness

W hen it comes to what people think or don't think about the afterlife these days, there is a fairly clear group of categories they fall into.

First of all, there are the materialists: the people who believe that human beings are carbon-based, biological organisms that the laws of physics and natural selection created blindly over the course of millions of years of evolution: no more, and no less. When we die, the holders of this view argue, no afterlife of any sort awaits us, and our consciousness will simply blip back into nothingness like the picture on a dropped television screen. And that, for this group, is pretty much the end of the discussion.

The rest—that is, the people who feel that we are in fact something *more* than our doomed-to-die bodies—can be divided into three general groups:

- Believers in traditional religious faiths—in America largely Christians—who doggedly hold to tenets and traditions born largely in times now long past, in the face of a modern world that is constantly threatening to pull these beliefs from their hands and discard them.
- Western converts to the Eastern faiths—primarily Hinduism and Buddhism—who struggle, with greater or lesser degrees of success, to marry ancient Eastern concepts like karma and reincarnation to the realities of modern life.
- Believers in the broad category of ideas covered by the term *new age*. This is the category that much of the contemporary writing and thinking about near-death experiences tends to fall under. (Though certainly not all of it. Moody and Hampe, for example, are both Christians, and Christian ideas penetrate much modern near-death imagery, even when the narrators don't style themselves as specifically Christian in their beliefs.)

Many more groups could, of course, be added to this list: students of occult and esoteric religious philosophies like the Kabbalah; followers of Native American, aboriginal, and other traditional/primordial belief systems . . . and so on. Needless to say, there is a lot of overlap between groups. There are new age Christians, there are Jews with some Buddhist beliefs. Nonetheless, these are the lines that come most immediately into view when we try to categorize the different things that people believe or don't believe about the spiritual world these days.

But the most important thing about these spiritual views is

precisely that they are different. In our pluralistic world, open-ness to multiple perspectives is essential if we are even remotely interested in getting along with the other people who live on the planet with us and engaging in meaningful interchange with them. But the fact remains that being genuinely open to other people's views of reality is inevitably to cripple one's own view of that reality, for to acknowledge the validity of other perspectives is to pull the rug out from one's own.

This, in a nutshell, has been the whole problem of religion and philosophy in the modern world, and it's no coincidence that when postmodern philosophers talk about the difficulty of reconciling different worldviews, it isn't long before the subject of death shows up in the conversation. For if the visible world alone can be truly known, and if arguments about what lies or doesn't lie beyond the physical are just that—empty talk, devoid of any solid grounding in reality—then death is always going to be what interrupts the conversation.

In the past, before the world became so hopelessly crowded with conflicting opinions and worldviews, many people were given, at birth, a single vision of the structure and meaning of human life, and a single picture of what waits beyond the body. Without such a single, believable map of the soul and its destiny, our chances for living a life that is in any genuine way happy become considerably slimmer. Yet we are told by many voices today that such a map is no longer possible.

Can we have our cake and eat it, too? Can we be open to and respectful of the philosophies and worldviews of other peo-ple, yet at the same time have a view of our own life that allows it to stretch out beyond the borders of personal death? Can we have, in short, a single vision of ourselves that shows us to be real spiritual beings within a cosmos that genuinely has larger plans for us, yet that also makes room for other perspectives? (Or at least spiritual ones. Straight materialism is another matter, for it is comfortable only in a single section of the world; a section that all other perspectives insist is not all there is but merely one among many other equally real ones.)

The key to answering this question might lie in adopting a single word into our vocabularies.

That word is *imaginal.*

Though *imaginal* doesn't appear in most dictionaries (and my computer underlines it in red every time I type it), the word has in fact been around since at least the seventeenth century. However, it first began to be used in the distinctively modern way that I intend it only in the late nineteenth century, by a poet and classical scholar named Frederic W. H. Myers. In the sense Myers used it, the word *imaginal* describes a kind of perception not defined by the simple distinctions between real and unreal, actual and imaginary, that we members of the materialistic modern world so often unconsciously let govern the way we think. It describes, instead, a state of things in which what we see in front of us is neither entirely real nor entirely imaginary, but *both at once.*

Most of us go about our day-to-day activities taking it for granted that the world is divided into two basic halves. There's the three-dimensional, rock-solid, "real" world that exists "out there," beyond our skins. And then there is another world, much more vague and mushy by comparison, that exists "in here"—inside our bodies, and in particular, inside our heads. The things that go on in our minds ("in here") might be more personal, and often more interesting, than what's going on in the physical world ("out there"). But those things are also, we tend to assume, less real. The "real world," after all, does what it does and is what it is, regardless of what we think or don't think about it.

At least, that's what we used to think it did. But, as physicists discovered at the beginning of the twentieth century with the advent of quantum mechanics, it turns out that the plain physical world that we think exists "out there" is actually a fiction. On a subatomic level, the observer is an active part of what he or she sees, and there quite simply is no such thing as completely detached observation.

The American philosopher and pioneering psychologist William James anticipated these insights when he pointed out that unprocessed perceptual data doesn't come at us ready-made, but is, in its unpackaged state, a "great blooming, buzzing confusion," which we assemble into something meaningful and coherent—something we can actually understand and deal with—by following rules of perception that the society we are born into teaches us virtually from the moment of our birth. (A clear and powerful illustration of this occurs when people blind from birth recover their sight as adults. Far from suddenly seeing the world around them with the clarity and coherence that people who can see from birth have, these people need to go through a lengthy, and often quite unpleasant, period of training in order to learn to interpret—in fact, to construct—a coherent picture of the visible world out of the raw data their eyes are suddenly transmitting to their brains.)

This doesn't mean that the physical world is a pure product of our fantasy. It's out there, all right. But it *does* mean that all perception is creative to some degree, and that in order to see the outside world in an ordered and meaningful way, we first need to do a great deal of stuff to it: stuff that we are normally unconscious of because we do it automatically. All experience is, to one degree or another, "generated" experience. Everything in the world that we see "out there" is actually manufactured by us, at least in part, through a collaboration between the secret, creative part of our minds and the unprocessed, blooming, buzzing raw material of the physical universe: a universe that is in fact not even made up of solid stuff at all, but rather of relationships between patterns of energy that in themselves, if we look deep and hard enough at them, dissolve from energy into something even more indistinct and hard to pin down, something that some scientists have suggested is itself akin to or even identical with consciousness.

The poet William Blake put all this more simply when he said: "A fool sees not the same tree that a wise man sees." What Blake meant by this was not just that we create, in part, what we see, but that as a result of this, our experience of the world is really much more personal and individual—much more *ours*— than we tend to realize. Everything we do, every person we see, every song we hear, every book we read, is experienced by us in a manner so uniquely our own that these things as we know them actually *need us to come into existence at all.* To a very real extent, a song I like and listen to again and again over the years, and that conjures up a world of familiar associations each time I hear it, only exists as the profoundly complex object that I experience it to be thanks to the individual work that I've done on it. (This is, of course, why it's often so disappointing to meet the creators of works of art—be they songs or books or poems or whatever—that have affected us strongly. We expect the creator of the work to be the creator of the work *specifically as we've experienced it.* But they can never be that person, for the simple reason that the person we *really* want to meet when we meet these people is, at least in part, that hidden part of ourselves that collaborated to make their work so personally meaningful to us in the first place.)

The only world that we can truly know is the world we know personally. The completely impersonal, completely objective, completely "out there" world just isn't there.

But what if, granting that this is the case in life, it is even *more* the case in death? What if in death, too, a world is waiting to encounter us, and that it too is partially independent of us and partially in need of our participation . . . *but to a greater degree than it is in life*? It may be that unlike the world we encounter "down here" in earthly life, the world up there is infinitely more malleable to our directing imaginations, infinitely more ready to take on the shape and nature we want it to. In this transphysical dimension, perceiver and perceived may interact in such a way that the mark of the observer lies much more strongly upon what he or she observes—even though in both cases, it remains true that there really is an observer, and there really is a world that he or she is observing.

In other words, it may be that just as we cannot live in the physical world in anything but a completely personal way, neither can we live in the world beyond this one in that way. Just as there is no such thing as a generic path through life—just as each life takes place in the first-person singular—so there is no such thing as an impersonal path through the worlds waiting after the death of the body. It is a journey that individuals take, and individuals alone.

The Tibetan Book of the Dead actually suggests as much itself. "For most Westerners," Sogyal Rinpoche writes, "the forms of the visions detailed in *The Tibetan Book of the Dead* may seem quite strange and unfamiliar. Everybody, being composed of the same psychological components and elements, will experience visions of one form or another. Western people, however, will probably experience them in forms that are more familiar to them, according to their cultural conditioning. The important thing about these visions is not what particular form they may take, but how a person *relates* to them. Their form merely provides a reference point for the practitioner, who is able to attune himself or herself to the energy, luminosity, and quality of the vision."

What's interesting here is that Buddhism, the supremely impersonal religion, ends up making the same basic point that all perception is absolutely personal and individual—that each of us, both here in the physical world and even more in the trans-physical world, perceives a world *that is his or her own and no one else's*. As the psychologist and near-death specialist David Fontana writes: "The *bardo* teachings are compatible to those of the West in that they insist the mind plays a major role in creating the experiences met with in the initial stages of the afterlife. However, there is no mention of the houses, countryside, trees and flowers in the *bardo* that we find in the Western literature because such things were not a feature of Tibetan culture, and even had they been the Bardo Thodol would have dismissed them as illusory memories of earth life, and insisted that instead of being attracted to them they should be disregarded so that the mind can concentrate upon the reality behind appearances."

In other words, whatever we make of the unfamiliar and often quite unsettling imagery in *The Tibetan Book of the Dead,* the last thing we should do is take these descriptions completely at face value. "If a Westerner were to find him or herself in the Buddhist *bardo,*" writes Fontana, "the result would be not only confusion but probably terror. Imagine dying in a Kentish village with white houses and apple orchards and the drowsy sunshine of a summer afternoon and then finding oneself in a rocky windswept landscape peopled with wrathful Tibetan deities brandishing bloodstained swords. The Westerner could hardly expect to realize that these visions are in fact helpful symbols, well known to Tibetans, of the forces that destroy ignorance. Similarly, imagine the Tibetan villager trying to make sense of an afterlife of white houses and apple orchards and a British summer."

But again, if this means that the world we enter after death can accurately be described as essentially a *mental* one, this doesn't mean that the stuff we find there isn't there at all. According, once again, to William Blake, who got many of his ideas on this subject from the seventeenth-century scientist and mystic Emanuel Swedenborg, the imagination is "the divine bosom into which we shall all go after the death of the Vegetated body." This statement is hard to get much of a purchase on until we realize that what Blake is talking about is not "imagination" in the sense of our ability to create unreal images within our minds, but rather a whole dimension of being: one which we enter when we leave the physical body, and which is less dense, less stubbornly immovable, *but equally real.*

When we die, in this view, we go to *another real place.* But the rules of this place are different from those that govern the material one we are in right now. Our active imaginations, after a lifetime of collaborating with physical reality, and doing so as the less powerful partner in the alliance, are suddenly much more free, much more in charge of things; they are in a realm of being in which, whether they want to be doing so or not, they are able to actively create much more of that reality than they did when they were in the physical world.

This can also be, however, where the problems arise. For after a lifetime in the physical dimension, we are so often out of touch with the large but generally unconscious part we play in creating our daily reality that when we die we can suddenly find ourselves at the mercy of this unconscious creative power in ourselves, watching—and actually finding ourselves *within*—its productions, without having any control over what is happening to us. We're driving the car, but because we don't know we're driving the car, we are unable to control where we go in it.

Life in the physical world is, from the perspective of these dangers that await us beyond it, both a curse and a blessing. In life we are at the nonstop beck and call of physical issues— having to clothe, shelter, and feed ourselves, having to negotiate the absolutely endless and incessant demands that the physical body and the physical world make upon us. When we die, the tables are turned. Suddenly the physical world has no more dominion over us whatsoever, and our interior being—that mysterious command center that throughout life we envisioned vaguely as lying just behind our eyes—is now handed the controls and left to run the show for better or worse.

All this explains the Buddhist emphasis on getting in touch with those hidden parts of the psyche while still alive: on learning to control those parts of our mind that really and truly produce so much of what we perceive, but that we so often allow ourselves to imagine just happen of themselves without our input. For if we are not in touch with those parts in life, in death we will find ourselves completely at their mercy.

The poet John Milton's observation that each of us has the power to make a hell of heaven or a heaven of hell is infinitely more the case when we cut loose from the stubborn anchor of physical existence. The world that waits beyond this one is, it would seem, a much more elastic place than the one we currently inhabit: in the world beyond, things don't "hold still" the way they do when we are in the physical world. Reality shifts and moves; the ordinary rules of time and space are collapsed, the way they so often are in dreams. Yet at the same time, what transpires there has nothing of the unreality of dreams. For though Buddhism describes the postmortem state as being fundamentally "unreal," we have to place this declaration within the general context of the *entire* Buddhist view of reality, which is a view that sees every level of existence as unreal save for the highest level—the level of *sunyata*. If the afterlife world is fundamentally unreal for Buddhists, and Hindus as well, so too, it should be remembered, is the fire hydrant at the end of the street. The bottom line is that the landscape of the afterlife is more malleable to our imaginations than this world is, but this does not mean that it is less real than the world we are in right now. Instead—and hard as this may be for us to picture—it is *more* real.

In the world beyond this one, what we see is a manifestation of who we are. Not who we are on the surface, but who we are in terms of that fathomless kernel of essential identity that Buddhism calls the indestructible drop, and that the gospels describe as the pearl of great price. In the Tibetan view, this inner essential self contains the results of all the good, all the not so good, and all the genuinely bad actions we committed while alive, and once we have died the nature of our inner character acts as the projection room for the series of intensely real and intensely personal mini-movies that the newly dead soul finds itself watching. The afterlife is a place where, as the poet and student of afterlife philosophies William Butler Yeats put it, "imagination is now the world." As such it has a novelistic depth and subtlety to it. The afterlife is, quite simply, *as complex as we are.* This is terrifying, but it is also the single most fantastically positive piece of news we could ever hear, and the cure for every variety of modern despair. For if the world beyond the body is a place where our full and fathomless interior complexity is allowed to emerge and truly exist, it means that we might actually be the secret larger beings that humans have, since the dawn of history, hoped to be.

Does the brain survive death? Clearly not. But does that then mean *we* don't survive? Only if we accept a dogma that, though it is constantly drilled into us, the members of cultures past were not at all as sure about as we are:

The brain produces thought.

What is the brain? Anyone wishing to uncover what does or doesn't happen to consciousness when life ceases has, in our modern world at least, to ask this question. This is because for the last few hundred years, it has become ever more obvious that the brain is the seat of consciousness.

This fact wasn't nearly as obvious to the peoples of the past as it seems to be to us. If asked to point toward his or her "center," to the place that is most *them,* many an individual from times and cultures past would have pointed not to their head but to their heart. Some people still do this today, of course, but the fact remains that the majority of us in the modern, science-dominated world identify ourselves with our brains much more than the members of previous cultures did. Without the brain, we have been taught, there is no consciousness—and with no consciousness there is no personality. The physicist Stephen Hawking spoke for much of the scientific community when he said in a recent interview: "I regard the brain as a computer which will stop working when its components fail. There is no heaven or afterlife for broken-down computers; that is a fairy story for people afraid of the dark."

But is it really as cut-and-dried as that? If pressed further—if asked, that is, just exactly how this extraordinarily subtle and sophisticated sense of "me"-ness that each of us feels manages to exist in the cramped and mushy darkness inside our skulls—most of us will conjure up a picture of brain synapses: of delicate, twig-like ganglia sparking little electrical connections between themselves. Millions upon millions of these, we will suggest, somehow not only generate our ability to be blurrily conscious of the world around us as infants, to do our multiplication tables as schoolchildren, to master feats of architecture or mathematics as adults, but also are responsible for all those inexplicably significant little feelings that drift though our minds every day. The minute little sparks of joy or dips of melancholy . . . all the impossibly subtle and personal sensations that go together to make up our inner existence: all this mysterious and fathomlessly magical psychic wilderness is, we will (if we are loyal members of the modern materialistic world) suggest, the result of those countless neuronal synaptic connections, firing away in our brains.

These neurons, and these spark-like connections, do of course exist. But when it comes to the question of whether all those billions upon billions of connections are in fact capable of creating the sense of personal identity that each of us feels so solidly and stably (at least if we are mentally healthy), the jury is actually very much still out: much more out, in fact, than most people realize. Work among scientists, primarily but not exclusively neuroscientists, increasingly suggests that the argument that consciousness is dependent on the body, and more specifically the brain, cannot be argued with anything like the immovable certainty that most scientists used to (and often, as Hawking shows, still do) believe it could.

Scientists have in recent years become very good at watching brain activity as it happens. The invention of the electro-encephalogram has allowed them to measure electrical activity in the cerebral cortex, while the functional magnetic resonance imaging technique, or fMRI, has allowed them to measure differences in rates of blood flow to the brain's 100 billion nerve cells. All this observation has taught us a number of surprising things about the brain. One is that the various styles of thinking of which humans are capable (analytical, emotional, etc.) are not strictly localizable to one or another section of the brain, even though certain sections of the brain may specialize in certain kinds of thought. Against expectation, it has been proved that people with severely damaged brains, or brains severely reduced in size due to birth defects, can perform mental tasks equal to or beyond those performed by people with normal brains. If the brain is imagined as a "wet computer," storing information along the same lines that a computer does, these people should not be able to do the things they do.

But the most surprising thing about the brain that this research has uncovered has been stated very clearly by a Dutch cardiologist and specialist in near-death experiences named Pim van Lommel. "There is no direct evidence," Van Lommel writes, "to prove if and how neurons in the brain produce the subjective essence of our consciousness."

Brain activity is measurable. And brain activity takes place when we think. It is clearly evident in the changes in blood flow and electrochemical activity that technology now makes it possible to monitor. Whatever consciousness is, it is correlated with brain activity. It is intimately tied up with these tiny physical goings-on within the gray matter in our heads. Not only that, but the process goes both ways. Thinking—or not thinking—certain things can affect the actual neurological structure of the brain, while damaging part of the brain can affect our ability to think correctly, or to think at all. But despite all that, scientists have had no luck in demonstrating that consciousness—that mysterious thing that each of us experiences every second of our waking and sleeping life, and that makes each of us ourselves—actually comes from the brain. *Brain activity isn't consciousness,* and all attempts at finding a neural basis for it have so far come up with nothing.

Not only can consciousness not be nailed down to one particular spot in the brain, however. Its origin can't be found anywhere in the physical world. Summing up his own research, Van Lommel comes up with the following extremely bold statement: "On the basis of prospective studies of near-death experience, recent results from neurophysiological research, and concepts from quantum physics, I strongly believe that consciousness cannot be located in a particular time and place. This is known as nonlocality. Complete and endless consciousness is everywhere in a dimension that is not tied to time or place, where past, present, and future all exist and are accessible at the same time."

The brain is the single most complex physical object known so far in the universe. But this does not mean that it is responsible for actually creating our identities, that it is the maker of who and what we really are.

But if the brain doesn't necessarily produce thought and consciousness, where else might those things come from?

Maybe from the place where the vast majority of peoples over the vast majority of time have always said they do: that same somewhere else that the soul itself comes from, before it builds up, from the elements at hand, the physical body that it uses during its time on earth.

The general name for the theory that consciousness comes from a transphysical source and is then mediated by the physical brain is called the transmission or filter model of consciousness, and has been around for a little over a century. According to this theory, instead of being a machine that generates the fleeting, temporary, and essentially insubstantial phenomena of our individual, interior identities, the brain actually functions as a kind of "reducing valve" (to use a term that Aldous Huxley came up with about sixty years ago), which, while it allows individual consciousness to function in the physical world, does not actually *create* that consciousness.

Though today more scientists than, say, fifty years ago are open to the question of whether there is more to human personality than the physical brain, such scientists are still very definitely in the minority. Psychologists, as a whole, aren't much interested in the question, either.

As a young man, David Fontana was obsessed with the question of what happens to one's inner self at death. Why, he wondered, weren't more people interested in this question? "My interest in such things," he writes, "was one of the reasons why, in due course, I became a psychologist, since I assumed that psychology was about the mind and just possibly had something to say about the soul (since the term 'psychology' in fact derives from *pukhe,* the Greek word for soul)."

He soon realized his mistake. The discipline of psychology, he writes, "has taught me a great deal about the brain, and about human behavior, emotions, personality and much more besides. For 40 years I have been in love with the subject and my love is as strong as ever. But as with all branches of science its approach is firmly based in the physical world, and as such it can only take us so far. Science and the scientific method pause before non-physical realities such as mind and the soul. Science studies the brain, which is a physical organ, but the assumption that the mind is no more than a function of the brain and therefore also physical is just that, an assumption. Certainly when the mind is active there are electrical changes in the brain, but electrical changes are not the mind."

It seems that if we in the modern world are going to insist upon looking at the brain as a machine, the evidence is growing that we need to envision it as a machine that consciousness "climbs into" for a time, somewhat (to use an oversimple but nonetheless apt image) like a soldier climbing into a tank. The brain, like the tank, is solid and substantial. Thanks to it, the individual may navigate the physical realm for a time, interacting with other objects in that realm and being acted upon by them in turn. Like the tank, the brain is useful for getting around, for making one's presence known, and in general for getting things done down here in the purely physical dimension. But it is also hugely limiting and constricting, and it is possible that it is only by virtue of our being so used to dwelling within the "tank" of our bodies and brains for so long that we have become accustomed to the really rather extraordinary limitations it places upon us. So accustomed, in fact, that like someone trapped in a dream, remembering certain things about the way things really are but inconveniently forgetting some others, most of us can no longer recall or even imagine that we ever possessed any other kind of existence at all.

If the filter model is right, we will eventually have to shake ourselves free of the idea that the brain produces thought. We will need to learn how to see our identities, and the thoughts and memories and feelings and personal ideas that define those identities, not as brain-created phenomena, not as the simple result of neurons firing within the gray matter encased in our skulls, but as *metaphysical* phenomena: that is, as phenomena that the brain and all the impossibly complex processes within it reflect, but for which those processes are not alone responsible. We will have to learn to conceive of consciousness, thought, emotion, and identity—everything, in other words, that we think of as most *us*—as something more than the brilliantly electrified mush inside our skulls.

We have, now, a concept (the imaginal dimension) and an idea (the brain doesn't necessarily produce thought) that, when brought together, give us an entirely new perspective on the fate not just of consciousness, but of our particular, individual, personal consciousness after the body has been left behind. A perspective that allows us to continue to believe in the existence of the spirit in the age of science, and that allows us also to appreciate different spiritual perspectives without insisting that one be right and all the others wrong. In this new view, when *The Egyptian Book of the Dead* describes the god Thoth as a tall, well-built man with the head of a bird, we are no longer forced to see this as either a) a description of an objective reality, pure and simple, or b) a totally fictitious product of the ancient Egyptians' highly fertile imaginations. The truth is that a god like Thoth is *neither* of these things. He is, instead, a being existing within the domain of the imaginal: a plane of experience that is every bit as real as the physical world we experience while "down here" in our physical bodies, but that is also much more elastic; a world that blooms and buzzes a hundredfold more vividly and intensely—and personally—than the one we are in right now.

If we can at least provisionally accept this pair of ideas, we become able to see that many of the things that before seemed obtuse, hard to understand, or just plain silly about what the peoples of times past have had to say about the afterlife are not so obtuse or silly at all. They allow us to take the afterlife descriptions of, say, an Inuit Eskimo and a Brazilian Indian seriously and respectfully, without having to literally envision the afterworld as a thick tropical jungle or a snow-covered stretch of northern tundra.

They are, in short, the key to understanding in a truly modern way the life that awaits us beyond death.

5

Different Kinds of Reincarnation, Different Kinds of Evolution, Why Flying Saucers Help Us Understand the Afterlife, and Why the Romantics Are Still Important

We are in the course of becoming individuals

—G. Rachel Levy

Reincarnation—the idea that people are primarily spiritual in nature and born into more than one physical body—is one of the most universal ideas there is. Though we tend to associate it with Hinduism and Buddhism, reincarnation in fact shows up in cultures at every historical stratum and in every part of the world. Plato believed in it (as my father liked to point out), as did his master Socrates. Jesus (as my father also liked to remind me) may have believed in it, and the Christian thinker Origen strongly felt its pull. Though most churches today deny it, the doctrine seems to have been accepted by a good number of Christian thinkers until at least 553, when it was strongly undermined thanks to the reforms introduced at the Second Council of Constantinople.

But the most important thing to understand about the doctrine of reincarnation for our purposes is that there are two basic ways of envisioning it: a more traditional one, and a more distinctively modern one. This difference is well illustrated in the following passage by the contemporary writer and philosopher Christopher Bache.

"If we live only one lifecycle on Earth," writes Bache in his book *Lifecycles: Reincarnation and the Web of Life*, "this constricts what we can expect to realize out of life. We are given just enough time to sort out our individual identity from our family's expectations, train ourselves in some trade, find a mate and raise the next generation, accomplish something professionally, and, if all goes well, relax for a few years with our grandchildren before we die. Along the way we may look up occasionally to marvel at the universe in which we live. We may cry in awe of the miracle of birth or the beauty of the Milky Way. We may even spend years contributing to our collective understanding of some aspect of its wonder. But always we know that however hard we try, we do not have the time to truly explore the extraordinary cosmos we find ourselves in or to participate to any significant degree in its grandeur. On the other hand, if we live many lifecycles on Earth all this changes. Our roles in the cosmic drama expand in proportion to the time we are on stage. Reincarnation weds our individual evolution to the larger evolution of the universe, and we become more significant participants in everything that is taking place around us. This inevitably will cause us to raise our philosophical estimate of the purpose of human existence."

The key difference between this new view of reincarnation and the older, more traditional Eastern ones—the difference that shows with real clarity that the view of reincarnation that writers like Bache have embraced is *not entirely* reincarnation as it has been understood by most of the peoples who have believed in it in times past—can be found in one key word, used pointedly by Bache in the above quote:

Evolution.

Most of us take it for granted that the universe evolves: that it is a very different place now than it was, say, ten million years ago, and that it will in turn be a very different place ten million years from now. But this idea, obvious as it seems to us, was not nearly so clear and unquestionable to people in the past. In fact, in the view of most of the traditional peoples who have lived and in some cases continue to live on earth, life for humans and for the cosmos itself was not a series of ever-changing and ever-new events, but (as we described above when talking about Buddhism) more like an ever-turning circle. In these older views, nothing ever really changed at all. Rather than leading anywhere genuinely new, the things that happened in life could be counted on to happen again, and again, and again, without end.

This circular vision wasn't necessarily negative. Indeed, it could be framed positively, as it was, for example, by the ancient Taoists, who saw the Tao as the ever-changing yet at the same time ever-*un*changing source of all existence. All life came forth from the Tao, vanished back into it, and came forth again . . . forever and ever. This is the kind of view reflected in the words of Ecclesiastes: "To every thing there is a season, and a time for every purpose under heaven." What's wrong with that?

Elsewhere in the ancient world, however, this circular vision of life was, again, a source of tremendous despair. It was so, for example, not just for the Hindus and Buddhists, but for certain schools of ancient Greek thought. The believers in the ancient Greek philosophy of Orphism (who provided those haunting lines of direction to the souls of the dead quoted in the preface) believed that the ever-spinning wheels of earthly life were a trap, pure and simple, and their doctrine of the soul's cyclical rebirth is so similar to the Hindu and Buddhist views that a number of scholars believe the Orphic philosophers must have originally picked the idea up in India and brought it back to Greece.

Despair at the circular nature of existence shows up in the Judeo-Christian world as well. Ecclesiastes, the book of the Hebrew Bible whose lines about the turning-and-turning world strike modern ears as so positive and celebratory, also contains the following, not nearly so positive ones:

What has been will be again,
what has been done will be done again;
there is nothing new under the sun.

Though seeing the cosmos as a vast, ever-turning wheel was a common practice in the ancient world, around 1000 BCE this attitude gradually began to change, with the birth of Judaism. Strange as it may sound, the new age would never have gotten started if it weren't for an inspiration about the true nature of time that first got rolling with the Hebrews some three thousand years ago. With them, the cosmos suddenly turned from the circular and essentially unchanging place it had been for countless thousands of years, into a *forward-moving* enterprise. Human history—the very specific things that happened to specific peoples and individuals in very specific times and places—suddenly started to *matter* to the Hebrews in a way they never had before in the ancient world, where what tended to be important were the ever-recurring great cosmic cycles, not the puny doings of humans. For the Hebrews it was hugely important to God what individual people—in particular, the Jewish people—did or didn't do, and the history they created by those doings wasn't at all circular (despite occasional lapses into the old thinking like that demonstrated by Ecclesiastes in the quote above), but more like an arrow. Life was, for the Hebrews, *a story with a plot:* one that began with the creation of the world and continued with Abraham's response to God's call to get up and leave the city of Ur behind, and that would culminate, far in the future, with the Hebrews' reentry into the Promised Land and the commencement of the Messianic era.

While this new idea got its start with the Hebrews (and, to a degree, with the sixth-century BCE religion Zoroastrianism, which saw world history as a battle between the forces of God, or Ahura Mazda, and Ahriman, the Zoroastrian version of the devil), it didn't stop with them. In the classical world around the time of Jesus, many thinkers were applying themselves once again to that greatest of Egyptian ideas: the potential divinity of the human being. These thinkers, who were focused around the Egyptian city of Alexandria, combined the conceptual tools of Greek philosophy with more ancient streams of wisdom to come up with a new vision of the true nature and destiny of human beings. In this new view, the universe itself was seen as a kind of giant, primordial man (a being known in mystical Jewish thought as Adam Kadmon), and each individual human being was seen as a fragment of this larger cosmic man that had fallen away from him when it entered the physical world. At death, this new philosophy suggested, each of us returns to the spiritual world to once again become part of this larger cosmic being. Humans (and again, the similarities with today's new age thought are clear) were fragments of divinity that had fallen into matter and needed to find their way back out of it so that they could recover the condition of primordial godhood that they had lost long ago.

What would human beings be like when they found their way back to this larger condition? Would they be the same beings as they had been on earth? If they were to be different, *how* would they be different? For most of its history, Judaism did not believe in a full, true afterlife for the human soul. Though each person was dear to God, it was the story of the Jews as a whole that truly gave glory to him. But with the birth of Christianity, all that changed. In the Christian view, all humanity had, like the Prodigal Son in the gospel story, wandered away from its original homeland, and would one day, after many a travail, return to it. But when it happened, that return would unfold person by person, and the redeemed earth the faithful would inhabit would be a more-than-simply-earthly place. By borrowing a few elements from Greek philosophy—in particular, the Platonic idea of the human being as participating in the logos, or divine idea, and of death as a release from the earthly clay of the body into a heaven of immaterial spiritual ideas or archetypes—Christianity developed the idea of an eternal soul that was destined to take a place in an equally eternal heaven: a heaven that combined aspects of the Jewish heavenly city with the Platonic idea of a more purely *spiritual* heaven.

The upshot of all this was that the afterlife became what up till then it had only been for the Egyptians (and for them only to a certain extent): a genuinely otherworldly place that nevertheless had room for *individuals.* Heaven, with the rise of Christianity, became a place full of earthly details. What Jesus's death and resurrection showed from this perspective was that every last thing that happens down here in the world somehow *matters,* and no matter how grim, grisly, or numbingly dull and pointless things might get sometimes, all will one day be made well when God fulfills the promise of redemption that Christ's death on the cross brought into being.

If the Hebrews kicked the historical cosmos into gear, the early Christians posited an endpoint of that history in which all the particulars of the present world might have a real, not a theoretical, place. Whether in heaven now or on the redeemed earth at the end of history, this early Christianity posited a world that was rescued in every detail. The redeemed earth that would arrive at the end of history, according to Christian cosmic speculation, was *spiritual,* yet it was also, paradoxically, *physical.* As such it was a continuation of that original Egyptian idea that when the cosmic story finally plays itself out, matter and spirit will no longer be separate categories but will unite in a single substance: one that has both a Platonic everlastingness and at the same time a Jewish earthiness and particularity.

The early Christian vision was deeply dynamic. It saw growth as a cosmic principle and envisioned the human soul as moving perpetually forward even after it arrived in heaven. "On account of the infinity of God," wrote the fourth-century Christian bishop St. Gregory of Nyssa, "the state of perfection is one of unlimited progress." Over the centuries, however, that initial focus on cosmic and individual growth, and that vision of history as a journey out of the innocence of Eden, through the trials of the fallen world, and then back into a new condition of divinity, slowly but surely degenerated. By the early Middle Ages, fear of the Christian hell had taken precedence over anticipation of the Christian heaven. The fiery horrors that awaited the hapless sinner served not to season and refine, as the fires of the Egyptian underworld had, but existed simply to torture the soul for offenses to God committed while in the body. The blessed in heaven, meanwhile, had so little to do that much of their time seems to have been spent looking down with disdainful approval upon the distant sufferings of their less fortunate brethren in the realms beneath them. One acted well in life so that, once it was over, one could avoid the fires of hell.

Unappealing as the more mundane, punishment-and-reward versions of Christianity are, they shouldn't be allowed to blot out the fact that in its original form, Christianity was a profoundly world-affirming religion, for it envisioned cosmic history as a U-shaped affair in which the world began as spirit, "fell" into matter, and, over the course of a long, hard struggle, made it back into a state where the perfections of spirit and the particularities of matter were rejoined in a new synthesis. In this "cosmic story" vein of Christianity, the "garments of skins" that God clothed Adam and Eve with after they bit of the apple of knowledge of good and evil are a symbol of the physical body itself. Thus the fall out of the original perfection of Eden was in fact the fall from spirit into the world of matter: a fall that, terrible as it was, was in the end a felix culpa, or happy fault, for by falling out of innocence, Adam and Eve initiated a process that would change human beings in ways that were both unexpected and in the long run good.

Whether in its more inspired and positive forms or its more negative and moralistic ones, the basic Christian vision of present history as the interval between the initial and the second coming of Christ dominated Western thought up through the end of the Middle Ages. Then came the birth of modern scientific thought and a sudden, shocking enlargement of our understanding of the real size of the stage on which human history is unfolding: an enlargement that we take so for granted today that it is easy to overlook just how much it shook things up when it first occurred.

Up until the nineteenth century, most people in the West believed that while human history changed constantly, all of natural creation had been made in six days some four thousand years previously. And other than the occasional flood or earthquake it had changed very little ever since. With the arrival of Charles Darwin's theory of evolution and natural selection, however, and the birth of modern geology and paleontology, earth suddenly became a much older place, one where many more things (the march of continents, the coming into existence and dying out of different species, the slow but steady transformations of those species over time) had happened than had previously been thought. The great unchangeable cycles of nature suddenly revealed themselves as not unchangeable at all, but rather as chapters in an ever-unfolding story, just as (on a much smaller scale) human history itself was.

But even as it gave nature a more central place within the ever-unfolding drama of cosmic existence, the new scientific perspective removed a player from the stage as well. In a word, that player was God. With Darwin's introduction of the idea that life grows and changes essentially as the result of blind accident, the spiritual underpinnings of the cosmic story fell away and the history of earth and the things that happened on it suddenly became a purely material one. Life, in this new view, was still going somewhere, but it was no longer doing so with the help of God or any kind of larger spiritual dimension. It just chugged along on its own steam.

This new earthly, secular, material understanding of life's progress through the vast ages soon gave birth to the doctrine of Progress with a capital *P*. Though nature itself had no inbuilt purpose, this doctrine declared, being instead a random affair that unfolded the way it did because that was just how things happened to have shaken out, science could now harness these pointless powers of nature and consciously direct them. This meant that for the first time, rather than being just another hapless passenger on the vast, blind steamship of Darwinian evolution, humankind could actually break into the cabin and, at least to a degree, steer the ship where it liked. Scientific knowledge and the technical power it placed in the hands of humans would, in this new picture of things, soon solve all of people's practical problems, making life in the physical world a far easier and more leisurely business than it had ever been in the past. Steady and unending material progress powered by the still relatively new institution of capitalism would ensure that the discoveries of science were translated into goods and services that would spread inexorably around the world. Every day in every way, things would just get better and better. More inventions, more progress, more modern comforts and conveniences . . . Human life, though now revealed to be completely without point or purpose in any deeper kind of sense, was to be an endless rise on an escalator of every-increasing quality, convenience, and contentment. Life might not mean anything much, but it would at least be pleasant and comfortable.

Of course, it didn't work out quite this way. Indeed, these days, after all the technology-aided horrors of the twentieth and early twenty-first centuries, and with the possibility of total planetary ecological collapse looming ever closer, the nineteenth century's easy, science-drunk optimism about the future of humanity sounds like a pathetically naïve dream. And yet, in spite of all the damage it has done, it may be that our Western passion for progress still contains something intensely valuable: something, in fact, that we can't do without. If we Westerners are enduringly and unstoppably attached to the "going-somewhere" feeling, we need now more than ever to appreciate the idea that we might just live in a universe where forward movement is both material and *spiritual*.

The vision of a universe that is evolving both physically and spiritually, and of a humanity that is evolving in terms of its consciousness as well, is a central tenet in the smarter zones of contemporary new age thinking. But this vision is actually far from new, having been born some decades before the appearance of Darwin's theory, in England and Germany at the end of the eighteenth century and the start of the nineteenth. The people who brought it to birth were the poets, painters, and philosophers of the Romantic movement.

The Romantics, by and large, were Christians. But they

were Christians of a different stripe from any the world had yet seen. Taking the core Christian imagery of humankind's fall from innocence and its slow but steady struggle back to a new spiritual condition beyond both innocence *and* experience, Romantic writers and philosophers like Samuel Taylor Coleridge and William Blake in England, and Johann Wolfgang von Goethe, Friedrich von Schelling, and Georg Wilhelm Friedrich Hegel in Germany, reenvisioned the Christian story of fall and redemption using the new, more accurate styles of nonmythological (that is, historical) thinking that were then emerging. In this new picture of the creation, fall, and redemption of the world, the old Christian story of fall and redemption was transformed into a more fluid, gradual event in which spirit slowly and perhaps even purposefully "fell" into the material dimension so that it might slowly but inevitably find its way back up into the world of spirit.

> We in our time are . . . the heirs of a very old and expanding tradition . . . that it is the lot of man to be fragmented and cut off, but haunted in his exile and solitariness by the presentiment of a lost condition of wholeness and community.
> —M. H. Abrams, *Natural Supernaturalism*

For several years during my midforties (before my knees started to give out and forced me to less jarring forms of exercise), I jogged a lot. Like many joggers, I both hated and enjoyed the activity, for while it was unarguably boring, there was no getting around the fact that if you did it for a while you'd start to feel . . . different. Often, when I'd been running for a while and was feeling more comfortable in my body because of the endorphins I'd coaxed it into releasing, and all those other nuts-and-bolts physical reasons, I'd get a strange but pleasant sensation that even as I slogged along down on the physical plane, I was being followed, somewhere just above and behind me, by someone—or something—else: a being that though I describe it using physical terms like "above" and "behind," isn't of the physical plane at all, but a higher, more mysterious one.

Higher . . . There I go again, using a this-worldly, physical term to describe something that I just finished saying isn't physical at all. Of course, it's almost impossible *not* to use physical terminology when describing the nonphysical world, and the fact is that though this entity was never there when I turned my head to look for it up in the sky, I would nonetheless get a strangely solid feeling that it really and truly *was* there, coasting along just above the trees, tracking my progress like a flying saucer sent down to investigate just what exactly it is that people on earth get up to.

What was this mysterious entity? My suspicion is that it was me. Not the mundane "me" I knew and felt myself to be on a day-to-day level, not the me that struggled and fretted and felt itself constantly swamped by the petty concerns of the world, but a larger, secret part of me. A part that never came down here to earth in the first place, but that drifts along far above it—serene, slightly imperious, gorgeously immune to all the clutter and idiocy of the world below.

Our whole culture, I sometimes think, is under the sway of this larger entity. I was fourteen when the original *Star Wars* came out, fifteen when Steven Spielberg's *Close Encounters of the Third Kind* arrived on screens, and even have a hazy memory of my first viewing, with my father of course, of Stanley Kubrick's

2001: A Space Odyssey, in 1969 when I was only seven. The first record I ever purchased for myself, the debut album by the rock group Boston, featured a garish, seventies-style flying saucer rising up above the earth. Flying saucer imagery was everywhere in my childhood, and especially my teen years, so it only makes sense that when I try to picture this mysterious larger part of myself that I feel hovering and brooding somewhere above me, a flying saucer is the first object that comes to mind.

Not that I'm the only one to have made this connection. Writing about the flying saucer craze of the forties and fifties, the psychologist Carl Jung argued that the swarms of flying disks suddenly being spotted in the skies around the world were manifestations in modern, technological guise of the mandala: the ancient Far Eastern symbol of the higher or total self. Mandalas (the Tibetan sand versions included) are typically circular, and circles are the most ancient and widespread symbol of wholeness—of *completion*—there is. It didn't really matter, for Jung, whether flying saucers were real or not. What did matter was that flying saucers carried a strong psychic charge for modern humanity because they stood for *totality,* for a condition of fullness that we moderns have stubbornly shut ourselves off from, and that we secretly—and sometimes not so secretly— long to recover. Whatever else they might or might not be, Jung suggested, flying saucers are a *psychic* reality: "an involuntary archetypal or mythological picture of an unconscious content, a *rotundum,* as the alchemists called it, that expresses the totality of the individual."

I didn't run into Jung's interpretation of the flying saucer phenomenon until I was an adult, but by the time I did, I'd been pretty well prepped for it by my father. Driving home from a viewing of *Star Wars* in the early summer of 1977, I asked him what he thought about the scene in which Luke and the other rebel fighters flew their spaceships down the trench that runs around the Death Star. As the camera hurtled along the impossibly narrow trench with the walls rushing by on both sides, I was overcome by a strange—and strangely pleasant—sensation. Why, I wondered, was the feeling of zooming through a narrow channel so attractive, and so oddly familiar?

"It's a memory of when you were a sperm cell, shooting into your mother," my father replied decisively.

It was, of course, a characteristic response for my father: irritatingly simplistic, patently reductive, and yet at the same time curiously interesting—curiously *right*. A sperm cell shooting toward an egg is, after all, a fragment seeking to become a whole. I suspect that *all* space objects stand, to one degree or another, for this lost and larger part of ourselves, floating along above and looking down at us as we negotiate the exhausting maze of material existence.

But can we ever find our way back to that lost wholeness? And, most important of all, what will that wholeness do with us once it has us again?

That was the primary question that Romantics, in their new vision of the shape and meaning of human and cosmic history, were asking. The scholar of Romantic literature and philosophy M. H. Abrams writes that "in the most representative Romantic version of emanation and return"—that is, the story of our fall out of oneness with the spiritual Source and our slow fight back to it—"when the process reverts to its beginning the recovered unity is not . . . the simple, undifferentiated unity of its origin, but a unity which is higher, because it incorporates the intervening differentiations." What this means, essentially, is that in the great unfolding of the cosmic story, when we finally get back to where we started from, *we will not be the same beings we started out as.* Or as T. S. Eliot put it, in what is perhaps the single most famous formulation of this philosophical idea in all of literature:

> *We shall not cease from exploration.*
> *And the end of all our exploring*
> *will be to arrive where we started*
> *and know the place for the first time.*

Is Eliot talking about the Eastern circle here? Hardly. He is talking about a vision of life in which the great circular motions of the universe—the changing seasons, the circling planets, the generations and civilizations that rise and fall—are framed within a larger movement in which the soul, and the cosmos itself, do not suffocate in an endless tumbling circularity but rather surge forward and ever forward, toward a culmination beyond the power of words to describe; a culmination that Eliot hinted at in the *Four Quartets'* famous last lines:

> *And all shall be well and*
> *All manner of thing shall be well*
> *When the tongues of flame are in-folded*
> *Into the crowned knot of fire*
> *And the fire and the rose are one.*

To oversimplify just a little, in the Romantic vision the reason for the universe's creation was so that God or the Di-

vine could give birth to an untold multiplicity of spiritual beings: beings who, in their journey away from and back to him,
would be allowed to grow into the truly autonomous spiritual
beings God desired them to be in the first place. Enfolded in
God's original unity, these beings had *potentially* possessed this
individuality right from the start, but they needed to embark
upon the perilous journey away from the divine and the spiral-
ing journey back in order that, far in the future, they might finally struggle their way once again into his embrace as finished
individuals: free and fully discerning beings who had won that
freedom through the long, hard, confusing, dangerous, and
quite often simply painful work of incarnate existence.

The implications of this new, revivified version of the great
Western story of departure and return that the Romantics told
(a story that, once again, didn't so much deny the basic Judeo-
Christian vision of fall and redemption so much as retell it in a
modern guise) were and remain today hugely positive. *Though
you may now feel alienated and alone,* the Romantic cosmic vision tells us, *you were not always so, and you will not always be
so. But your aloneness must be conquered through a brave, earnest,
and full development of your individuality—through becoming
the complete spiritual being you implicitly are already, and were
always meant to fully become.* If many of us in the modern world
today find ourselves cut off from the rest of a universe that
seems like a dead and dull machine, a landscape full of zom-
bies rather than a vibrant theater in which living spiritual beings play out their destinies, this does not mean that the world
has always looked this way, or that it will look this way in the
future, either. In fact, the alienation so many of us feel—the
sense of cut-offness from the spiritual Source—is, the Roman-

tics would say, the surest sign that we have attained the beginnings of true spiritual adulthood. For just as each individual human life involves a journey out of the innocence of childhood into the harder, colder, more demanding world of adult experience, so too does the cosmic journey of humanity at large contain a "childhood" period of original innocence, one that was eventually lost as humanity began to grow toward its ultimate goal of true spiritual maturity.

There was a time, wrote William Wordsworth in the classic Romantic formulation of this journey out of innocence as reflected in the loss of the innocence of childhood,

> . . . *when meadow, grove, and stream,*
>   *The earth, and every common sight,*
>   *To me did seem*
>   *Apparell'd in celestial light,*
> *The glory and the freshness of a dream.*
> *It is not now as it hath been of yore;—*
>   *Turn wheresoe'er I may,*
>   *By night or day,*
> *The things which I have seen I now can see no more.*

The Romantics were keen students of myth and legend, and they often read such stories with this universal story of descent and return in mind. They found it, for example, underlying all the fairy tales of princes or princesses exiled in foreign lands, their true stature either forgotten or concealed. The homecoming, after many adventures, to the castle where the prince or princess had always belonged to begin with is, in the Romantic interpretation of these stories, a camouflaged version of the homecoming that each and every human soul will one day experience when it recovers the memory of who and what it really is: a spirit currently exiled in the realm of matter, but destined, someday and somehow, to return to its true home, carrying the treasure of an individuality earned by completely entering into and submitting to the transformative ordeal of physical existence.

Here, then, in the Romantic description of what the universe looks like and what we are doing in it, are the first inklings of a genuinely modern vision of the soul and its destiny. It's one in which the individual human being is not defined— and ultimately gobbled up—by the material dimension, as it is in materialism. Nor is it eclipsed by an impersonal metaphysical absolute, as it is in most Eastern faiths. Nor does it get stuck in a static heaven or hell that leaves no further room for development, as in the more conventional Christian view. Instead it is a view in which each human soul is shown to be on a *genuine journey*.

A journey that, it began to be suspected, might feature not just one but multiple passages down into the material sphere, and back out of it as well.

6

The Transcendentalists, Reincarnation Reenvisioned, and What the Universe Was Really Created For

The love of life is out of all proportion to the value set on a single day, and seems to indicate . . . a conviction of immense resources and possibilities proper to us, on which we have never drawn.

—RALPH WALDO EMERSON

In the second half of the nineteenth century, when the Romantic period in Europe was in its waning years, this new Romantic revisioning and retelling of the old Western idea of fall and redemption started occupying the minds of a very different group of thinkers on the other side of the Atlantic. When it did, an idea that was constantly present in the background in the musings of the European and British Romantics came to the foreground—for in truth, the whole Romantic cosmic vision couldn't really work without it.

This idea was, of course, the doctrine of reincarnation.

Owen Barfield, a British barrister and writer who early in his life became a student of the ideas of Rudolf Steiner, was one of the twentieth century's most eloquent advocates of the Romantic philosophy. Barfield felt that the ideas of the Romantics were not dusty literary relics but were still vital and living. New age thinking, at its sharpest and most responsible, is, Barfield would suggest, really just, to use a term he was fond of, "Romanticism come of age." But to really take those Romantic ideas seriously, Barfield felt, we also need to take seriously the idea of what he liked to call "repeated earth lives."

"If the idea of [spiritual] evolution . . . has become attractive to many minds," Barfield wrote, "there is nevertheless one awkward obstacle in the way of its acceptance; and particularly of its acceptance as a ground for believing in my own existence." This belief, said Barfield, is "that the self really evolved, not just the vehicles of it." In other words, if we are to take the spiritual/developmental worldview initiated by the Romantics seriously, we must realize that this also entails taking seriously the idea that the personal being we experience ourselves to be right here and now did not come into existence with the birth of our present bodies, but has been around for a much, much longer time.

This was precisely what that new group of thinkers on the other side of the Atlantic was beginning to suspect. In the life we know here on earth, we find ourselves, wrote Ralph Waldo Emerson, "on a stair; there are other stairs below us which we seem to have ascended; there are stairs above us, many a one, which go upward and out of sight." Emerson is using a poetic image here, but he is not doing so just because the image sounds pretty. He very much means, with this came-from-somewhere, going-somewhere imagery, what he says, just as he does in another, more direct passage from his writing on this subject. "The soul," wrote Emerson, "comes from without into the human body as into a temporary abode, and it goes out of it anew. . . . It passes into other habitations, for the soul is immortal."

Emerson viewed our true larger life as a kind of forward-moving yet also spiral drama in which one life follows another, each to some degree imitating the shape and trajectory of the one that came before yet also introducing new material. And this, of course, meant that Emerson accepted an extremely personal and individual version of the concept of repeated earth lives. For if the soul is really and truly to grow over time, if it is on a genuine journey through the temporal and physical dimensions, then in order for that journey to lead somewhere really valuable, not only must the same individual soul keep on returning, time and again, but it must bring with it all the accumulated memories of what happened to it in lives past, even if, while on earth, they typically remain unavailable to the conscious portion of the mind, appearing only in otherwise inexplicable likes and dislikes, and various and sundry other quirks of character.

The difference here from most Eastern versions of reincarnation is that with the Eastern models, it is the ethical residue of a life that lasts from one life to the next. That is, if you did something bad in one life, then you'll have to pay for it in the next. This is a hugely important insight, of course, for the idea that the universe actually possesses an ethical component that is as real as the energy patterns of which it is made up is perhaps the central insight of all Eastern philosophy. Not only that, but the thinkers of the East didn't just hypothesize this fact: through intensive meditative techniques, they experienced it as a living reality. If the first and greatest shock that an individual experiences at death is that they are "still here"—still themselves—the second, more gradually dawning shock is that the universe is a place where good and bad exist as more than simple cultural designations but actual metaphysical categories; in other words, that the goodness or badness of an action is as real as an atom collision.

But this insight tended, in the Eastern visions of the reincarnation drama, to remain focused purely on the ethical side of things. Still, if the universe is capable of retaining and remembering our every thought and action, this also might mean that the more personal aspects of our existence can survive, too. The atmosphere of a certain summer afternoon, the particular words of a particular person, spoken on a particular day, when a particular tree was moving in just a certain way outside a half-open window, the paint on which was ever so slightly chipped . . . in this vision of the reincarnation drama, this stuff survives as well. The kind of things that, in our day, are included in poems and novels and treated there usually as magical but tragically singular ephemera: the glimmering bits that float on the surface of a universe that, seemingly for no real reason, gives birth to them for a moment and then gobbles them up forever. All these tiny, complex, and hugely mysterious details of an individual personal life, lived once and once only . . . In this new vision, this is all saved, too. Human meaning, in this view, isn't just a distraction to reentry into the divine, or *sunyata,* or whatever one might choose to call it, but in large part *the reason for the journey.* We are born, and born again, not because we are stuck in a pointless circular honey pit of fear and desire, but because each of us is a complex being, growing and changing not in spite of but precisely by means of the very real individual experiences that happen to us. This doesn't change the key Eastern idea that the universe is a moral place, but it adds something crucial to it: something that changes the reincarnation process from a trap and a machine of despair into a process productive of, rather than antithetical to, true human meaning.

The American Transcendentalist movement was a further chapter in the dawning of this new perspective. For Emerson, a person's individual character was everything. If we live one life after another, it could only be, in his view, in order that this individual, personal self that we are at essence could continue to grow and develop—could continue to become, in short, ever *more* personal, ever *more* the true larger self it was destined to be.

There is a further way that this journeying transearthly being is different from the "indestructible drop" that reincarnates in Buddhism. For in this new view that was coming to birth in Emerson's day, the soul that enters into and leaves the material world *can only realize its full individuality when out of the body, between lives.* Down on earth, according to this view, the soul is doomed always to be but a fragment of the greater self that it was before incarnating and that it will be again when it leaves the body. But though we can never see all of this "above" part of ourselves while within the grips of the material world, we can, if we are paying attention, catch occasional glimpses of it: the kind of glimpse that Emerson famously described in his essay "Nature," when he talked about how at certain moments, walking in the woods, his perception of himself changed and grew larger. "I become," Emerson wrote of these moments, "a transparent eye-ball; I am nothing; I see all; the currents of the Universal Being circulate through me; I am part or particle of God."

Emerson coined a name for this larger self. He called it the "Oversoul"—a term still very much alive in contemporary new age writings about the larger fate of the human person.

"If our ego-self is our natural identity in the physical world," writes Bache in *Lifecycles,* "the Oversoul is our natural identity in the spiritual. . . . When we leave our physical bodies behind at 'death' and return to the spiritual domain, we (ideally) exchange our ego-identities for the larger identity of the Oversoul. This larger identity consists of all the lives we have ever lived. To be reunited with the Oversoul, therefore, is to experience simultaneously a profound expansion of our being and a coming home to a deeper identity."

In this emerging view, there is an ever-increasing emphasis on the value of all the small things we engage in and experience while down here on earth. Rebirth becomes, in it, not a trap, but a tool for the soul's development.

In *The Drama of Love and Death,* the early twentieth-century writer and proto-new-age philosopher Edward Carpenter summed up this idea with exceptional clarity. "Limitation and hindrance," wrote Carpenter, "are a part of the cosmic scheme in the creation of Souls because limitation calls the spirit out of itself." The physical body, in Carpenter's view, is at once hopelessly limiting yet strangely conductive to the development of personality. The limitation that physical incarnation places upon us serves what he called "the evolution of self-consciousness and the sense of identity." Why? Because "it is only by pinning sensitiveness down to a point in space and time, by means of a body, and limiting its perceptions by means of the bodily end-organs of sight, hearing, taste, etc., that these new values could be added to creation—the self-conscious self and the sense of identity. Through the development of identity, mankind must ultimately rise to a height of glory otherwise unimaginable."

In the famous words of the British Romantic poet John Keats, the physical world is a "vale of soul-making." But what's really crucial to understand about this statement is that, just as with Emerson's staircase passage above, Keats did not mean it as a pretty but impotent poetic idea. The physical world was, Keats and his fellow Romantics suspected, a place where spiritual beings come in order to *grow in specificity* before returning to the spiritual world where they reassume their larger spiritual identities. To state all this as compactly as possible: the physical dimension is, in this view, *a limited, difficult, but crucial area of the evolving spiritual-and-material cosmos, where we, as evolving spiritual individualities, accomplish a key portion of our becoming true individual spiritual beings.*

The familiar idea that we are "here to learn" (which I got so sick of hearing from my father's new age friends as a kid and was so surprised to hear from my near-death survivor interviewees at *Guideposts*) ends up having to do not just with learning about the physical world and ourselves as we endure it, but with the whole impossibly slow process of *getting used to it down here:* a process that we begin at birth and which takes, for most of us, our entire lives. In a sense, to be born into the physical world really *is*, as I sensed during my nightmare-plagued years as a child, *to be kidnapped.* It is to be taken away from

where we truly belong. Yet at the same time, this line of thinking suggests, in being thrown into the material dimension and
subjected to the crippling amnesia and the general diminishment of ability that goes with it, we are given the opportunity
to *become ourselves* in a way that the purely spiritual world can't
provide us with. Separation, unsureness . . . all those qualities that are most difficult about life, are, in the end, *giving* us
something. Something we can only fully understand when we
are back up in the spiritual world, and (to take it a little further)
perhaps only in that impossibly distant point that the Egyptian
and Abrahamic religions postulated when the worlds of matter
and spirit will be once again fully and finally united. It is precisely by way of the maddening combination of limitation and
possibility that earthly life presents us with that we move ever
forward, ever closer to a condition that Egyptian religion, and
Christianity as well for that matter, was not afraid to describe,
at least in their bolder moments, as godhood.

What *is* a god, exactly? It is a being that is at once completely individual and completely cosmic: a being that is at
once completely personal, completely itself and no other, yet
at the same time completely and consciously at one with the
universe that gave it birth.

If we can manage to train our gaze on this idea of the universe as an arena for the gradual development of such beings,
and if we can see these developing spirits as moving back and
forth, into incarnate existence and out of it; and if we can
manage to take this picture of things seriously enough that we
can actually carry it around with us as we go about our daily
business, something fundamental changes. Suddenly the great
sweep of cosmic evolution becomes not a distant and abstract

event, but something that is going on *now*. Being aware of this cosmic evolution, and of the fact that our ordinary, everyday consciousness is the breaking wave of an event that has been proceeding for some four billion years, can genuinely change our focus on what our life means. Suddenly the "me" that we feel ourselves to be is not some meaningless little blip, susceptible at any moment of being swallowed up by the universe, but *the very point of the universe itself.*

Emerson was not the only member of his circle to be attracted by the first glimmerings of this new, huge-yet-intimate, cosmic-yet-personal philosophy, and by the doctrine of reincarnation that lay at its center. "As far back as I can remember," wrote his friend and fellow Transcendentalist Henry David Thoreau, "I have unconsciously referred to the experiences of a previous state of existence." Elsewhere, Thoreau writes: "It is unavoidable, the idea of transmigration; not merely a fancy of the poets, but an instinct of the race." The lesser-known Transcendentalist James Freeman Clarke, a contemporary of Emerson and Thoreau, made the point even more specifically: "Evolution has a satisfactory meaning only when we admit that the soul is developed and educated by passing through many bodies. . . . If we are to believe in evolution, let us have the assistance of the soul itself in this development."

Thus did some very old ideas end up taking on a decidedly new form. By blending the traditional Eastern doctrine of reincarnation (that in Emerson's and Thoreau's time was just making its way to the West via the first translations of Eastern sacred texts) with the Western vision of creation as a story proceeding in vast chapters or movements from innocence to experience to a yet-to-be-known condition beyond our present human experience, Emerson and the Transcendentalists, and the European and British Romantics who preceded them, raised the curtain on a genuinely new way of looking at the universe and the human place within it. To state the upshot of this new vision as plainly and boldly as possible, we might borrow the words of the French philosopher Henri Bergson, who concluded his final book, *The Two Sources of Morality and Religion,* with the startlingly bold suggestion that the universe itself is, in essence, "a machine for the making of gods."

This hugely positive scenario of descent and return is our new spiritual narrative, the synthesis of East and West that so many have been groping toward, especially in the last century and a half or so. It's the "transcendent narrative," the meta-story of all meta-stories, that really and truly *is* the cosmic story of our time.

It's our design in the sand.

The early versions of this new vision of the cosmic story and the true human place within it took deep hold in the imaginations of thinkers far beyond the narrow circle of the Transcendentalists. In fact, it shows up in some authors who one might think would be the last in the world to be concerned with such things.

"I did not begin when I was born," wrote *Call of the Wild* author Jack London, "nor when I was conceived. I have been growing, developing, through incalculable myriads of millenniums. . . . All my previous selves have their voices, echoes, promptings in me. . . . Oh, incalculable times again shall I be born."

Here, meanwhile, is Thomas Wolfe, from his 1929 novel *Look Homeward, Angel:* "Each of us is all the sums he has not counted; subtract us into nakedness and night again, and you shall see begin in Crete four thousand years ago the love that ended yesterday in Texas. . . . Each moment is the fruit of forty thousand years."

And here, perhaps most surprisingly, is that quintessential embodiment of American *material* progress, Henry Ford: "Genius," Ford wrote, "is experience. Some seem to think that it is a gift or talent, but it is the fruit of long experience in many lives."

Though they are certainly indebted to them, the differences between these new visions of the soul's journey and the older, Eastern visions of incarnate existence as an ever-spinning wheel are always there, if one looks for them. It's a difference that, of course, was expressed with particular force in the work of another of Emerson's and Thoreau's contemporaries (and the accidental initiator of this particular book), Walt Whitman.

"I know I am deathless," Whitman wrote:

> *I know this orbit of mine cannot be swept by a carpenter's*
> *   compass . . .*
> *And whether I come to my own today or in ten thousand or*
> *   ten million years,*
> *I can cheerfully take it now, or with equal cheerfulness I can*
> *   wait . . .*
> *I laugh at what you call dissolution,*
> *And I know the amplitude of time. . . .*

"Whitman," wrote the literary critic Malcolm Cowley, "believed that there is a distinction between one's mere personality and the deeper Self," and that "we are all involved in a process of spiritual evolution that might be compared to natural evolution." All of Whitman's work is imbued with this intuition that the soul is the hero in a vast cosmic adventure, moving ever forward through great earthly and cosmic cycles, which, though they turn round and round, nonetheless also move forward, ever closer to some final consummation beyond the current power of words to convey.

Though the concept of evolution was central to his writing, Whitman was, of course, speaking from a much larger perspective than that of the conventional Darwinian evolutionists of his time. Whitman's evolution proclaimed itself loudly as both material *and spiritual*. This "double process" of material and spiritual evolution, says Cowley, "can be traced for ages into the past, and . . . will continue for ages beyond ages. . . . All men are divine and will eventually be gods."

This new picture of the soul's place in the great drama of forward-moving cosmic existence wasn't confined to America and England. "As we live through thousands of dreams in our present life," wrote Leo Tolstoy in a letter to a friend, "so is our present life only one of many thousands of such lives which we enter from the other, more real life . . . and then return after death. Our life is but one of the dreams of that more real life, and so it is endlessly, until the very last one, the very real life,—the life of God. . . . I am not playing, not inventing this: I believe in it, I see it without doubt."

That humans are destined to become gods is, as we've already seen, an idea at least as old as ancient Egypt. But in these new visions of the soul's long journey toward its ultimate destiny, there is an unprecedented emphasis on the individuality—the richly and contemporarily psychological *humanness*—of this godlike being that each of us will one day become. In this new, more psychologically focused vision of the soul's journey, it is up to each of us to realize that our present personalities are not obstacles on the way to that condition of godhood, but rather the seeds that will, one day, allow us to fully blossom into it: to become, in short, the true and larger selves the cosmos always intended us to become.

It isn't hard to see, in this amalgam of Eastern and Western wisdom that came to full birth more than a hundred years ago, the roots of the basic view of reality that is at the center of today's new age movement, and of course the scenarios my father so enthusiastically spun for me. An easy thing to parody, it is also, however, a hard vision not to be moved positively by, provided one can allow it the space to unfold in one's imagination without denying it out of hand before that has had a chance to happen. This vision of the human soul as real, substantial, personal, immortal, and destined someday for a truly godlike existence is one that takes some of the best spiritual intuitions of the East (chiefly, the idea that the soul is capable of living on earth more than just once and in more than just one single body, and that the soul is inextricably woven up with the rest of the cosmos rather than separated from it) and combines these insights with the best spiritual intuitions of the West (chiefly, the idea that life is not a circular round but a story that moves forward with ever-new chapters, in each of which the soul grows larger, deeper, and more complex).

But perhaps most important of all, this is a view of life and death that, though it does not entirely cure the profound sense of alienation that is so endemic to the modern world, nonetheless makes that alienation easier to bear. How? By explaining *why that alienation exists in the first place.* If limitation is, paradoxically, the chief tool of soul growth, the horrors of the world are not explained and excused outright, but they *are* placed within a context that allows us, with great relief, to honestly and openly see all of physical existence for what it truly is: *an arena of interaction between two different levels of existence that is defined by possibility, but also by limitation and frustration at every turn.* What is growing up about? It's about learning that the physical world won't satisfy all our desires. Why on earth should a universe exist in which we have to learn this lesson? Perhaps because the part we are in right now is just one little wedge of that universe. From the child's exit of the mother's womb, to his gradual discernment of the separate objects that surround him but refuse, most of the time, to do what he wants them to do or be what he wants them to be, to his increasingly complex and problematic relationships with other people and other things over the course of his life, the individual who enters into the troublesome testing ground of earthly life has become, by the time he reaches adulthood, a being so inured to the fact of separation and frustration that he scarcely believes that the essential feeling of loneliness that physical embodiment creates can ever be completely left behind.

But it may just be that he is wrong to feel that way. For when all else fails there comes, according to this still-emerging tradition of insights into the nature of the soul and its destiny, a moment when the endless dead ends and frustrations that souls on earth are forced to meet cease once and for all.

That moment is death.

To use a simple but nonetheless accurate image, death returns us from the small, cut-off, lonely little pizza slice we generally feel ourselves to be on earth, to the full whole pie of our transearthly personalities: the larger, infinitely more connected beings that we always remain on a deep level while here on earth, but that we nonetheless in large part forget about in the course of incarnation.

Traveling down to earth in the partialness of a new earthly incarnation, we leave, in this view, our true and total selves behind for a time, until the day when, at death, we once again return to those selves, thus adding a further "volume" to the vast library of experiences possessed by our larger, spiritual self. The Anglican poet John Donne once wrote that "death is an ascent to a better library," and there is indeed, in this picture of the soul and its place in the universe, a sense in which our larger selves contain a kind of library of all our experience over time. As the higher self drifts along above, the smaller self goes down into the world to gather—to use an analogy from the natural world that started with the Romantics but has been used a number of times since—the pollen of earthly experience. Experience that, once back in the "hive" of the world above this one, will be distilled into the honey of true and lasting transearthly *personal* character.

If we can get ourselves to take this view seriously, all the various breeds and varieties of life pessimism that have come to the fore in modern times will be rendered infinitely less threatening than they currently appear to be. Life is no longer something that begins—as it is seen to do, for example, in modern novels beyond counting—with youthful promise and ends with old age and black, bitter disappointment. The term of a human life transforms from a recipe for heartbreak and disillusion into what it has always in fact been, secretly or not so secretly: a single chapter in a much larger, much *better* story. For no matter how badly one particular chapter might end, the fact of that larger story's existence allows whatever happens now, in this life, to be seen in a more charitable and understandable light.

7

The Age of Science and the Age of Spiritualism, the Unsung Discoverer of the Human Unconscious, the French Schoolteacher Who Spoke to the Dead, and the Botanist Who Mapped the Afterlife

As the nineteenth century advanced, science of course did as well—at a rate never before seen in the world's history. The enormous discoveries in technology and industry taking place in America and Europe in the late nineteenth century made many feel that all belief in "the whole so-called spirit-world" (as the poet Rilke called it) would soon die a quiet and largely unmourned death. Given the momentous breakthroughs then being made on all fronts of scientific endeavor—breakthroughs that were seemingly making human life easier, more efficient, less painful, and more full of leisure and enjoyment than ever before in history—who could be so foolish as to want to continue to believe in the existence of a domain that one could neither see, hear, smell, touch, taste, or reap any measurable benefits from? Religious superstition (which all talk of "souls" and "spiritual dimensions" was inevitably tied up with) had kept human civilization shackled in ignorance for centuries. At last those shackles were beginning to fall away, revealing to humankind *the world as it actually was.* In this new vision of the universe, the proponents of positivistic science argued, the "spiritual" had no place whatsoever.

Just how serious were the majority of scientists in the nineteenth century about ousting all notions of a spiritual world from their maps of reality? Robert Watson, an early advocate of the highly materialistic behaviorist school of psychology, set the general tone when he announced loudly that science had "rooted out every theory that involved such relics of Judaic superstition as mind, consciousness, or soul." No one, Watson confidently asserted, "has ever touched a soul or seen one in a test-tube; and what can be neither touched nor seen and so eludes objective verification must be dismissed as non-existent." How could the invisible world that Emerson, Whitman, and the Romantics had experienced and written about with such passion possibly be defended against attacks like this?

Almost as if in answer to this question, in the spring of 1848, in a small (and no longer existent) suburb of Rochester, New York, called Hydesville, a series of loud raps began sounding within the walls of the farmhouse of a family named Fox. What was causing them? Nobody knew. But the family's two youngest daughters, Catherine and Margaret, noticed that the knocks didn't seem to be random, but came in response to the family's activities in the house. Deciding that the knocks wanted to communicate, they devised a simple system of reading them (two knocks in answer to a question meant yes, while one meant no). Soon the girls were having elaborate exchanges with an entity they playfully named "Mr. Splitfoot" (a then-popular nickname for the devil).

These question-and-answer sessions eventually convinced the girls that Mr. Splitfoot was in fact not the devil, but the ghost of a peddler who had been murdered in the house prior to the family's arrival. (The body of what appeared to be a murdered man was later discovered under the floor of the house's basement, lending credence to the girls' story.) Word spread of the farmhouse's ghostly inhabitant and its willingness to communicate with the girls, and soon reporters arrived to investigate.

Ghost stories are, of course, as old as humankind, and stories of mysterious noises sounding in old houses were hardly a new phenomenon in 1848 either. So on the surface it's curious that the "Hydesville Ghost" became the hugely newsworthy sensation that it in fact did. In a time when the media machine moved at what by today's standards would be the speed of a horse and buggy, the Fox sisters and the Hydesville Ghost nonetheless managed to become nationwide news, drawing droves of tourists to the town, and ultimately transforming two unassuming farm girls into national celebrities.

Why did people care so much about it? One possible explanation is timing. In America in 1848, the invisible world was badly in need of a representative—of someone, or some *thing*, that would speak up for those aspects of the world that refused to sit still and be measured by science. Regardless of whether Mr. Splitfoot had some basis in reality or was a simple hoax (people interested in these kinds of things are still arguing about it), the Hydesville Ghost came along at just the right time to become this spokes-entity, and its appearance was met not just with interest but something closer to relief. America was, at that time, entering one of the most radically disorienting periods of change in human history. While these changes were largely physical (railroads, factories, revolutions in medicine, and an almost daily plethora of other new inventions that changed life in ways small to large), they also brought along a wealth of psychological effects, most of them negative. For along with the new material inventions and comforts that human ingenuity was suddenly producing in bulk came a new and hugely disorienting set of tenets about what human life—be it comfortable and disease-free or otherwise—actually *meant*.

In this new view, all the old consolations of religious faith were tossed out the window. Human beings were not, as had been comfortably believed in the West for centuries, spiritual beings created by God and dear to his heart, but mere biological organisms: *machines,* in essence, that, like the rest of life on earth, had arisen from the mud purely by accident. Special as all our inward dreams and desires might feel to us, this new perspective assured us that all that happened within our minds and what felt like our souls or spirits was just an evanescent—in fact, essentially *nonexistent*—result of the inbuilt, evolutionarily created desire to live and to propagate. The mind and all it contained was a very fragile and limited electrochemical by-product of the body and brain, and basically possessed no truly solid existence whatsoever. The universe, in this new view, was still a vast and awesome place, and it was certainly a wonder that beings as intelligent and resourceful as humans had arisen within it. But that they had done so still didn't mean very much, for in the end *nothing* meant anything, as the universe itself was devoid of values or consciousness. It may (by accident) have created us, but this didn't mean it cared about us, or how we felt about the matter.

The poetic charter for this new and cripplingly grim view of what human life was, and was not, all about, is Matthew Arnold's celebrated 1867 poem "Dover Beach."

Listen! you hear the grating roar
Of pebbles which the waves draw back, and fling,
At their return, up the high strand,
Begin, and cease, and then again begin,
With tremulous cadence slow, and bring
The eternal note of sadness in.

Sophocles long ago
Heard it on the Ægæan, and it brought
Into his mind the turbid ebb and flow
Of human misery; we
Find also in the sound a thought,
Hearing it by this distant northern sea.

The Sea of Faith
Was once, too, at the full, and round earth's shore
Lay like the folds of a bright girdle furl'd.
But now I only hear
Its melancholy, long, withdrawing roar,

Retreating, to the breath
Of the night-wind, down the vast edges drear
And naked shingles of the world.

The "eternal note of sadness" in that "grating roar" of the rocks on the beach combines two of the bleaker but also more powerful and durable human insights into life and what it is all about. Not only do we live in a world where, as many of the ancients believed, we "begin, and cease, and then again begin." We also, this poem suggests, now live in a world where no true spiritual consolations exist for this grim earthly fact. The turning and turning of the world, and of the wheels of misery upon it, will never change; in fact, the only true change in human life that has occurred in a long time is the emergence, here in the modern age, of the realization that there is nothing larger behind all this: no invisible spiritual wheels spinning behind the universe's all-too-visible material ones.

One important side effect of this new, distinctively modern, and postreligious perspective on the meaning—or rather the complete and total *non*meaning—of life was that Americans and Europeans at the middle of the nineteenth century were finding themselves increasingly trapped in a world that, while physically much bigger than it had been in ages past, was at the same time strangely confining and claustrophobic. This was because the world was now, as Owen Barfield once put it, a place with no *insides* to it. When the world becomes a physical place only, rather than a physical *and* a spiritual/mental place, something strange immediately happens to people's inner experience of themselves, to their sense of what had until recently been known as their souls. For the vast majority of peoples over the vast majority of history (and prehistory), the human being has been understood to be *at the very least* a twofold creature. He possessed a physical body visible to all, but also an invisible spiritual body: one that contained the thoughts and emotions, and perhaps most important, was responsible for the mysterious but nonetheless very real sense of *me*-ness that each of us feels. This invisible spiritual body left the physical body temporarily each night during sleep, and left it permanently at death, when it voyaged to realms that, like the spiritual body itself, were not (at least most of the time) visible to physical eyes because they were of another, higher nature than the merely physical.

When, with the arrival of the modern scientific perspective, the spiritual world was declared to be nonexistent and the physical world was declared to be the *only* world there is, this inner "me"—the spiritual person—was declared to be nonexistent as well. And there was no time when this declaration rang out more loudly or strongly than in the America of the late nineteenth century.

Few people could argue that the old religious views, with their naïvely concrete heavens crowded with saints and angels and their even more concrete hells crowded with smoke-choked sinners and laughing devils, needed some drastic upgrading. In the dawning age of science and technology, many people justifiably celebrated the fact that along with the comforting promise of heaven, the scientific perspective had banished all the old threats of eternal damnation, of roasting in fire and suffering the pokes of Satan's trident for eternity. Clearly, leaving all that junk behind was an entirely good thing. The problem was that when the older, hell-and-damnation models of the spiritual world (and the inner mental-emotional world of the human mind/soul) were thrown out, *they were not replaced by any new ones.* Instead, the inner world of psychological/ spiritual reality that all of us experience and live within *was simply declared to be unreal.* Rather than getting an upgraded description, like the physical world did through the revolutions in scientific knowledge that were then taking place, the spiritual landscape was simply cancelled as a topic worth thinking about. With no spiritual world to connect itself to, the inner "me"—that person-inside-the-person that most people simply can't help but feel themselves to be—was declared to be a part (and in essence an unreal, completely insubstantial part) of the physical body and nothing more. When the body died, so did the inner person, because that person had had no existence in and of itself to begin with.

> **We are all prisoners of the outer man.**
>
> —Jakob Böhme

An important fact to keep in mind regarding all of this shifting around in terms of the belief in a soul beyond the body is that for the greater part of history and prehistory, in most parts of the world, *people didn't naturally experience themselves as actually being bodies at all.* They experienced themselves as *spirits or souls inhabiting bodies.* This was so patently obvious and apparent for most peoples that it scarcely demanded discussion. So when the arbiters of wisdom in our culture suddenly proclaimed that the body is all there is and that the real inner person that we intuitively know ourselves to be doesn't really exist at all, it was inevitable that people would react strongly against this news, whether they were conscious of the fact that they were doing so or not. For there continues to be, in most of us at least, something that quite simply *knows* that our inner, extra-bodily essence is real and substantial and not simply an imaginary phantom. To be told that one is in fact not a soul in a body but a body alone is like going to a costume party in a cumbersome getup and mask and discovering, when the party is over, that you can't take the costume off. Suddenly you simply *are* the costume. This close, uncomfortable, and in certain respects rather absurd thing that you had been happy to wear for an evening has become something you can't remove or escape from, because—terrifyingly and ridiculously—*you have become it.*

All of which puts those superficially not-all-that-interesting knocks that allegedly sounded within the Fox farmhouse in 1848 into something more like their proper perspective. In the America of 1848, they amounted to a declaration that, whatever the scientists of the day had to say to the contrary, the spiritual world wasn't dead, wasn't nonexistent, and wasn't going anywhere, no matter how much anyone might want it to.

So was born the age of spiritualism and psychical research. Within a few months of the appearance of the story of the Fox girls, people all across America were experimenting with séances, automatic writing (that is, writing done by one's own hand but not consciously controlled by oneself), trance mediumistic communication, and other technologies for finding and taking the measure of the invisible world of spirit that had been so summarily thrown out of the picture by the new scientific worldview. As Americans found their lives transformed almost daily by ever more scientific discoveries and inventions—and ever more arguments from scientists that the physical world is in fact the only one that exists—they countered by launching an all-out search for evidence that the world of spirit was as real and consequential as it ever had been, and that if the age of science had in fact arrived, then science would have to make room within itself for the spiritual dimension whether its chief spokesmen wanted to or not.

Many of the investigations and discoveries related to the spirit world that took place in the years following the appearance of the Hydesville Ghost have not aged very well. The chief reason that most of us (if we know about it at all) look back today on the great age of American spiritual investigation that began in 1848 as a frivolous and silly rather than a serious chapter of American spiritual history is that much of it actually *was,* in fact, pretty silly. A typical late-nineteenth-century séance, with its materializations of "ectoplasm" (a semispiritual, cotton-candy-like substance that supposedly emerged out of thin air or from the mouths of mediums), its floating furniture, and its disembodied hands reaching out of the darkness to grab at unsuspecting participants, seems to offer little of value to someone trying to decide if the spiritual world is real rather than a mere fancy.

For decades, in fact, most remotely thoughtful people have been embarrassed to go anywhere near this stuff. But the fact remains that whatever its (certainly numerous) faults and just plain silly aspects, the explosion in spiritual exploration that took place in the latter half of the nineteenth century actually had quite a bit more going for it than many people realize. The more responsible of those investigators were involved in what was in fact an altogether laudable project: to examine certain areas of human experience that science could not yet explain, and to do so with an open mind and *without* a hidden agenda to simply explain them away.

From the start, the idea of examining spiritual events and experiences scientifically struck many people as deeply misguided. Most scientists thought it was simply absurd, for the obvious reason that the spiritual world had been proved not to exist. Meanwhile, on the other side of the fence, many members of the clergy felt that trying to pin the truths of faith down and pick at them as if they were laboratory cadavers was the height of human arrogance. If, as Plato originally suggested, like can only be known by like, to bring the arrogant and objectifying attitude of science into the realm of spirit was to drive the subject from the room before a single measurement could be made.

But despite the hostility with which it was greeted, the urge to look at the spiritual with the mind of science could not, once it had started, be held back. The first inklings that the new vogue in spiritual investigation would produce discoveries of genuine scientific value began in 1852, when a French math and science teacher named Hippolyte Léon Denizard Rivail became interested in the spiritual investigations taking place over in America (and increasingly in England, France, and the rest of Europe as well). Fascinated as he was by the new vogue in communicating with disembodied spirits, Rivail was equally unimpressed by what most of these spirits had to say. If the spirits were real, Rivail reasoned, they should be able to do more than just move furniture around and guess what numbers séance participants were picturing in their heads. He therefore, with a combination of open-mindedness and intellectual rigor that would set the model for the best investigations into the spirit world that were to come in the years to follow, set himself to finding a group of mediums willing to ask the spirits some genuinely weighty questions, and to record their answers.

Rivail focused his initial investigations on table knocking, a practice that developed in the wake of the Fox sisters' communications with Mr. Splitfoot. In a standard table knocking session, a group of people would sit around a table with their hands placed lightly on it. Spirits were summoned, and after a while the table would begin to tilt and tremble, its legs tapping out answers to questions put by the sitters.

Rivail soon discovered, however, that a far more efficient way of communicating with the spirits came via writing mediums. Mediumistic communication was widely practiced in the ancient world and is the ancestor of today's channeling. Whether the results produced by it are seen as emanating from the world beyond or merely from the subconscious minds of the people involved, in a world where consciousness itself can't be proved to be produced by the brain to begin with, mediumistic phenomena simply cannot be explained away as merely imaginary. Weird or not, mediumistic phenomena are real, and powerful, and in the late nineteenth century this long-known fact was revived with a vengeance.

The phenomenon tended to take one of a handful of basic forms. In a full-fledged trance mediumistic session, the medium lost consciousness and allowed a spirit or spirits to make full use of his or her body to write, speak, and gesture. A partial trance medium, on the other hand, remained semiconscious and sometimes was even able to remember all or part of what had transpired when the session was over. Still other mediums remained completely conscious, and repeated or wrote out the words of the spirits as they sounded silently within their heads. The writing mediums that Rivail favored scribbled out the spirits' communications while either partially conscious or in full trance, while a helper stood by, ready to replace the paper he or she wrote on as each page filled up.

In 1857, after five years of collecting material, Rivail published *Le Livre de Spirits,* translated into English soon after as *The Spirits' Book.* Written under the pen name of Allan Kardec ("Allan" and "Kardec" being two of Rivail's names in previous incarnations, according to his invisible informants), *The Spirits' Book* is structured as a series of just over a thousand questions (put by Rivail/Kardec) and answers (provided by a virtual army of disembodies spirits).

Kardec's spirits proved more than willing to discuss with him larger issues like God, the universe, and the ultimate destiny of the human being, and if it is hard for most people to get their heads around the idea that Kardec might really have received this mass of material from an actual bunch of spirits anxious to instruct humanity on the true nature of the universe, the fact remains that the answers he received are strangely and suggestively coherent. Again, if the results he obtained were simply from the unconscious of the numerous people involved, this still ends up suggesting that the unconscious minds of many people at that time and place (a number of them not terribly educated by today's standards) housed an extraordinarily streamlined and provocative theoretical understanding of the nature and shape of the evolving spiritual/material universe.

In addition to their interesting consistency of tone, Kardec's spirits have a refreshingly un-pat quality to them. They don't (for me at least) induce the almost instant feeling of grogginess and vague unease that so much of today's channeled material does. At the same time, they also manage to paint a picture of the shape and nature of the universe that is profoundly optimistic and (again, for me at least) curiously believable. The world, according to Kardec's spirits, is in essence precisely what the poet Keats had suggested it was just a few decades beforehand: a material-spiritual arena intentionally designed for the development of individual beings. Each of these beings, said Kardec's spirit informants, is distinct, unique, and irreplaceable. It possesses a specific personality that makes it different from every other being in the cosmos. It is itself and no other. It is also immortal. It will outlive the very universe that gave it birth, and its true calling is to develop its individuality to a degree that is, from our present earthly perspective, very hard to imagine because it is as distant from our current evolutionary state as humans are from the unicellular organisms that first populated earth.

Interestingly enough, one of the central tenets of *The Spirits' Book,* and without which none of its descriptions of spiritual evolution would hold together, was quite new and shocking when the book came out—even to readers open to its generally provocative and unconventional ideas. That doctrine is reincarnation. If the whole point of the universe is spiritual progress, Kardec's spirits explained, that progress is impossible unless individual souls can take birth, again and again, in physical bodies. It is by means of that process, they explained—of that repetitive and voluntary submission to the struggles, limitations, and frustrations of the physical—that spiritual beings are able to evolve in the first place. In much the same way that Edward Carpenter would do a few decades later, Kardec's spirits present physical life as an arena conducive to spiritual growth that functions in this capacity not *in spite of,* but *because of,* the profound limitations it forces on the beings that submit to it.

The picture of the universe that emerges from Kardec's material is, of course, the same general one sketched by the Romantics and Transcendentalists. It was a picture that was, as they say, "in the air" at the time—but perhaps in a deeper way than this expression is usually meant to signify. It's a picture that once again argues that if the creation and development of individual spiritual beings is the primary purpose of the universe at large, productive limitation is the primary purpose of that part of the universe made up of physical matter (a part that Kardec's spirits suggest, correctly as it turns out, makes up but a very small wedge of the universe as a whole). Though painful, confusing, and comically limiting and confining compared to the larger worlds of spirit that surround it, the physical world is, Kardec's spirits stated unambiguously, *the place where individual growth can occur as nowhere else.* All spirits, in Kardec's cosmos, are evolving (even if many get stuck and fail to move forward for shorter or longer periods). Evolution, by its very nature, demands that there be such zones of frustration and struggle in addition to the infinitely larger realms of freedom and unimpeded forward movement.

Following the indications of his spirit informants, Kardec came to see *growth* as the primary reason for the existence of the universe, and individual consciousness as the thing that does the growing. Individual, embodied consciousness (as opposed to the more generic and impersonal consciousness framed by the Eastern traditions) is what, in the view of Kardec's informants, is real, and in the long run is what truly matters. And the physical dimension is the playing field in which that consciousness, in the form of numberless particular spirits, moves toward the far-distant goal of unity-in-multiplicity: of a universe where a single soul can be both entirely and uniquely itself, and at the same time completely and seamlessly melded with the rest of creation.

Gone completely from this philosophy is the ever-turning wheel of the older Eastern reincarnation models. In its place is a vision of the universe as more of an *event* than a thing: a vast, journey-like movement from an original point when all was contained in God or the divine ground, toward another point, inconceivably far in the future, when all the individual spirits in the universe will be with God again, but as *individualized beings*. It is, according to the views of Kardec's spirits, because of this movement toward individualization—toward each and every separate spirit becoming its own fully realized self, unlike any other in the universe—that evolution on all levels, be it physical or spiritual, exists to begin with. This way of thinking suggests that the whole physical universe is necessary for the existence of a single individual human soul, and that such a soul is in fact the most important and advanced thing in the universe. A corollary of this is that each individual soul takes on repeated bodily form less as the result of imperfect actions committed in the past than because possibility by nature entails limitation, and the development of agency entails the correction of that limitation from inside rather than out. In other words, in order to become, in the far distant future, the fully realized beings that we were destined from the very start to be, we essentially need to break and fix ourselves times past counting.

Here then, about 160 years ago, were the beginnings of a vision of universal evolution that was large enough to accommodate the physical aspect of the evolutionary process, *without being confined to it*. It's the real beginnings of the better and smarter side of the new age. The part that people can make fun of if they want, but that might nonetheless hold the real key to an understanding of the spiritual nature of the universe that takes the evolving cosmos of science into full account. It's a perspective that goes completely beyond the small and tired arguments between an evolving universe that's purely material in nature (in other words, the picture laid out by the more materialistic members of the scientific community) and a spiritual-material universe that's nonevolutionary (in other words, the picture laid out by most traditional, prescientific religions). In this new vision, the universe is indeed evolving (as the material evidence discovered in the eighteenth and nineteenth centuries so irrefutably suggested), but in a larger and deeper manner than a merely material one.

All of the deepest and best ideas of the new age, in short, were present, and present in an extremely coherent form, in the communications of a bunch of (apparently) disembodied spirits, given to a French schoolteacher a century and a half ago. Kardec's was a picture of the universe that, in its details, was never quite seen before, but it would appear again and again in the decades to come: a picture that, it can be argued, is the central emerging spiritual narrative of our time. Kardec's is the first and still one of the most completely and coherently worked-out examples of what we might simply call the Narrative: a new model of the nature and fate of the soul in a universe that is spiritual as well as physical, but also distinctively *evolutionary* in nature, both on a physical and a spiritual level. The Narrative paints the nature and destiny of the soul in a way that takes the best of the wisdom of the ancient East and the ancient West and combines it with the best and most compelling insights of modernity, without being robbed of its spiritual depth, and—most important—its optimism. It is a modern story of the soul and its fate that we can both believe, and be glad that we can believe it.

In 1901 a Canadian psychiatrist named Maurice Bucke published a book, *Cosmic Consciousness,* that argued that the world was on the cusp of a new age of heightened spiritual awareness: one that in the past only rare individuals had attained, but which would now be available to many more. In a famous passage, Bucke (speaking of himself in the third person) described an event that occurred one night as he was on a carriage ride home after an evening spent reading and discussing poetry with friends.

"All at once, without warning of any kind," wrote Bucke, "he found himself wrapped around, as it were, by a flame-colored cloud. For an instant he thought of fire—some sudden conflagration in the great city; the next he knew that the light was within himself. Directly afterwards there came upon him a sense of exultation, of immense joyousness, accompanied or immediately followed by an intellectual illumination quite impossible to describe. Into his brain streamed one momentary lighting-flash of the Brahmic splendor which has ever

since lightened his life; upon his head fell one drop of Brahmic bliss, leaving thenceforward for always an after-taste of
heaven. . . . Like a flash there presented to his consciousness
a clear conception in outline of the meaning and drift of the
universe. . . . [He] sees and knows that the cosmos, which to
the self-conscious mind seems made up of dead matter, is in
fact far otherwise—is in very truth a living presence. . . . He
sees that the life which is in man is eternal as all life is eternal;
that the soul of man is immortal as God is; that the universe is
so built and ordered that without any peradventure all things
work together for the good of each and all; that the happiness
of every individual is in the long run absolutely certain."

This became the classic description of what happens when
a temporary rupture occurs between the smaller, day-to-day
"down here" self and the larger, more encompassing "up above"
self. "We live our lives," wrote William James at right around
this same time, "like islands in the sea, or like trees in the forest. The maple and the pine may whisper to each other with
their leaves. . . . But the trees also commingle their roots in
the darkness underground. . . . Just so there is a continuum of
cosmic consciousness, against which our individuality builds
but accidental fences, and into which our several minds plunge
as into a mother-sea or reservoir. Our 'normal' consciousness
is circumscribed for adaptation to our external earthy environment, but the fence is weak in spots, and fitful influences from
beyond leak in, showing the otherwise unverifiable common
connection."

A central idea of the Narrative is that ordinary consciousness is not complete in and of itself, but is a smaller, truncated
part of a much larger consciousness, one that James here com-

pares to an ocean. This is an invisible sea within which we float without (for most of the time at least) knowing it, and which allows us, at times at least, to communicate and connect with other island-identities also afloat in it. Though neither states it outright in these passages, both writers hint that what holds us back from experiencing this sea of spirit more directly is *physical embodiment*. To have a body, in this view, demands of us that we become, for a time, *less* of who and what we truly are, in order that we might ultimately become *more*. Bucke and James were trained scientific thinkers, not idle dreamers (though both were and still are often accused of being such), but it was definitely the dream of both that the new century would witness a marriage of scientific understanding with spiritual insight that would do justice to the true size and grandeur of this vision of what the human being really is.

> If you wish to upset the law that all crows are black, you must not seek to show that no crows are; it is enough if you can prove one single crow to be white.
>
> —William James

This feeling that the insights of science and of spirituality could no longer be cordoned off from one another—that the two could not profitably continue to move forward as separate narratives addressing mutually exclusive realities—was in the air at the end of the nineteenth century every bit as much as it is in the air today. In 1882, it led a small group of people to form an organization called the Society for Psychical Research. Though the name sounds stodgy and old-fashioned to our ears, the society was in no way the arcane collection of oddballs it is so often represented to be these days (on those rare occasions when it is mentioned at all), but a group holding a large number of brilliant, accomplished, sensible, but unapologetically open-minded people dedicated to investigating the less tangible aspects of the human being using modern scientific methods. Those aspects included many that, up until then, science had refused to look at. Hypnosis, telepathy . . . even communication with spirits. But these phenomena were not just examined for their own sakes. In *Irreducible Mind: Toward a Psychology for the 21st Century,* the contemporary parapsychologist Emily Williams Kelly writes: "The larger purpose of psychical research, as conceived by its most prominent founders, was to examine such phenomena in light of their bearing on questions about the nature and place in the universe of mind or human personality."

One of the society's most talented and energetic members, and its head for more than ten years, was a poet and classical scholar named Frederic W. H. Myers—the same Myers who first brought the term *imaginal* into modern English use. Myers died in 1901, the same year that Bucke's *Cosmic Consciousness* came out, and spent the last decade of his life working on a mammoth, posthumously published volume titled *Human Personality and Its Survival of Bodily Death.* Though largely forgotten today, *Human Personality* is, like *Cosmic Consciousness, The Spirits' Book,* and James's *Varieties of Religious Experience,* a foundational text for the emerging evolutionary vision of what lies beyond the death of the body. A work of psychology much more than its title suggests (its original and more accurate title, changed by the publisher at the last minute, was *Human Personality in Light of Recent Findings*), Myers's book sought all but single-handedly to lay the groundwork for a genuinely modern spiritual psychology: one that would establish the human being as a creature composed of both matter and spirit, *but whose primary identity was spiritual.*

Myers was one of those people whose lives have very clearcut themes right from the start. As a boy of five, he discovered the body of a mole in a field and was scandalized when his mother told him, first, that the mole would not come back to life and second (and more distressingly) that it had no soul. Myers's interest in the existence of the afterlife was personal, passionate, and consuming. Married at an early age to a difficult and demanding woman, he developed a deep, if apparently platonic, relationship with a younger woman who then died, leaving Myers emotionally shattered and even more intellectually fixated on discovering what had happened to the living, breathing person who had left him behind. Myers was interested in highly metaphysical questions for entirely human reasons—the chief of which was his inability to believe that the human personality could simply come to an end with the death of the body.

"The question for man most momentous of all," Myers wrote, "is whether or no his personality involves any element which can survive bodily death. In this direction have always lain the greatest fears, the farthest-reaching hopes, which could either oppress or stimulate mortal minds." Myers was convinced that the time he was born into was one in which the question of what, if anything, survives the death of the body would have to be tackled by science, and the result would be a genuinely revolutionary shift in our perception of the universe and the place of human beings in it.

Myers was also, along with James, one of the original developers of the concept of the unconscious. Though we tend to attribute to Sigmund Freud the discovery that most of us, most of the time, don't really know what we're thinking on a deep level, the fact is that a number of thinkers around Freud's time were also wrestling with this idea. Myers (though the typical introductory book on psychology mentions him briefly if at all) was one of the most important.

Ordinary consciousness always struck Myers as somewhat disappointing. Was the space within the perimeters of the everyday self that we all woke up to and lived within each day really all that was available to us? "There seems no reason to assume," he wrote, "that our active consciousness is necessarily altogether superior to the consciousnesses which are at present secondary. . . . We may rather hold that *super-conscious* may be quite as legitimate a term as *sub-conscious,* and instead of regarding our consciousness (as is commonly done) as a *threshold* in our being, above which ideas and sensations must rise if we wish to cognize them, we may prefer to regard it as a *segment* of our being, into which ideas and sensations may enter either from below or from above."

The language here is dense, but in simpler terms what Myers is arguing is that our ordinary consciousness, useful as it is, is also (as we saw James state) a kind of island on which we in the modern world are at present marooned. Beyond it stretches another kind, or kinds, of consciousness, and rather than being primitive and simple, this surrounding unknown ocean is actually full of all kinds of complex and sophisticated stuff, and we suffer deeply in being shut off from it. Shifting the metaphor, this means that these regions of ourselves that we are presently shut off from are not *beneath* our ordinary selves, but *above* them. Beyond the shores of our individual, personal identities lies not darkness but light: a whole *world* of light and intelligence that we can enter if we but learn how to pass over the psychological barriers currently set up to keep us satisfied with our limited, ordinary, everyday selves.

"For Myers," writes his biographer Trevor Hamilton, "the unconscious was not a mere repository of rubbish or the source of psychological disease. It contained gold. The subliminal had elements of the sublime. From the subliminal emerged the insights, the skills, the inspirations, that one associates with genius and the highest creative achievement." Most of the decisions we make, in other words, are not really even made by "us" but by another person standing directly behind and above us: the larger, and largely hidden, person that we in truth are, but that we are often all but completely out of direct touch with while in the physical body.

Voicing an idea that in the 1960s would become the nucleus of the human potential movement, Myers suggested that everyone has the capability to be *more* than they are at the moment. Most of us are walled off from this greater potential, but geniuses and savants, he suggested, are less so. Myers felt that exceptional individuals do what they do because they have broken down, at least a little, the door to the attic where their true and total selves are stored, and have put those larger parts of themselves to use.

To illustrate this concept of the larger, secret self who was really in charge, Myers liked to point out that when people are hypnotized, they often remain perfectly conscious of their normal, everyday selves and what they've been doing, but when they are brought out of trance, they typically have no knowledge of what went on while they were hypnotized. What this suggests is that it is only when we are brought out of our smaller selves that we come into contact with the person who is really directing our life: a person we would assume we know well, but who in fact, for most of us most of the time, remains a stranger.

If Myers had gone no further than suggesting the existence of this secret, larger self while we're alive, he would have irritated far fewer members of the scientific community than he did—though he still would have irritated plenty. But he did go further. He insisted that one of the most important challenges facing science was to address the question of whether the human personality continued to exist after bodily death. "There exists," Myers wrote, "a more comprehensive consciousness, a profounder faculty, which for the most part remains potential only . . . but from which the consciousness and faculty of earth-life are mere selections . . . [No] Self of which we can here have cognizance is in reality more than a fragment of a larger Self,—revealed in a fashion at once shifting and limited through an organism not so framed as to afford its full manifestations."

Imagine inhabiting a huge, person-shaped building: a building that allows one to travel from the leg to the heart to the head to the foot, but in which it is impossible to be in all the rooms at once. That's really, suggested Myers, the way all of us are forced to experience ourselves while alive. But at death the walls separating one room from another in this structure break down, while at the same time the little person we were in life, who had been forced to inhabit one or another room of this larger self at a time, suddenly grows larger, so that we are able to inhabit the whole of the building at once. Likewise, where in life we only caught glimpses of other people's larger buildings, in the state beyond death we can suddenly see much more of them, just as they, at the same time, can see much more of us.

Such was the landscape that Myers became convinced awaited one when the physical body was left behind.

In *Irreducible Mind,* Edward F. Kelly and Emily Williams Kelly write that while "the engine that drove all of Myers's thinking and work was his passionate desire to learn whether or not individual consciousness survives death," he knew also that the age he had been born into demanded that he pursue this question in a scientific spirit. "As a scientific naturalist in the broad sense," they write, "he fully recognized that such an enormous question cannot be answered until that problem, and any empirical phenomena relevant to it, can be situated in a framework that makes them theoretically continuous and congruent with other psychological and biological phenomena. This does not mean *reducing* the unknown to the already known, the approach taken in so much scientific psychology, but instead *linking* the unknown to the already known in a continuous series. Developing such a series, from normal to abnormal to supernormal psychological phenomena, formed the methodological and organizational basis for all of Myers's work."

In the service of establishing this link, or series of links, between the known and the unknown, of breaking down the walls separating us from knowledge of the multicompart-mented buildings of our true larger selves, Myers collected evidence from both sides of the life/death divide. On the "death" side: ghosts, apparitions, and messages from the dead received through mediums. On the "life" side: feats of mind on the part of the living, like telepathy, precognition, and various and sundry forms of superlearning such as we are familiar with today from math and memory savants; feats that, he felt, could simply not be accomplished by a mind confined to the physical brain. (He would no doubt have been interested in the suggestion made by some brain researchers today that the neuronal capacity of the physical brain is incapable of storing anything approaching the amount of memories an average individual has access to, and that the true storage system for this material must lie "outside" the brain in something like the way that the websites that show up on a computer screen are not all contained by the computer itself.) The two-pronged argument that ran through all of Myers's research was that a) all of us are, right here and now, much more than we think we are and b) at the hour of our death, we will experience not a diminishment or extinguishment of our personality, but a triumphant return to those fuller and larger selves that we have, at least potentially, been all along.

> It may all be true, for anything that I know to the contrary, but really I cannot get up interest in the subject."
> —scientist T. H. Huxley, in response to a
> question about his reaction to the evidence
> that the human spirit survives death

If it sounds strange that so many respectable members of intellectual society could have allowed themselves to become so deeply engaged in questions about the human soul and its possible survival of death, this is only because we are so used to being told that these aren't ideas that people with any intelligence would ever spend time with—that in the modern age they're simply not worth asking.

Myers never guessed that things would turn out this way. There is, as Colin Wilson points out, a tone of barely contained excitement running through his writings, especially *Human Personality*. "He was quite convinced," writes Wilson, "that man was at some crucial turning point in history, and that this new 'science of ourselves' would transform human existence as completely as the science of Galileo and Newton had transformed it since the seventeenth century."

This, of course, turned out not to be the case. Myers's huge and vocal optimism about the ability of science to discover the larger geography of the soul and its existence beyond the body ensured that as the twentieth century ground to a start and psychology became more and more materialistically oriented, his work, and that of the society he headed for ten years, would fall all but completely by the wayside. After all, who could take seriously someone who maintained that we are actually *more* than our physical bodies—that we are in fact spirits moving about momentarily, but *only* momentarily, within the physical world? "Astonishingly," writes Wilson, the work of the Society for Psychical Research "did little or nothing to influence public opinion."

One big reason for this was, Wilson suggests, the very diligence with which the society had gone about collecting its evidence. Precise and exacting as they are, the voluminous *Proceedings* of the society often make for dull reading. Meanwhile, as psychical research put more and more people off for precisely the hairsplitting exactitude that its scientific opponents had complained that such a discipline could never possess, spiritualism, the popular quasi-religious movement that had grown out of the initial sensation created by the Fox girls, put people off for the exact opposite reason: it was a magnet for the credulous and the simply foolish. Tarred with the brush of what spiritualism had become within a few decades of the Fox girls' appearance, psychical research had little chance but to become a figure of fun as well. "Preposterous scandals—mediums in their underwear and ghosts with double-jointed big toes—had," writes Wilson, "the unfortunate effect of suggesting that the SPR was a collection of bumbling crackpots."

However, writes Wilson, looking back from our perspective one can, if one suspends snap judgment, see that "its achievement during those first two decades was monumentally impressive. It had set out to answer the question: Can the paranormal be taken seriously, or is it a collection of old wives' tales and delusions? What undoubtedly surprised those pioneers was the sheer mass of evidence for the paranormal. It must have seemed incredible that one person in ten had experienced a hallucination, and that so many people had seen apparitions of dying relatives or had out-of-the-body experiences. Newspaper scandals about fake mediums may have impressed the public, but what impressed the SPR was that so many mediums were obviously genuine, and that so much evidence for life after death stood up to the strictest examination."

Citing *Phantasms of the Living*, a massive book of evidence of the paranormal collected by Myers and two other members of the society and published in 1885, Wilson writes that though *Phantasms* "may be one of the most boring books ever written, its two thousand pages of cases finally batter the mind into the recognition that [the reality of the spirit world] is something that has to be faced." One could almost say that the real mistake of the initial scientific researchers into the afterlife in the late nineteenth century was that they did their job *too well.*

Ignored or not, the work of Myers, Kardec, and their associates shows that at the same time that materialistic science was preparing to exert an all but complete stranglehold on belief in any world beyond the one immediately visible to ordinary eyes, there occurred the first glimmerings of a spiritual-psychological framework in which the spiritual world, and the larger spiritual identity of the incarnate human being, could be *affirmed scientifically:* a framework in which the real story of the place and destiny of the human soul in life *and* in death could for the first time be laid out in a truly modern way. But this framework, while sketched, was never completely drawn out. Not in Myers's time, and not—at least so far—in our own time, either.

> I know now that revelation is from the self, but from that age-long memoried self, that shapes the elaborate shell of the mollusk and the child in the womb, that teaches the birds to make their nest; and that genius is a crisis that joins that buried self for certain moments to our trivial daily mind.
>
> —William Butler Yeats, *Autobiography*

Though public interest in spiritualism and psychical research faded in the early years of the twentieth century, the quest on the part of certain of the smarter and more responsible psychical researchers to chart a new map of the soul and its movements through the evolving cosmos did not disappear entirely. While scientists in large numbers continued to work at eliminating all hint of the spiritual dimension from its maps of reality, Westerners seeking an alternative to materialism on one side, and the clouds-and-halos visions of the afterlife presented by conventional Christianity on the other, tended more and more to find it in the wisdom of the ancient East. The classics of Hindu spirituality, like the Vedas and the *Bhagavad-Gita,* and of Far Eastern spirituality like the Chinese *Tao Te Ching* and Japanese Zen literature, gained more and more translators, and more and more readers as well. In comparison to the Western faiths, those of the East were older, more logical, more aesthetically appealing, and more psychologically satisfying. They were also free of the seemingly arbitrary laws and dogmas with which Judaism and Christianity were so loaded, and they embraced the beauties of the natural world in a nonconfrontational manner that the Western faiths very definitely did not. With the great age of spiritualism and psychical research over, the future of the afterlife in the West seemed to belong to the sages of the East.

Not that there wasn't a fair bit of kookiness at work among the new Western purveyors of these Eastern religions as well. Many influential Eastern ideas first found their way to the shores of Europe and America at the end of the nineteenth century courtesy of that controversial Russian mystic (and great heroine of my father's) Helena Blavatsky. Blavatsky brought these ideas to the West wrapped in the doctrines of Theosophy, a quasi-religious mix of Eastern and occult ideas focused on the central

concept that the universe was in a process of spiritual development that had unfolded over a series of cycles, each of them
encompassing long historical epochs. Blavatsky's Theosophical
Society was one of the first places where the Eastern concepts
of karma and reincarnation were married to the more modern
ideas about a universe that was actually in evolution, moving
forward on both a physical and a spiritual level. But Theosophy
and its offshoot anthroposophy, started by that other hero of
my father's, the Austrian mystic Rudolf Steiner, also brought
with them a mass of ideas that, far from being clear and easy to
understand, were profoundly and self-consciously obscure and
confusing. A person coming to either theosophy or anthroposophy with a simple desire to figure out what might or might not
happen to them after their bodies were laid to rest encountered
a hugely complex and occasionally outright inconsistent mass
of theories about cosmic epochs, lost civilizations like Atlantis
and Lumeria, enlightened masters speaking clairvoyantly from
secret hideouts in the Himalayas, and any number of other
weird and alienating ideas. Other occult and esoteric groups,
like the Golden Dawn, an influential group that flourished
in Europe in the early part of the twentieth century and that
boasted a number of famous members, such as Yeats, were also
heavily bound up with secret and extremely obscure doctrines
that stood little chance of shedding light on the spiritual nature
of man to any but a small group of adherents.

One of the main things that appealed to Westerners about
Eastern spiritual ideas was their no-nonsense quality. But the
price for accepting those doctrines in their entirety meant
abandoning the profoundly Western idea that the individual
human personality was irreducibly valuable, and that it would

survive death intact. What continued to be really needed was a view of the fate of the human soul that combined the cosmic sweep of the Eastern traditions with the focus on the individual that the Western traditions possessed. To state the situation in a general, but nonetheless accurate, way: For the Eastern faiths, the universe was, quite simply, not the factory for the creation of gods that Bergson so daringly suggested it might be, but a trap to be escaped from, pure and simple. The Eastern faiths are circular, and what the West was searching for was an evolutionary perspective that did not lock the universe into a no-exit, circular, rinse-and-repeat cycle of lifetime after lifetime after lifetime.

What the West wanted was actually present, in nascent form, in the spiritual vision inaugurated by the Romantics and the Transcendentalists, and continued in a new and genuinely scientific spirit by James, Myers, and their like. Though not nearly enough people knew this fact, some nonetheless did, and in the new century the work of this energetic minority— their quest to develop new styles of approaching the invisible and questioning the beings it might or might not contain— carried on, though now with considerably less fanfare. Quietly but doggedly, certain curious individuals continued with the idea championed by Kardec that if you want to know what happens to the soul in the world beyond the physical, if you want to make a map of the cosmos that includes more than just the physical body, the first place you should look for answers are the souls who have already entered that part of the cosmos.

Very often, these researchers were not self-proclaimed occultists, not holders of any particular doctrines, bizarre and secret or otherwise. They were simply intelligent, open-minded people with a strong need to know more than the modern world was ready to tell them about the world beyond the senses. Very often they were, like Myers had been, people who had proved unable to accept the passing of a loved one; people who were not prepared to believe that so complex an entity as the human personality could be reduced, in an instant, to a dead mass of matter. People who, in short, could not accept death as the end.

And so, whether they were supposed to or not, and whether the people they knew thought it was silly or not, these people continued to research the question of what happens when you die by questioning the individuals most likely to have answers on this matter.

And on certain occasions, at least, they received answers.

One member of this new group of twentieth-century after-life investigators was a British World War I widow named Jane Sherwood. Following the news that her husband, Andrew, had been struck down in a trench in France, Sherwood set out on a quest for a medium who could help her get in touch with him.

Disappointment followed disappointment. Then one day Sherwood met a "table medium"—that is, someone who received messages from the other world via the taps of the legs of a table on the ground, such as Kardec had encountered in his initial investigations, and whose results impressed her as none of the professional mediums and seers she had met with so far had.

"I attended one of her sittings," writes Sherwood, "and was surprised at the power with which the table appeared to be rocked and the speed with which a message could be put together. Hearing of my efforts she suggested lending me a planchette, a triangular piece of wood about the size of an outspread hand with a hole at one end for the insertion of a pencil. It ran on two small ivory wheels and the hand was placed lightly palm downwards on the board. Any movement was registered by the pencil as it moved over a sheet of paper. I remember how my own poised pencil had shown signs of independent activity and thought that this device might help in overcoming the inertia of the hand. She placed the toy on the table and rested her hand on it. With a slight creak of its wheels it moved up the table and then stopped. I thought that unconscious pressure must have been applied but when I tried it myself it was uncanny to feel the determined jerk with which it responded. I had heard of such gadgets before as adjuncts to a parlor game and had a vague theory about magnetic influence from the hand, but I took the thing home with me and that evening, as soon as I was alone I took a large sheet of paper, drew a circle on it, placed the letters of the alphabet around it and started to experiment. One placed the pencil at the center of the circle, put one's hand gently on the rest and waited for signs of movement. Almost at once it stirred and began to walk across the paper and as it reached a letter I noted it down and replaced the pencil at the center. I was intrigued and curious and persevered although that first evening I failed to get any significant grouping of letters. On succeeding evenings I tried again sometimes getting series that made words but these were only stray and meaningless. Then one evening on scanning the record I saw that one set of letters had recurred several times and the thought came to me that they might be initials. 'GFS' meant nothing to me. I could think of no one for whom they might stand. But when next I tried the planchette the mysterious letters recurred twice more and I paused, puzzled and at a loss. I again put the pencil to the center and this time it walked right out of the circle and wobbled about on the white paper outside. This had never happened before and with the utmost care lest I deflect its course I relaxed my hand until it scarcely touched the wood. The pencil moved into a series of recognizable letters. They made a name, a signature—'G. F. Scott.'

"Curiously, not a doubt assailed me that an actual identity was represented by that signature. Its very unfamiliarity was reassuring. I had my response at last but from an unknown source. There was the seal of certainty about it, impossible to doubt. I knew that the first part of my search was over and after years of lonely experimenting the shock of success halted me wordless. I felt, too, the impact of an emotion, a surprise and joy that matched my own. But who was this stranger?

"For a while I could do nothing but sit back and wait for the realization of this to quieten and steady. Then I took another sheet of paper and set the planchette free to write what it would. Writing came slowly at first and with anxious care I steadied and relaxed my hand feeling the letters forming underneath though I had to move the frame aside to read them. The writing was large and sprawling but quickly became more legible and the stupid little ivory wheels creaked and stuck under the effort to force them into faster action. Again and again a flood of relief and joy stopped the busy pencil and seemed to fill the room where I sat, no longer alone but strangely aware of an unknown friendly presence as though this stranger had indeed quietly walked into the silent room and was making himself known to me."

So began a years-long conversation between Sherwood and several invisible figures—a group that eventually came to include an individual who Sherwood became convinced was her disembodied husband. Sherwood produced a series of books detailing these investigations, one of a surprisingly large number that came out in the early decades of the twentieth century. Not all of these books are good, but many of them are much more intelligently put together than someone who hasn't read them might imagine. The best of them all sketch out the same general geography, and tell the same general story. If we take what these books say, and if we combine it with the life-and-afterlife geographies sketched by Kardec, Myers, and their peers, a curiously coherent picture emerges: a picture of the cosmos as a place that has given birth to human beings not as a random accident but for a very specific reason; one in which the individual lives, and lives again, not pointlessly and circularly, but in order *to rise* and *develop:* to become the true superbeing that all of contemporary new age thought is always alluding to and thinking of, even if often only in a backhand manner. It is a view that combines the best of the Western traditions, the best of the Eastern traditions, and anticipates the best of contemporary new age thought as well. It is the most coherent, the most convincing, and the most profoundly positive philosophy of life and death that has ever existed. It is a truly modern, truly useful, and—even, it should again be underlined, if we attribute all "spirit communication" not to actual spirits but to normally inaccessible parts of our own minds—truly *believable* map of the soul and its larger destiny.

One of the first people to notice the surprising number of these new books describing the world that waits after death, and the curious coherence of the world they describe, was Robert Crookall, a retired British botanist, geologist, and specialist in the taxonomy of coal-forming plants. Crookall ceased his plant studies in 1952, but rather than spending his retirement years relaxing in his garden, he threw himself into the task of reading and organizing this huge shadow cargo of books on the afterlife and what happens in it. To Crookall's list of already published works, which in the years before his retirement included *Fossil Plants of the Carboniferous Rocks of Great Britain,* he now added *The Supreme Adventure, Intimations of Immortality, The Mechanism of Astral Projection,* and half a dozen other titles on similar subjects.

Crookall's approach was disarmingly straightforward. Sorting through the strange mass of spirit communication books, out-of-body adventures, near-death narratives, and other paranormal material that appeared in the decades since the early days of the modern boom of spiritualism and psychical research, he tried to make sense of the data they provided in the same way he would have studied the fossil evidence for the morphology of an extinct species of plant. "The writer," he wrote in his 1960 book *The Supreme Adventure,* "has advanced no new evidence, cited no new or startling cases; on the contrary, most of our evidence has been extant for approximately half a century. We have merely subjected it to systematic analysis, bringing into relief truths that are otherwise obscure."

How could a seasoned and respected scientist like Crookall have brought himself to place so much credence in these books? By placing the same kind of basic faith in what his senses and intellect told him that anyone must have if they expect to learn anything at all about the world around them. This, Colin Wilson has suggested, is what any sensible investigator of the subject should do. "I do not," writes Wilson, "decide that a person is trustworthy because I have solid, incontrovertible proof of it. I decide it on the basis of dozens of experiences of that person, which finally fit together like a mosaic, giving me an 'overall' picture of his character. It could be compared to a newspaper photograph which, when looked at through a magnifying glass, turns into a series of black and gray dots. Nobody looking at those individual dots could believe that they would really build up into a recognizable face. The strange thing is that when we look at the picture from a certain distance, the dots vanish, and we can not only see a recognizable face, but even the expression in the eyes."

In other words, Crookall could not help but see that the data made a picture, and that that picture made too much sense of too many otherwise disparate facts to be ignored.

Of what the "dead" actually had to say in this material, Crookall said (with his characteristic amusing bluntness): "when their opinions are both a) practically unanimous and b) supported by extraneous evidence, we suggest that they are worth considering by mortals." In scientific research, the answers usually aren't just sitting around waiting for someone to come along and notice them. They're hidden. They're fragmented. And they're often so mangled by circumstance that they can appear to tell the unwary investigator exactly the opposite of what they really signify. So it was in the case of the material Crookall was now investigating. Along with a mind well suited for collecting and examining mind-numbing statistics and minutiae, Crookall possessed a courageous indifference as to whether the material he was concentrating on contradicted the dictates of materialist science. If it didn't, fine. If it did, that simply meant that those original dictates would be in need of rewriting. Ignoring the discomfort and occasional outright scorn of his colleagues, Crookall wandered off into this thicket of taboo material in search of patterns and consistencies: keys to a larger picture that was currently hidden from view.

He found them in abundance. Taken together, Crookall's books comprise an entire taxonomy of the life that awaits beyond this one. It anticipates by decades the work done by the near-death investigators of the seventies and eighties, but underlines and reinforces just about everything those investigators have to say and places it within a larger context. The departure from the body, the tunnel, moving with dizzying speed toward a white light . . . Crookall had all this material well covered decades before Raymond Moody's book made it popular in 1975. On top of that, Crookall's work tells the rest of the NDE story, moving far beyond the initial glimpses of the beyond that the majority of near-death narratives focus on.

Why is Crookall's work so little known, even by people who like this kind of thing? The short answer would seem to be his dryness. Crookall was, first and foremost, a details man, and his books, while full of documentation of what is arguably the single most consequential human experience there is, read very much like the plant taxonomy books that he cut his teeth on. But dry or not, in his books a new master narrative of life beyond the body can be seen assembling itself, a narrative that we do not need to see as just another story among stories, but as *the* story: the single spiritual narrative for our time.

Since I died I have not remained stationary.

—Frederic Myers (postmortem)

Two of the books that Crookall made most use of in his researches and felt were among the most coherent, eloquent, and suggestive sets of communications from a transphysical source were *The Road to Immortality* (1932) and *Beyond Human Personality* (1935). Both were dictated to a retiring Irish playwright named Geraldine Cummins. Cummins discovered, more or less by accident, that she had a talent for automatic writing, and over the course of a long and in the worldly sense, at least, quite uneventful life, she produced, by this method, thousands of pages written by her hand in a series of highly distinct writing styles (both in terms of how the letters looked on the page, and in the sense of what the words they formed actually had to say). Cummins herself wasn't entirely sure of where this material came from. Were disembodied entities really communicating through her? Was it instead just her "subconscious"? She never fully claimed to know. But there seems to have been little doubt among those who knew her personally that if Cummins had in fact produced this material out of her own head, then she was, both intellectually and stylistically, a much more talented and versatile person than she appeared to be on the surface. The words that came from her through this method did not sound, in short, like her.

The Road to Immortality and *Beyond Human Personality* were both authored by a disembodied spirit that called itself "Myers." Was it Fred Myers? Since his death at the turn of the century, Myers had been showing up among more mediums than just about any other disembodied spirit save for perhaps William Shakespeare—a fact that isn't surprising given the earthly Myers's passion for the idea that postmortem survival would one day be proved. If the soul did survive the death of the body, no spirit would have desired more ardently to swim back down against the current and let the earthly community know, once and for all, that this was the case.

Some of Myers's communications were more convincing than others, and one series of them, given to a number of mediums in widely separated parts of the globe over a series of years and called the "Cross Correspondences," is believed by many researchers to constitute the single most convincing proof for the reality of the survival of the human mind in an extrabodily form. The theory behind the Cross Correspondences was that if a disembodied spirit communicated one fragment of information to one medium, another related piece of information to another medium, and still a third piece of information to a third medium, and if, when these three separate recipients brought their information together they formed a whole that made sense in terms of the concerns of the communicant but that the separate recipients could claim no knowledge of . . . then the source of these fragments would have to be someone, or something, other than any single one of these separate recipients of the information. The problem with the Cross Correspondences, however, is their extreme obscurity. Like many a classics professor, the earthly Myers had taken great pride in his learning, and most of the communications given in the Cross Correspondences are so impossibly arcane that they have proved too taxing for most people to even bother reading through.

Mediumistic communications can often be like material received through many another communications medium: patchy, unreliable, and ambiguous in terms of precisely where they're coming from and precisely who is talking. In the case of mediumistic communications, this is so chiefly because the device used to receive these messages—the human mind and brain—is a notoriously patchy device in and of itself. Whether the subconscious creates these messages or receives them from somewhere else, in either case it plays a large role in determining the shape and nature of what comes through. Entities communicating mediumistically, if they really do exist separate from the unconscious, need nevertheless to "climb into" the unconscious of the receiving individual to get their messages across, and they are hence limited, to a large but not complete degree, by the abilities of that receiver. The smarter and more learned the medium, the better the equipment for the communicating entity. But people who are good mediums aren't necessarily either the smartest or the best educated. So from earliest times all the way up to now, the quality and even to a degree the content of the mediumistic message seems to depend heavily on whom it's coming through.

None of the bigger problems that came with the Cross Correspondences, however, occur with the Myers communications that came through Cummins. Rather than work to convince Cummins, or anyone else, that it was in fact he who was communicating (the principal thrust of the thousands of pages of the Cross Correspondence material), Myers—or whoever it was—simply launched into a strangely clear and no-nonsense description of what the afterlife is actually like. Reading this material, one gets the sense that whoever or whatever produced it really doesn't care what people will or won't make of it, and is simply laying out, in as swift and compact a manner as possible, the information that the earthly Myers had for so long felt that humanity was in greatest need of hearing. Forget all that other junk, the message seems to be, and pay attention to *this*.

If few people these days talk about the work produced by Myers while he was alive, even fewer choose to go near the material he produced after he died. Crookall, however, paid plenty of attention to it, for the same reason he paid attention to the rest of the sources he focused on in his books describing the afterlife state. Wherever it came from and however it got here, it *made sense*, and when combined with the communications received by other spirits through other persons, it made even more sense. As Raynor C. Johnson, an English-Australian physicist who worked on similar subject matter at around the same time Crookall did, pointed out: "in what are believed to be good sources there is a remarkable measure of general agreement." And when things agree, they should be of interest.

Johnson too had a basic sensibleness that makes his work hard to discount if approached with a genuinely open mind. "It has always been to me a matter of surprise," Johnson wrote, voicing what should by now be a very familiar argument, "that people, who on religious grounds claim to believe in their survival of death, are apparently content to hold vague and unsatisfactory views about the nature of the life they will then confront. If they knew that in a few years' time they would be going to live permanently in another country, they would take an intelligent interest in learning what they could. . . ."

The material collected by Crookall and Johnson, and laid out by people like Cummins and Sherwood, isn't, in many ways, dissimilar from the channeled material that is available in such quantity today. But it is often, quite simply, better. The first models of a new vision are very often the clearest, and it's a commonplace in spiritualist and channeling circles that the best communications come in first, with a gradual loss of clarity between here and there occurring afterward. This seems very much to be the case with this general body of material: the basic stuff that came down years back is the real armature of everything that has come along later.

Thanks to Raymond Moody, Kenneth Ring, and the other near-death researchers who started their work in the seventies, the beginnings of a genuinely modern picture of the afterlife—one that is both similar to but also subtly and significantly different from conventional Eastern and Western religious narratives—has been coming more and more into the light. But the funny thing is that there are, and have been for some time, considerably more sections of this map available than many people with an interest in these matters realize. A genuinely new Narrative, a new story of the soul and its fate that respects and takes cognizance of the maps of the past but also takes into meaningful account the discoveries and the truths of the modern world, has been emerging for more than a century now. It is a genuinely modern geography of the afterlife. It is coherent, it is consistent, and it is also, last but not least, in no way unscientific. The world of multiple dimensions it describes, in which the seemingly solid world of matter we move within is really just a singularly dense field of energy, in a hierarchy of such fields that consciousness can shift gears and move up and down in, is showing itself to be ever more similar to the universe that modern physics describes.

Most important of all, this new view of the universe is also overwhelmingly positive. If we open our minds to the possibility that it might just be accurate, it can change our perspective on both the joys and the sorrows of the life we know in countless ways, all of them good.

8

Death on the Slopes, the Initial Stages of the Afterlife Journey, the "Silver Cord," "Ghost Clothing," and What It's Like to Emerge from Physical Space

The near-death experience is at least as old as Plato, who in the tenth book of the *Republic* tells the story of a soldier named Er who was killed in battle and thrown on a pile of bodies slated for cremation, but who then regained consciousness before the torches were lit. Back among the living, he recounted how while out of the body he journeyed to a land above the earth where the good were separated from the evil, and where souls on their way back to earth were made (as my father had first explained to me) to drink from the river Lethe to blot out their memories in preparation for a fresh go-around in a physical body.

Similar stories—though typically with fewer or no allusions to reincarnation—come from medieval Europe, not to mention countless primordial shamanic cultures (where the reincarnation element often shows up strongly). So many stories like this exist that an argument could be made that the near-death experience is in no way an exclusively modern phenomenon, and that the afterlife geographies of all peoples at all times owe at least some of their details to the experiences of people who have made near escapes from death and returned, like Er, to report on what happened.

But in the nineteenth century, just as the Narrative was really gaining momentum, these stories suddenly seemed to become much more common.

One reason for this was clearly the fact that such narratives were suddenly receiving greater attention, as the question of whether the soul could possibly survive death was, as we've described, being asked just about everywhere.

But there were other, less direct reasons for this sudden boom in near-death narratives. Toward the end of the nineteenth century, for example, mountaineering became a major vogue in Europe. Adventurous individuals began traveling to faraway peaks, scaling them and quite frequently dying on them. Along with a high accident and mortality rate, the rage for mountaineering also produced a large number of narratives by individuals who courted but evaded death on the slopes.

Near-death experiences (though not yet called such) undergone by mountain climbers were so common that in 1893 a Swiss geologist named Albert Heim published an entire collection of them called *Notes on Deaths from Falls*. Heim had suffered such a fall and was astonished to discover, in the few brief seconds it took to occur, that his frame of reference shifted gears dramatically, allowing him to suddenly see his entire life as if from the position of a spectator: a spectator who was at once completely involved, and just as completely disinterested, in what was happening.

"I saw my whole past," wrote Heim in classic NDE fashion, "take place in many images, as though on a stage at some distance from me. I saw myself as the chief character in the performance. Everything was transfigured as though by a heavenly light and everything was beautiful without grief or anxiety, and without pain. The memory of very tragic experiences I had had was clear but not saddening. I felt no conflict or strife: conflict had been transmuted into love. Elevated and harmonious thoughts dominated and united the individual images, and like magnificent music a divine calm swept through my soul."

Another mountain climbing narrative with many classic NDE features comes from a clergyman named J. L. Bertrand. While on a journey up a mountain in Switzerland, Bertrand, who was not a young man at the time, felt tired and decided to stop his ascent and allow the younger members of the party to pick him up on their way back down.

"I sat down," recalled Bertrand, "my legs hanging over a precipice, my back leaning on a rock as big as an armchair. I chose that brink because there was no snow, and because I could face better the magnificent panorama of the Alpes Bernoises. I at once remembered that in my pocket there were two cigars, and put one between my teeth." Bertrand lit the cigar, sat back, and considered himself "the happiest of men."

Suddenly a kind of paralysis came over him. The match he had lit for his cigar burned down to his fingers, but he was unable to release it. Though his body was immobilized, Bertrand's thoughts were crystal clear. "If I move," he reported thinking to himself, "I shall roll down in the abyss; if I do not move I shall be a dead man in twenty-five or thirty minutes."

Unable to do anything else, Bertrand studied the sensations he felt as his body temperature slowly dropped. First his hands and feet froze, then "little by little death reached my knees and elbows. The sensation was not painful, and my mind felt quite easy. But when death had been all over my body my head became unbearably cold, and it seemed to me that pincers squeezed my heart. I never felt such an acute pain, but it lasted only a minute, and my life went out."

Bertrand's tale then starts to take on the lyricism so common in descriptions of near-death events when the protagonist suddenly discovers that though "dead," they feel more alive than ever.

"'Well,' thought I, 'at last I am what they call a dead man, and here I am, a ball of air in the air, a captive balloon still attached to earth by a kind of elastic string, and going up and always up. . . .'"

Looking down, Bertrand saw his half-frozen carcass sitting on the snowy ledge.

Like so many a near-death narrator to come, he was not impressed by the sight.

"What a horrid thing is that body—deadly pale, with a yellowish-blue color, holding a cigar in its mouth and a match in its two burned fingers. . . . If only I had a hand and scissors to cut the thread which ties me still to it!"

Floating above his body, Bertrand looked down the mountain and saw one of his party's guides. With the high-focus exactitude so characteristic of these types of experiences, Bertrand zoomed in on the guide and saw that, out of sight of the rest of the party, he was drinking Bertrand's bottle of Madeira wine. The guide then went into Bertrand's supplies and took out a chicken leg. "Go on," thought Bertrand to himself, "eat the whole of the chicken if you choose, for I hope that my miserable corpse will never eat or drink again."

With the feeling of joy and lucid calm that are also so often mentioned in the context of these experiences, Bertrand felt his vision expand, so that he could suddenly see far beyond the mountain his body was on. He saw his wife traveling to the village of Lucerne—though Bertrand recalled that she had told him she was not going there until the following day.

"My only regret was that I could not cut the string. In vain I traveled through so beautiful worlds that earth became insignificant. I had only two wishes: the certitude of not returning to earth, and the discovery of my next glorious body, without which I felt powerless. I could not be happy because the thread, though thinner than ever, was not cut, and the wished-for body was still invisible to my searching looks."

Then, all of a sudden, the fun stopped. Bertrand, bobbing in the ether, suddenly felt a tug from below. "Something was pulling and pulling the balloon down." The guide had discovered Bertrand's body and was rubbing it with snow to shock him back into consciousness.

Bertrand's reaction was once again the same as that of countless near-death narrators who have found themselves in similar situations: unhappiness and outrage.

"My grief was measureless. I felt disdain for the guide who, expecting a good reward, tried to make me understand that he had done wonders. I never felt a more violent irritation."

Once conscious again and back in his cold, wet, miserable body, Bertrand railed at the guide.

"Ah," he shouted at him, "if only you had simply cut the string."

"The string?" said the guide. "What string? You were nearly dead."

"Dead!" Bertrand shouted back. "I was less dead than you are now, and the proof is that I saw you going up [the mountain] by the right, whilst you promised me to go by the left."

"The man," recalled Bertrand, "staggered before replying, 'Because the snow was soft and there was no danger of slipping.'"

Not taken in, Bertrand responded: "You say that because you thought me far away. You went up by the right, and allowed two young men to put aside the rope. Who is a fool?" Bertrand then demanded to see the bottle of Madeira. Stunned, the guide staggered backward and fell down.

"'Oh,' said I brutally, 'you may fall down and stare at me as much as you please, and give your poor explanations, but you cannot prove that my chicken has two legs because you stole one.'

"This was too much for the good man. He got up, emptied his knapsack while muttering a kind of confession, and then fled."

This early narrative is a veritable catalog of the kinds of details of the initial portion of the NDE that would be repeated later in countless others: the triumphant feeling of buoyancy and release when one has left the body; the growing feeling of vision and power, of rising further and further from the world and being able to see more and more of that world with super-

sharp clarity; the movement up into other worlds of continu-
ally intensifying beauty and strangeness; and, of course, the
final, resigned return to the abandoned body, going back into
which is like climbing into a heap of freezing wet clothes that
one has dropped on the bathroom floor just before stepping
into a hot shower.

But perhaps the most suggestive aspect of this early NDE
story from our perspective is its cinematic quality. Dying, the
Reverend Bertrand's narrative strongly suggests, is strangely
movielike. Even though the event took place long before movies developed the kind of swoop-and-zoom effects we now take
for granted, it is impossible not to read his story without using
the kind of visualization techniques that most of us know from
the cinema. This suggests something surprising yet at the same
time (given the feelings of pleasure that the moving camera
gives us) almost obvious: that the cinema might not really represent a new experience at all, but is instead an unconscious
technological approximation of one that all of us know intimately already: that of movement, in a body both weightless
and all-seeing, through a world of luminous color where all
appears in razor-sharp focus.

But perhaps it isn't even enough to call these experiences
cinematic and leave it at that, for cinema is nothing but a technological extension of the human ability to tell a story in a
manner that mirrors actual experience while remaining all-
powerfully above and apart from it. Personal yet impersonal,
universal yet specific, the writing that most affects us often
tends to have the quality of being somehow *free* of the story it is
telling, even as it also remains right at its heart. A good writer,
it is often said, is one who is both distanced and completely *un-*

distanced from his or her material. Or as André Maurois once said: "The true artist always ends in giving up real life in order to see it better, and from outside."

One of the strange joys of a really good novel is the almost physical sensation it gives of omniscience—of seeing the world and understanding it from multiple levels and angles that allow one to be both everywhere and nowhere. This "from outside" experience that art gives, and the deep appeal it exhibits for those who know it, suggests that knowing and experiencing a situation from more perspectives than just the single, shut-in, behind-the-eyes one is something that could potentially become natural and normal to all of us. Advocates of the theory of the evolution of consciousness like Owen Barfield and Jean Gebser have suggested that humankind is even now moving toward a point when more people will be able to experience this "from outside" sensation while in their bodies. Gebser, in his book *The Ever-Present Origin,* called this state of consciousness the "integral aperspectival," which means, basically, a condition in which everything is perceived at once, without the single, point-in-space perspective that became so pronounced when artists discovered perspective in the Renaissance.

What makes all this important from the perspective of near death-experiences is that when we leave our body, we seem to slide immediately into the integral-aperspectival mode, seeing things going on all around us, and perceiving ourselves as well, from a point of view that is not a single point at all. Just as quantum physics has discovered that subatomic particles only appear to be in one single place at a time but are in fact in many places at once, so too does the essential experiencing self appear to have, once out of the body, something of this everywhere-at-once quality. That's what allows people, once out of the body, to so quickly cease to identify with it as the source and guardian of all that is truly "them." The world beyond their skins, it is discovered, is every bit as capable of containing them as the physical body had been, and in fact does a better job of it, for it doesn't constrict and control the individual consciousness in the way that the body and especially the brain did.

> **The act of dying is absolutely painless. The contortions frequently witnessed are purely muscular: the dying man does not feel them as pain. . . . Occasionally, the spiritual counterpart, when released, assumes a perpendicular position, but more generally it floats horizontally above the dying form. It may remain some time in this position, for it is attached to the body by a fine filmy cord. Death does not take place until this cord has been severed.**
>
> **—mediumistic communication,**
> **early twentieth century**

Another characteristic feature of Bertrand's story is the cord he makes such frequent reference to. Named for a passage in Ecclesiastes in which it seems to appear (". . . if the silver cord be broken . . ."), the silver cord shows up in many early near-death narratives, where it tends to act as the spiritual equivalent of the umbilical cord. Once it is broken, power to the body ceases instantly—as when an electrical cord is yanked from a wall. Deprived of the transphysical energies that it needed in order to maintain its organic coherence, the physical body then begins the process of disintegration. At the same time, the spiritual body, free now of the need to keep the physical body energized and coherent, undergoes an immediate increase in power and intensity of consciousness: one that Bertrand seemed to have been at the beginning of when rather than breaking free of the cord, he was "pulled back" by it.

Other narratives, meanwhile, suggest that it is possible to die with at least some of this cord still attached. When this happens, a kind of dual consciousness can occur, in which, though free of the physical body, the now transphysical person is still aware of what is happening to it. Postmortem communications from women still attached to their bodies by this cord have included complaints about their jewelry being removed in preparation for burial or cremation.

There may be, in addition, not one but two of these cords, attached to different parts of the body. The deceased Frederic Myers, via Geraldine Cummins, echoed many other communicators when he referred to the departing soul as a kind of spiritual "double" of the physical body: one that is "in appearance, an exact counterpart of the physical shape. The physical and spiritual bodies are bound together by many little threads, by two silver cords. One of these makes contact with the solar plexus, the other with the brain. They all may lengthen or extend during sleep or during half-sleep, for they have considerable elasticity. When a man slowly dies these threads and the two cords are gradually broken. Death occurs when these two principal communicating lines with brain and solar plexus are severed."

This all sounds weirdly materialistic, of course. "Cords" and "threads," surely, are items from *this* world, not the next, and descriptions of the spiritual world that contain them must be products of the imagination and nothing more.

Then again, maybe not, for though this concreteness can put us off, it may actually be pointing up a shortcoming on our own part: the inability to think of the spiritual world as a place that *contains specific things.* We tend to assume that, in the highly unlikely event that there really is a world beyond this one, it is airy and misty, not solid and concrete. But why is this necessarily the case? The widespread traditional idea that we live in a graded universe that moves from the material up to the immaterial (a perspective that, in a degraded form, has given us our cartoonish modern idea of a heaven of clouds above the earth) does not necessarily carry with it the idea that the higher you go in these worlds the vaguer they are. In fact, for most of the authors who described these ascending realms, what is lost as one moves up is not concreteness but *density.* The objects one encounters in the worlds are still objects, and the persons one encounters are still persons, but they are so in something like the way a tree in a Cézanne painting is a tree. Through Cézanne's ability to present the tree in terms of its multivalent inner core, the tree has become more than the single image that appears to the ordinary, mundane eye. And yet . . . it is still a very specific object. An object that, while remaining itself, has opened itself so that its inner, essential being unfolds for whoever views it with the proper eyes. In his book *Spiritual Body and Celestial Earth,* the French author Henry Corbin described what the Iranian mystical tradition calls the "Earth of Visions," a world "above" this one that appears to those who travel to it as an "external world" that, at the same time, is not the physical world we know. "It is," Corbin wrote, "a world that teaches us that it is possible to emerge from measurable space without emerging from extent, and that we must abandon homogeneous chronological time in order to enter that qualitative time which is the history of the soul."

It is this difficult but essential idea that when we leave the body we "emerge from measurable space" without "emerging from extent" that we need to keep in mind when we come upon the disconcertingly physical details that pervade the accounts of Crookall, Myers, Johnson, and others like them. The world beyond this one is, according to these representative modern tellers of the after-death story, crowded with very specific things and particular people. But those things and people are free from the tyranny of the purely physical perspective that material existence forces upon us. In the world beyond the physical, both time and space are recalibrated, so that we can appear as the people we are now, yet also, paradoxically or not, *the people we used to be as well,* and we can be perceived in such a way that our subjective essence shines forth rather than hiding invisibly beneath our (in this world) all-too-solid flesh.

Jean Gebser once suggested that just as we come into the world crying, we should leave it smiling, and there is a considerable body of evidence that many people follow this suggestion. While birth into the physical body is traumatic, exit from it is often just the opposite, even when it doesn't look that way to an outsider. Death was, for Helen Salter, a classics lecturer at Cambridge who spoke to her husband through Geraldine Cummins, "such a short journey . . . so incredibly easy and painless." For a moment, Salter said through Cummins, she panicked and tried to get back into her physical body, but when that brief moment of panic passed, there came what she calls "the unimaginable moment," the moment described by so many communicators, when she realized that she was still "there," still herself—and that in dying she had, in fact, lost nothing of the self she really was. Nothing, that is, except for the physical body, which in the instant of her leaving it revealed itself fully as what it always had been: a temporary vehicle gathered from the elements of earth and that now, with its animating power gone, would be returned to that earth.

Another vivid early NDE account featuring the silver cord comes from a doctor named A. S. Wiltse, who had a near-death experience in Kansas in 1889. Wiltse "died" and then came to again, still inside his body but unable to move it and no longer possessing the desire to do so. "I learned," he reported, using some medical terminology from his professional life in a decidedly new way, "that the epidermis was the outside boundary, so to speak, of the soul." Wiltse then felt a sensation of being rocked to and fro, and "the innumerable snapping of small cords." As one "cord" after another snapped, he left his physical body feet first, finally snapping fully free at the head. Before completely leaving his body, Wiltse reported that he "peered out" from it, hesitant for a moment as to whether to proceed. He then found himself lighter than air and bobbing up and down in the room attached by a single cord "like a soap bubble . . . until I at last broke loose from the body and fell lightly to the floor, where I slowly rose and expanded into the full stature of a man."

Like many a posthumous communicator and NDE subject, he found himself naked but immediately upon noticing this fact was clothed. Moving among the people in the room around his body, he found that he was interacting with the physical dimension in the kind of half-here, half-there manner characteristic of NDE subjects. He stood on the floor and could walk on it, yet when his arm brushed against someone else in the room it went right through.

Again like many such narrators, he now became giddy and amused at the sheer fantasticalness of the situation. Deciding to see what things looked like beyond the room where his body lay, he noticed that he was being trailed by a thin cord "like a spider's web."

Losing consciousness for a moment, he woke up to find that he seemed to be moving forward without effort from himself. Then, in front of him, appeared three imposing rocks. Clouds gathered overhead. A voice then told him that if he went beyond the rocks he could not come back. He got the sensation that even if he tried to pass through the rocks he would be prevented from doing so. Then, the next thing he knew he was back in his body, wide awake, and trying (unsuccessfully, of course) to tell the people around him about what had just happened.

Much as the Reverend Bertrand's story stood out for its cinematic quality, this one stands out for its naturalistic details. The gentle rocking of the innumerable small cords (often mentioned in the context of the one or two larger cords) as Wiltse gradually freed himself from his body; his peeping out beyond the body's edges like a child hesitating on the edge of a boat before jumping into the water; and finally, the three rocks: details that are at once earthly yet clearly more-than-earthly, and that indicate the narrator has entered at least the outer edges of a realm both concrete and symbolic. A realm where, as Yeats said, "imagination is now the world."

And of course, there is the matter of the clothing. The Egyptians, when they suggested that everything in the physical world possesses its double or counterpart in the spiritual world, voiced an idea that has shown up numerous times in afterlife discussions ever since. How can we make sense of this idea (the very opposite of the conventional wisdom that "you can't take it with you") that when we die we might find ourselves wearing a favorite shirt that we've had for years, and that it is (in report after report) the *exact* shirt, right down to the buttons?

The fact that the newly disembodied dead seemed often to find themselves not only dressed, but dressed in items of clothing they'd possessed in life, early on struck critics of this kind of narrative as final and irrefutable proof of their absurdity. For consciousness to survive death in any form is, from this perspective, absurd enough. To survive it personally, with one's entire earthly sensibility intact, is more so. But to survive it in one's favorite slacks and T-shirt is the last straw. As David Fontana, in a discussion of the related phenomenon of apparitions appearing in familiar clothes to people in this world, writes: "people often seem more surprised by the references to clothes than they do to the references to the apparitions themselves, and use the idea of clothes as a reason for dismissing everything as the observer's imagination."

Like it or not, though, the clothing issue is just too widespread to be ignored. Crookall, who wasn't one to look away from a consistent theme in afterlife material no matter how ridiculous it might strike others, even devoted an entire monograph to the subject (titled, appropriately enough, "Ghost Clothes"). He there wrote the following: "If the physical body has an objective etheric double, then presumably all other physical objects, including of course clothes, must have etheric doubles."

Etheric derives from *ether,* a word that, before its modern use in organic chemistry, referred to a mysterious intangible substance that ancient philosophers hypothesized permeated the entire universe. The spiritual body closest to the physical body (the one described in narratives like the ones above, that acts as a kind of battery supplying transphysical energies to the physical body before the "cord" connecting the two is severed) is often called the etheric body. For many readers, the name has a kind of kooky/occult sound, but the concept behind the name (and the numberless narratives that attest to its reality) becomes easier to accept if we return to the basic image of a nonphysical world that exists in level upon level above this one and that is susceptible, throughout, to our individual shaping imaginations—just as the world we currently inhabit is, but *much more so.* After all, to suggest that at death we simply enter the formless, transcendent realms where all things material are left behind in their entirety is, in a way, like arguing that immediately upon birth into the physical world we should start drinking beer, get married, and find a job.

By positing the existence of a world just as real as or even more real than ours, but more susceptible to our unconscious perceptive/creative abilities, the imaginal can help us see that the world we enter at death might hold not just things like ethereal, semiphysical cords and threads but far more familiar and personal items as well. The basic idea here (and it is an idea stated again and again in postmortem literature both ancient and modern) is that when we die we remain, first and foremost, *ourselves*—with our same habits and limitations, our same quirks, and our same strengths. We have bodies, we have perceptions, we are capable of movement and decision and indecision . . . And, because the doors of the fantastically intricate treasure house of earthly memory are thrown open, every object we ever came into contact with while alive is capable of being resuscitated.

Though the idea that human beings possess several additional nonmaterial bodies in addition to their physical one is a universal idea, what's also universal is disagreement on exactly how many of these bodies there are. But a designation of four is common, and if we follow this number of divisions up from the etheric, the next body we encounter is the astral.

Just as the etheric is a kind of "battery" body that acts as a storehouse for memory and semiphysical energy, the astral body is associated most often with the emotions. The term *astral*, which sounds as kooky/new agey as *etheric* sounds kooky/occult, came originally from the Greek philosophical school of Neoplatonism, where it suggested that there is a part of our earthly body that was originally "stellar" in nature. That is, its true home is what the Orphic fragment that we quoted at the start of this book called "the starry heaven," rather than the earth. Beyond these two is the even more rarefied "spiritual" or "celestial" body, which is associated most often not with energy or emotion but with values: that is, the sense of what traditional philosophy usually calls the true, the good, and the beautiful. Beyond these three superphysical bodies there is only the core, that absolutely essential center of centers that all the real arguments about postmortem existence inevitably circle on: the "indestructible drop" of Buddhism and the "pearl of great price" of the gospels: the thing-that's-not-a-thing that, however successfully or unsuccessfully we manage to describe it, is the true point of it all.

However many or few spiritual bodies we may actually possess is not so essential a question as it may first seem, if we remember that the extraphysical dimensions can appear differently depending on who is looking at them. A spiritual tradition that describes the human being, for example, as having eight bodies (as a number of North American tribes do) is looking at human extraphysical experience from its particular earthly perspective, with that perspective's particular assumptions and traditions. But whether four in number, or five, or eight, these extraphysical bodies always convey the idea of a central being who manifests through a number of more exterior bodies, each of which is appropriate to a particular level of the multistoried physical-material universe.

Walt Whitman speaks eloquently for this basic intuition that the self we truly are resides, like a Russian nesting doll, within this series of ever more subtle spiritual vehicles. *My real body*, Whitman wrote, was

> . . . *doubtless left to me for other spheres,*
> *My voided body nothing more to me, returning*
> *to the purifications, further offices, eternal uses*
> *of the earth.*

In this vision of things, the material body that we move around in while on earth will, for all of us, inevitably fall away one day, and the bodies that live beyond it will fall away in their turn. But the core identity where live the soul's deepest thoughts and hopes and feelings will remain through all these transformations, educated and deepened by them, but otherwise untouched.

What all these perspectives have in common is the insight that, no matter how few or many of these bodies there may be, once each has served its purpose it is no longer a tool but an obstruction, and the core identity seeks to escape from it with the kind of immediate intuition of its uselessness that the Reverend Bertrand so vividly displayed that day in the Swiss Alps. Each body is first a tool and then, if not discarded, a hindrance and an anchor, holding us back from where we are supposed to go and preventing us from becoming what we are now supposed to be.

To leave one body behind is, again universally and regardless of the fine points, to undergo a death that is, at the same time, a birth. When, on the earthly plane, we see an animal emerge from a shed skin, or a butterfly emerge from a chrysalis, what we are seeing is the earthly version of a process that continues to occur in the dimensions beyond this one, an idea that Henry Corbin explained by saying that the worlds beyond our own *symbolize with* this world. What this means—and it's an idea that while at first seemingly alien actually makes a deep intuitive sense—is that the stuff that goes on in the dimensions above this one bears a similarity to this one, even when that stuff appears at first glance to be completely unrelated to it. Different as the worlds are, they are levels of one single cosmos, so that what first appears strange will, if we linger with it, eventually cease seeming so.

I came into a strange clearness and could not believe that I had died.

—mediumistic communication,
early twentieth century

It is as if I were extracting the real "me" from the unreal "me."

—mediumistic communication,
early twentieth century

I am where I am, yet I am everywhere! I am a self that is far greater than what I thought and felt myself to be.

—mediumistic communication,
early twentieth century

Intimately related to the idea that we possess multiple bodies is the idea that each of these bodies has a spiritual landscape or set of landscapes that corresponds to it: a world, that is, in which it moves and in which it truly belongs. Traditionally, there are said to be seven of these, though again, the numbers can and do differ depending on whom you listen to. "Seven immediate 'spheres,' 'planes,' 'realms,' 'conditions,' 'mansions' or environments, are described," Crookall writes, "but communicators insist that they are not sharply marked off from each other and that there are others, whose nature is indescribable, 'beyond.'"

Again, this all sounds preposterous on the surface but actually makes quite a bit of sense once one considers it using a few of the basic insights bequeathed to us by modern physics.

Physicists now often talk about the universe as being made up of different vibrational levels. The electromagnetic spectrum is, of course, the closest and easiest example of this. We walk around all day immersed in a sea of electromagnetic information that we are completely unaware of, but which our computers, cell phones, and televisions are capable of picking up. This idea is all we need to get a basic grasp of the concept of how worlds entirely beyond our present comprehension might be right around us right here and now. Our ideas about here and there, above and below, are all developed from the perspective of our apprehension of physical reality, and have little or no meaning whatsoever from the perspective of subatomic physics, where locality becomes ever less of an issue. As Pim van Lommel stresses, the worlds beyond this one are nonlocal, just as consciousness is as well.

If one's level of consciousness is geared to a lower level, one will not be able to perceive the beings or the landscapes of a higher level, even though spatially speaking these two levels might "exist" in one and the same place. So it is, then, that someone who has just exited the material body will find him or herself in a dimension where the laws of the physical world are partially obeyed. This is how we might arrive at a situation in which an individual newly freed of their physical body is capable of moving around the room where it has just died, of going through doorways, etc., but also of walking right through the still-living people standing in the room.

Some of this can be clarified by looking at what the discarnate spirit of a woman named Betty White had to say to her husband, Stewart, who recorded her mediumistically received thoughts in a series of books in the thirties and forties.

"There is in you, as I think there is in me," said Betty through a medium, "a final point below which there is no need of underpinning. That point is our ultimate foundation, supporting by its own sheer strength all the vast structure of our senses, emotions and thoughts—the manifold of our perceptions, instincts, tastes, our loves and hates, our very response, and even obligation, to the world of things, forces and people about us." This "deep-down, ultimate core of you" Betty calls the "I-am," and it is, of course, identical to that core of cores we've been describing throughout the book as the key to the whole business.

"Psychological experience," Betty continues, "is that which is most closely related to the I-am . . . which will carry on forever; the I-am which is the core of you, the purpose of consciousness expressed in the individual." Betty liked to refer to the physical world as the "obstructed" universe, and the world we move to at death as the "unobstructed" universe. When we shift up from the obstructed to the unobstructed one (a shift that she too liked to describe as a shift, primarily in frequency), we bring with us not only our core selves, but, via the imaginal capacity, much more of our exterior trappings than we most likely ever imagined we would, and it is this specific personal stuff—from a body with clothes, to familiar objects and surroundings from our old lives—that can foster the illusion that we are still simply alive and on earth.

The idea that the dead often don't initially realize they are dead is universal. While many near-death, out-of-body, and postmortem narratives describe the newly dead person floating off almost immediately into other dimensions like the Reverend Bertrand did, others linger longer on the old familiar earth, or what at least feels like the old familiar earth. In these kinds of narrative, the individual wanders about the earthly world, going through doorways, walking down roads, only gradually finding him or herself in a world that, though it still looks familiar, is clearly no longer the exact physical world they were in while alive.

When, exactly, does the world the individual is moving in shift frequencies? It's an all but impossible question to answer from our perspective, but the concept of the imaginal allows us to conceive of a consciousness that seamlessly transforms from the earthly to the transearthly, filling in the perceptual picture in essentially the same manner that our minds fill in the picture in ordinary life. Everyone knows the experience of seeing an object that one thinks is one thing, only to then discover that it is something else. Driving along the highway, we see a small brown animal, struck but not killed by a passing car. The closer we come, the more details of the struggling animal we see—and the clearer it becomes that it is indeed just that . . . until finally we are so close that the object resolves into what it really is, and has been all along: a brown paper bag, moving from the wind created by passing cars.

Experiences like that remind us that our minds are constantly creating our reality, constantly taking creative/interpretive liberties with the raw material coming in via the optic nerve and the rest of our senses. So to see this process of collaborative creation continuing all but seamlessly as our consciousness shifts vibrational levels is really not so far-fetched at all. So it is that, oblivious to the fact that they are no longer in their physical bodies, the newly dead proceed through the outskirts of the afterlife landscape as if they were still alive—only gradually coming to realize that they are no longer fully part of the physical dimension.

While they framed the reasons for it in different terms than we do, primal cultures were often very aware of this danger of initial confusion on the part of the newly deceased individual. Such cultures often held ceremonies in which, during the first

three days after death, a person's spirit was strongly encouraged
to leave the community of the living and head off to its new
home in the lands of the dead. It wasn't, in the case of these
ceremonies, that the dead person's friends and relatives didn't
miss him or her. Rather, the ceremonies were held because it
was understood that the newly deceased individual might not
realize where he or she was, and that he or she *now belonged
elsewhere.* Though the newly disembodied person may feel so
much the same that it seems ridiculous to have to leave the
human community at all, there is now a larger world that calls
to them, and further challenges that need to be faced. Because
when one dies one remains initially so much who one was
when alive, the tendency can be to simply hang around and
keep on pretending to *be* alive—unless one gets a little push
in the right direction from the living. (This may have been one
of the original reasons for the invention of cremation. Burning
the old bodily anchor of the newly disembodied spirit lets it
know in no uncertain terms that its old home is gone and it is
time to move on.)

Primal cultures often referred to the newly dead soul as a
grub or chrysalis, an idea that makes sense for two reasons.
First, the newly dead soul is *a being in transit:* a creature that
was one thing before and is now *on its way* toward being something else. The other reason is that the etheric body is, according to many modern sources and some ancient ones as well,
itself very much like a cocoon, in that if it is not broken out of,
it can constrict and eventually smother the new being within it.
For a time it is essential . . . but after that it is a trap.

Because we identify so completely with the physical body,
because we grow, while alive, to believe that it is both all we

have and all we are, individuals often initially refuse to believe that the world of vibrant detail they have entered at death could be anything but a further continuation of bodily life. Paradoxically (from the "commonsense" viewpoint that death means an end to all these things), it seems that in many cases the only thing that tends to finally convince the newly dead person that he or she really is dead is the superior power, knowledge, and vision that he or she now has. The sensation of being able to move about as a specific, personal, empowered being, yet without the anchor of the physical body, is, it seems, similar to those moments we get as children when we suddenly pick up a new ability: when we suddenly find ourselves—in the shallow end of a swimming pool or on an older sibling's two-wheeled bike—doing what a moment ago seemed impossible. Childhood is full of these moments, and though the common wisdom is that such experiences die out at a certain point as we move into adulthood, the emerging Narrative gives us the immensely sensible and cheering news that such shocks of new ability actually continue once the physical body is left behind.

9

The Removal of the Coat of Images, More on Life as a Movie, and the Real Significance of the Life Review

I n its capacity as a storehouse of memory and vitality, the etheric body is like a combination of a battery and a fully loaded DVD of a favorite film, complete with deleted scenes, mini-documentaries about the making of the movie, and directors' commentaries. When the etheric body starts to fall away, the "panoramic" review of the life just lived begins; a review that account after account tells us is very much like a movie. As Jane Sherwood puts it, the etheric body "is essentially the vehicle of the clear-cut, detailed earth-memory, and as the real being [in the soul body] draws away from it, the memory-record is exposed." Or as another source puts it, "when therefore, anyone goes out of this life and enters the etheric, where everything, the good and the bad, is intensified beyond measure, the storehouse of the brain is opened and he is confronted with the record made. Nothing is forgotten." Philip

Gilbert, a young man who served in World War II, died from an accident soon after returning from service, and then began communicating with his mother, Alice, describes the panorama released by the etheric body as a kind of "photographic mesh." The life just lived becomes, in these descriptions, a kind of coat of pictures that, as it is removed, can be read not just by the individual whose life it was, but by others with the right eyes to see it.

Of course, none of this is completely imaginable from our present perspective. The idea of stepping outside the parade of experiences that make up one's life and seeing it as an object floating free, like a boat that one has jumped from, is only conceivable to a certain degree while we are alive, for it takes place in a dimension in which we are allowed to experience more of time than we typically do on earth, where experience tends to be confined to the present moment only.

But while it's hard to imagine, such an experience is certainly not inconceivable from a scientific perspective. For if consciousness is capable of existing outside the body, the movement out from its condition of embodiment would logically take the form of a vision of more of one's experience in the form of living memory, rather than the simple muted one-dimensional form we typically are stuck with in physical life.

Though many commentators agree that this movement out from one's experience forms the initial portion of the afterlife journey, there is considerable disagreement on how long the process can take. For some esoteric teachers like Rudolf Steiner, it can take not days but actual years. Focusing on these differences is problematic—for how do you describe a process of escaping from the borders of linear time while one is oneself still stuck within those borders? It's more useful simply to appreciate all the descriptions that come to us from these multiple narrators as metaphors for an experience that, from our perspective, can only be described in a limited and self-contradictory way.

Whether we strain to imagine what it might really feel like to perceive our entire life as a movie happening all at once, or whether we simply imagine the newly dead soul climbing out of the life just lived like a butterfly crawling out of a cocoon or like a child kicking and squirming his way out of a wet snowsuit, the full experience will remain one that is, from our current perspective, unreachably beyond our ken. But what's important no matter how we specifically imagine this experience is that we see it as a kind of *getting outside* our life so that it becomes *separate* from us in a way that was never possible when we were alive. Our life, while as deeply and personally familiar as it ever was when we were in it, becomes like a garment we can remove and inspect.

But even as we look at it from outside, we can also—as happens in the shifts in perspective that occur in dreams—see it from within. "Descriptions of the life review," David Fontana writes, "indicate that it is not like *thinking about* what has gone before, it is like being back within the experiences and emotions concerned, like entering a picture book instead of just turning the pages." To use Corbin's idea that the worlds beyond this one and the one we presently inhabit "symbolize with" each other, one could say that while the folds of the brain do not actually hold our earthly memory, they are analogous to the "folds" of the etheric or vital body, within which the intricacies of the whole vast whirling snow globe of our lives are held in perfect suspension. The appreciation wine enthusiasts feel when a good bottle of old wine is opened and the contents comes alive upon emerging into the open air—this is another earthly approximation of the kind of feeling one's consciousness must get as the events and atmospheres of times long past are resurrected, as fresh and new as in the moment they first were experienced.

"It suffices," wrote Marcel Proust in his seven-volume novel *Remembrance of Things Past,* "that a sound once heard before, or a scent once breathed in, should be heard and breathed again, simultaneously in the present and the past, real without being actual, ideal without being abstract; then immediately, the permanent essence of things which is usually hidden, is set free, and our real self, which often had seemed dead for a long time yet was not dead altogether, awakes and comes to life as it receives the heavenly food now proffered to it. One minute delivered from the order of time creates in us, that we may enjoy it, the man delivered from the order of time."

What Proust is talking about here are those rare but intensely memorable moments in life when another, secret self—the *total* self, a being vastly larger than the hopelessly limited individual we usually feel ourselves to be—comes back to consciousness as a result of experiencing a moment of what we might call *transcendent recall.* The single most famous such moment in all of literature occurs when, in the first pages of *Remembrance of Things Past,* the adult protagonist describes what happens when he tastes a madeleine, a small shell-shaped cake that he ate often in childhood. What comes back to the narrator in this moment is not just a flood of memory of the past—as smell and taste can of course convey so vividly—but a sense that this past is, in some mysterious sense, still present, still somehow *in existence.* This past moment turns out to be part of a whole *landscape,* one that we can, on occasion, catch a wider glimpse of, like someone in a dense forest who is lifted suddenly upward so that he can see the vast sweep of the forest stretching out in all directions. But one can only fully encounter this landscape when one has oneself expanded into the larger, superspatial and supertemporal self who, though we are largely unconscious of it, is actually the true protagonist of the lives we live down here on earth. The "I" that is not trapped by the tyranny of mundane physicality and the constricted mundane present moment but instead floats, flying-saucer-like, above it.

What Proust describes being recovered here is, in the words of the scholar of religions R. C. Zaehner, "the sum total of life in time and space, not one moment of which is permanently lost." And that is almost exactly what the near-death literature of the late nineteenth and early twentieth centuries describes as happening when the etheric body moves away from us after the death of the physical body.

None of this, actually, is miles from *The Tibetan Book of the Dead.* The chief difference is that in these more modern descriptions, the focus is not on getting shed of the life just done and the karma that inevitably is attached to it, but more on appreciating dimensions of that life that we hadn't been able to fully appreciate the first time around. Imagine someone like Proust or Gauguin, or for that matter Whitman, undergoing these initial afterlife experiences. Would they seek simply to atone for the wrong actions done and hope for the chance of a future incarnation in which they could behave more correctly? Such interpretations of the life review are exceedingly one-dimensional when we take into account the kaleidoscopically varied nature of the human psyche. Who knows what would draw one in or put one off upon seeing one's life again, complete and from the outside? To me at least, that such an experience might really exist is far less hard to believe than that all it really amounts to is the simple tallying of good and bad actions that morality-centered religious texts so often make it out to be. For if we live in an age of novels and movies, of the art of character analysis and development, of the appreciation of the aesthetics of the moment, then it makes sense that we might also be living in an age when those who die and look back upon those lives and experiences may do so with these long-cultivated sensitivities intact.

10

A World Much Like This One, the Waning of the Etheric, the Rise of the Astral, the "Second Death," and Connectivity, Spiritual-Style

I awoke from a deep sleep. Bewildered, I got to my feet, and, looking down, saw my body among many others on the ground. I remembered the battle, but did not realize I had been shot. I was apart from, yet I still seemed held in some way to the body. My condition was one of terrible unrest; how was it that I was alive and had a body and was not yet apart from the covering I had thought constituted my body? I looked about. Others of the seeming dead moved. Then many of them stood up and, like me, seemed to emerge from their Physical Bodies, for their old forms still lay upon the field. Soon I found myself among thousands in a similar mental state: none knew just what had happened. I did not know then, as I know now, that I always possessed a Spirit Body and that the Physical Body was only the garment it wore in earth life.

—MEDIUMISTIC COMMUNICATION, EARLY TWENTIETH CENTURY

"What is the matter with me, with us all?" I asked. He said, "Bob, we're dead!" I didn't believe it at first. I felt all right. The soul leaves the body as a boy jumps out of a school-door, that is, suddenly and with joy. . . . The easiest thing in life is death.

　—MEDIUMISTIC COMMUNICATION, EARLY TWENTIETH CENTURY

Something struck hard. . . . I fell and found myself outside myself! What a small incident this dying is! One moment I was alive, in the earthly sense, looking over the trench parapet, unalarmed, normal. Five seconds later I was standing outside my body. You see what a small thing death is, even the violent death of war! . . . It was as if I had been running hard until, hot and breathless, I had thrown my overcoat away. The coat was my body.

　—MEDIUMISTIC COMMUNICATION, EARLY TWENTIETH CENTURY

T he quality of one's consciousness at death, most of the early modern mediumistically received texts agree (once again also agreeing with Eastern sources including *The Tibetan Book of the Dead*), depends at least to some extent on the conditions in which one leaves one's body. "Those whose death is enforced," Crookall tells us (for example, a soldier killed in battle), "tend at first to be 'confused.' Such individuals enter the next world 'bewildered' by the dream-like quality of consciousness." Their surroundings are "'indistinct,' 'unreal,' 'misty,' 'foggy.'" This is because they have not left the physical body slowly, transitioning bit by bit out of it, but all at once, and as a result have arrived in the spiritual world still largely "immersed" in the etheric body. Its presence thus distorts their perceptions of their new surroundings, as well as their ability to understand them. They cannot get their bearings because they are partially blinded by the continuing presence of an organ that's no longer necessary, like a child (to use yet another analogy from the physical world) born with a caul. (Inevitably, hearing descriptions like this, our tendency is to imagine something preposterously concrete, like a child stumbling around with a half-removed sweater on its head. Such images are of course wrong, in that all this happens in a higher and hence not completely describable dimension; but at the same time, if we keep their limited and provisional nature in mind, these images are probably quite accurate as well.)

But however clearly or dimly they make it out, the dead, in the Myers model and the other contemporary and near-contemporary texts that mirror it, now find themselves in a world much like this one, if not exactly the same as it. A world that is often described as "earthlike." The capacity of the etheric body to act as a kind of storage unit for psychic energy means that if we die when we are young and vigorous, the images that it releases are so supercharged that they can overwhelm us. People who die young, and suddenly—as in war—are in particular danger of being in the situation that *The Tibetan Book of the Dead* spends so much time with, of having forgotten who one is and where one is, and of being, as a result, at the mercy of one's own creative imagination, within which one becomes stuck like a person in a kind of nightmarish gigantic movie house that never closes and never stops showing the same (alternately alluring and terrifying) movies.

As the etheric body dissolves, the astral body "wakes up." The more the etheric body falls away, the more clearly the astral body can take in its new surroundings, which now stabilize into a consistent landscape. Once again, the general consensus is that they are shockingly similar to earth. The loss of the etheric body, whether it takes a short time or long, is often referred to as the "second death." Once it is completed, we are in our astral and spirit bodies alone—though the presence of the astral makes it hard to experience the spiritual body in any but the most vague and attenuated way.

The astral body is, again according to countless late nineteenth- and early twentieth-century reports, as well as a fair number of reports from antiquity and the primordial world, just like the body we had on earth, only better; and this is true in an emotional/psychological as well as a physical sense. "What remains of us," the poet Philip Larkin wrote, "is love." Larkin, not a great believer in the idea of the afterlife, didn't mean it this way, but with the advance to the astral level this in fact seems to become the case. Jane Sherwood called our present world a "kingdom of *externals*." It's a world of surfaces. But when we die, "the voices of this world grow dumb," and we are no longer in a world of surfaces but a world of interiors. The deceased individual is now inhabiting its *body of emotion*—emotion that is, at the same time, expressed or bodied forth in that individual's actual appearance. A person in the form of the astral body appears as they did when they were in their very best shape, both mentally and physically, on earth. "I think," writes Raynor Johnson, "there is good reason to suppose that the astral body bears a close resemblance in form to the physical body at its best. . . . We all possess this body in our earthly life, but seldom consciously use it."

This again sounds absurd, unless we are able to accept the fundamental premise that the initial levels of the afterlife are in certain ways like the physical world, only more elastic and susceptible to thought. Again, while different from the Tibetan model, none of this material hugely contradicts it. What we have to keep in mind when processing this material and trying to see it in the context of world religions is that *the afterlife is not the possession of any particular religion or culture.* It is not Tibetan, any more than it is Polynesian, Australian, or Roman Catholic. We have to see the traditional texts that describe the afterlife as doing their best, within their specific linguistic and cultural contexts, to describe a landscape that is *real* but changes its features depending on who is moving through it.

One useful tool that we have in the modern world for trying to envision all this is the Internet. One of the chief reasons people love the Internet is the feeling of connected simultaneity it delivers. We long for the everything-at-once feeling that cybernetic connectivity provides, in its limited way, because we intuit that the life we currently live, in which objects hold completely still and one thing happens at a time, isn't the full world we want, at heart, to live in, and isn't the world where, as soul beings, we have in fact spent most of our time and where we really and truly belong. It may then be that once out of the physical body, one is "live" in a way similar (if vastly larger and more satisfying on a deep level) to the way one is "live" when one is online. In the movie *The Social Network,* when Jesse Eisenberg's character says, in that curiously analytical-yet-mystical manner, "the site is live," he is expressing in modern technological form an ancient—in fact, timeless—desire: the desire to shift from the cutoff state of physical embodiment to the plugged-in state of the body-beyond-the-body, where we are simultaneously in touch not only with our true inner selves, but the true inner selves of countless others as well.

Outlandish as all this may sound, it also has a completely familiar ring to it. To use Corbin's term once again: these strange experiences *symbolize with* the experiences we have in this world, even while being profoundly different from them. Nature is full of examples of the shedding of the outer by the inner. The hard, stiff, and unyielding falls away, and the soft, pliant, and responsive emerges. "On earth," says one early twentieth-century communicator, "we were as buds with our possibilities folded tight within us. . . . Now we are like flowers that have expanded from those buds—try to imagine that expansion."

11

Private and Public Postmortem Worlds, the Zone of the Earthbound Spirits, the Dangers of the Lower Astral, and the Continuing Power of Thought

I am where I am, yet I am everywhere! I am a self that is far greater and vaster than what I thought myself to be.

 —MEDIUMISTIC COMMUNICATION, EARLY TWENTIETH CENTURY

I am going out of myself. . . . I want to be *enlarged*.

 —MEDIUMISTIC COMMUNICATION, EARLY TWENTIETH CENTURY

I have never been awake before!

 —MEDIUMISTIC COMMUNICATION, EARLY TWENTIETH CENTURY

It was not long before I wanted to take an interest in things. I was aware of great joy and revelation, of new possibilities, and yet I was supposed to be asleep. That again comes to people who have lived in a particular way, who have clear minds and know what they want and think. The very stupid, unimaginative and dull people and those who have had some illness that has weakened them, need the heavy sleep from which they partly awaken when friends tell them some fact they can digest.

—MEDIUMISTIC COMMUNICATION, EARLY TWENTIETH CENTURY

Once thoroughly free of the etheric body and inhabiting only our astral and spiritual bodies, we live in a world that we create, in large part, with our own imagination, but that nonetheless overlaps with the worlds created by others. This is, again, supremely hard to envision from our perspective, but at the same time it makes an enormous amount of intuitive sense. In much of the more boldly detailed literature of spiritualism and psychical research that we're using as our imaginative model here (Kardec, Crookall, Myers, etc.), the dawning world we see as we emerge from the mists of the etheric and enter the astral dimension is given the unlikely (and confusing) name of "Hades." Hades is, according to the postmortem Myers texts, "a place of half-lights and drowsy peace," and he compares the soul's movement into it as "passing from active life into a still, sleepy world which resembles, in its anaesthetising qualities, the high noon of an English summer's day when the sun shines and the air is heavy with unshed rain."

"The ordinary person," Raynor Johnson theorizes in his book *Nurslings of Immortality,* "awakens in surroundings which give him friendly welcome, in a country not unlike his own but more beautiful than he has ever seen before. This landscape is, in fact, not a pure dream from the released unconscious of the newly dead individual but—like much of what one encounters in the postmortem dimensions—a collaborative affair. Specifically, it is the product of the creative imagining of beings on higher planes. . . . From *their* point of view, this environment would be counted an illusion: from the point of view of the astral plane dweller it is as real as trees, flowers, and houses are to us. In this setting he finds himself with some of the persons he loves, who have passed over before him. Their local environment is modified, though not always consciously, by the deeper minds of this community of individuals."

How do the specifics of this initial landscape that the soul finds itself in come to be? The Myers texts use a hypothetical newly dead individual, a middle-class Londoner named "Tom Jones," to explain it as follows: "An image is drawn from the young soul's memories. It is of a country considerably more beautiful than—but not unlike—the country Tom Jones and his comrades have known. This country is not real. It is a dream. But to Tom Jones it is as real as was his office desk and the alarm clock that roused him in the morning, summoning him to his work. It undoubtedly presents a more attractive appearance than his little gray London world, but in essentials it is of the same familiar stuff from which his England is made."

The key line here: "It is not real." This accords with the basic Buddhist perspective on the true nature of what the postmortem soul encounters, while at the same time placing it in a slightly different context. This ordinary man, the Myers texts continue, convincingly enough, "does not want a jeweled city, or some monstrous vision of infinity. He craves only for the homely landscape he used to know." He will not find that, says Myers, in the concrete sense. "But he will find, if he so desires, the illusion." Again, the Eastern tenet of Maya, or illusion, isn't contradicted, but *seen in a different light.* "Within this dream," say the Myers texts, "he will find his friends, some of his own people, and those two or three persons he really loved; that is, if they have already gone before him, been summoned by death at an earlier time." Are those people illusions? No. They are the actual souls of the actual people that individual had known on earth, moving now in an environment where, as Yeats said, "imagination is now the world" and the personal imagination is like a vehicle that at once surrounds the individual with a world of his or her creation, and facilitates the overlap between this private world and those of all the others present on that level.

It seems that one of the more confusing things about life in the postmortem realms for those who have only been there a short time is that while our mental powers increase enormously, most of the issues we have become so used to devoting those powers toward dealing with no longer exist. In physical life, the needs and demands of the body tug at us every second of our existence, dictating our moods and influencing the course and character of our thoughts so constantly that we soon find it impossible to imagine a life in which this is not the case. At death, the emerging Narrative suggests, all of this changes. Food, shelter, sex . . . the voices in our head incessantly demanding that we seek these out now all fall silent. But at the same time, our psyches, by the time we are at the end of even a comparatively short earthly life, are so thoroughly conditioned to pay constant attention to these needs that our natural inclination is to continue to try to satisfy them, and to co-create a world where that satisfaction can continue. Hence, source after source reports, the immediate afterlife realms are full of villages, of tables and chairs, of food, and of sex.

As one gradually makes one's way out of the mind-set of earth, however, the desire to fulfill these needs diminishes. If the physical world is a beautiful but at the same time terrible and exhausting place, one may now find oneself stopping, looking around, and taking in the beauty part without being distracted by the exhausting and terrible part. In short, one can relax.

> There are great cities over here for people who like cities. Harold has taken me on a short visit to . . . another London. . . . But this etheric London isn't all purgatory. There were some lovely people living contentedly in small houses in rather grubby streets. They were good souls, but such streets were their idea of heaven, so they found it. . . . They will gradually be weaned from this shabby idea of paradise when they learn to throw themselves more outward, when they use the wings of their minds and visit other peoples' worlds.
>
> —mediumistic communication,
> early twentieth century

If we are unable to shake off the etheric body completely, we can get stuck on the lower fringes of the Hades level—a level so close to the earthly that it in part overlaps it. Postmortem individuals unable to shake off the etheric are often called "earthbound" souls. They are, in a number of ancient as well as contemporary sources, described as being in a chrysalis condition, wandering around like larvae, their vision vague, their consciousness of where they are and what is happening to them unsure. They are, as Crookall put it, "in a half-world of confusion—a world caught between waking and sleeping, where the dream-experience becomes a reality and too often a nightmare." There is something unapologetically *Twilight Zone*–ish about many descriptions of this in-between realm. It is, as Jane Sherwood puts it, "a dim and formless world . . . peopled by the miasma of earth emotions and the unconscious projections of its inhabitants." It's the place where all the inner mental muck that is a part of every human psyche is exteriorized, rendered into a landscape as real as the physical world, but it is at the same time infinitely more plastic and changeable. (It's also, unfortunately, the source of much of the more questionable channeled material that comes through in such quantity these days—which is natural enough as the realm of the earthbound is the realm closest to and most similar to earth. Contemporary channeling literature contains some highly convincing—and unsettling—accounts of what can happen when one listens too eagerly and uncritically to these "earthbound" voices, for though they tend to package themselves as wise and all-knowing, the beings who speak from this level are usually no more wise than we on earth are, and are more interested in manipulating the living and preying on them psychologically than actually helping them. The definitive book on this negative side of channeling and of the problems that can come from interacting with entities on the "lower astral" zones is Joe Fisher's *The Siren Call of Hungry Ghosts*. Fisher, a talented writer on spiritual subjects who was seduced and then victimized by a group of disembodied spirits, ultimately killed himself by jumping from a cliff.)

All of this haze and fog clears up once and for all with the passage out of the initial "Hades" world, and into what is often called the "Paradise" level. As its name suggests, this world is cleaner, clearer, and all around better. At this level, which bears a strong resemblance to what in Buddhism is called Avaloka or the Lotus Flower Paradise, we get still more of our super-terrestrial memory back, and we lose the last of what a number of modern commentators call "brain memory"—that is, the kind of memory that we possess on earth, while enclosed within the no-longer-necessary envelope of the physical body. Referring to the frequency with which the newly dead are compared to grubs, Crookall writes that "many communicators independently liken the after-death 'sleep' phase to the chrysalis stage in insect development: they suggest that earth-life corresponds to the caterpillar stage (the 'nutriment' absorbed being represented by experience), the 'sleep'-and-dream phase to the chrysalis stage and the 'awakening' to the 'butterfly' stage in 'Paradise' conditions."

In other words, if, as has so often been suggested in world myth and literature, the soul is like a butterfly, it has now completely emerged from its chrysalis and is unfolding its slowly drying wings against the winds of that realm that Iranian mysticism called Hurqualya, the "earth above the earth."

In a good example of the kind of pointless confusion that gets layered onto the modern afterlife picture by an excess of terminology, the paradise level is also sometimes called the Plane of Illusion. This is doubly problematic, as what happens on the Paradise/Plane of Illusion level is *not* illusory, except in comparison to the hyperreal levels of experience that lie above it. Compared to our current world it is, by common consensus, an entirely *more* real place. On this level there is a reality common to all, while at the same time each individual soul there continues to possess its own personal interior reality, one that overlaps with but doesn't cancel out the individual reality worlds of the other souls there.

"The fact that individuals 'create' their own realities," writes Fontana, returning once again to the ever-recurring clothing issue, "makes possible sense of the descriptions of the Plane of Illusion that include references to people wearing clothes and living in houses and indulging in some of the pleasures enjoyed on earth." More than ever, this is a world that makes one think of what we are currently trying so hard to recapture through the Internet. To make a slightly ridiculous yet nonetheless apt comparison, it would seem that the afterlife is a lot like Facebook, with the difference that the simulacrum of connection with others that Facebook *partially* provides is here actually *provided in full.* The higher we move in this supremely interactive domain, the more able we are to communicate with others while remaining, at the same time, ourselves and no other. All of cyberspace may just be a kind of flattened, introductory version of what life beyond the body actually is.

Fontana writes that the fact that people seem to go about very earthlike business on the Plane of Illusion may suggest that it is "composed of a subtler version of the quantum reality that underlies our own visible world. If it does, then maybe there is more of a continuum between this world and the next than we might suppose. We are even told that in the next world some people open shops and that others enjoy shopping in them, which adds to the impression that the Plane of Illusion may be a form of make-believe existence in which individuals continue to think of themselves as they were on earth. . . ." Once again: imagination is now reality, and the idea only sounds stupid when we ourselves fail to have the imagination to conceive of an environment in which our inner psychological furniture can overflow its boundaries and interact with the furniture of others. Imagining heaven as a small town with a butcher shop and plenty of park space to walk your dog is idiotic. Imagining reality as being mental as well as physical in its construction, and hence allowing for "exterior" environments containing parks and butcher shops to be generated by the imaginal capacity of the mind once it is free of the directives of the physical body, is not.

Focus is the equivalent of power in this world. The sharper our focus, the more we are able to remain anchored in our particular reality and not get sucked into those of others. Fontana writes of a young woman living with other deceased family members who explains "that if they fail to concentrate sufficiently they find that rooms previously in their house have puzzlingly ceased to exist."

Once again, this in certain ways contradicts and in certain ways completely meshes with the tenets of traditional Buddhist thought. "The more closely we study the Bardo Thodol," writes Fontana, "the more we recognize that in itself it possesses similarities with the Plane of Illusion. Once again we are confronted with an illusory mental world in which experiences are created from the memories, the attachments, aversions and ignorance that the unenlightened mind brings with it from earth. The hallucinations seen in the *bardo* are 'real' in that they represent genuine mental propensities on the part of the viewer. . . . Even visions such as the peaceful and the wrathful deities are seen only through the veil of the viewer's ignorance, and not as emanations from the Ultimate Reality."

We are told by the Myers texts and other modern and semi-modern sources that use this particular terminology that people typically spend a long time on the Plane of Illusion, because it functions, among other things, as a transitional level, allowing for the slow development of the individual toward higher levels not so totally dominated by the rules of earth perception. "The large majority of human beings when they die," report the Myers texts, "are dominated by the conception that substance is reality, that their particular experience of substance is the only reality. They are not prepared for an immediate and complete change of outlook. They passionately yearn for familiar though idealized surroundings. Their will to live is merely to live, therefore, in the past." The texts' hypothetical Tom Jones character, for example, "will desire a glorified brick villa in a glorified Brighton. So he finds himself the proud possessor of that twentieth-century atrocity. He naturally gravitates towards his acquaintances, all those who were of a like mind. On earth he longed for a superior brand of cigar. He can have the experience ad nauseam of smoking this brand. He wanted to play golf, so he plays golf. But he is merely dreaming all the time or, rather, living within the fantasy created by his strongest desires on earth."

But the cigars and golf don't, even for the most unimaginative postmortem soul, go on forever.

12

Seven Planes, the Judgment, to Be Reborn or Not to Be Reborn, Life as a Movie Worth Watching, and the Concept of the Group Soul

S
even is a number with a particularly strong spiritual pedigree, and the idea that the heavens are divided up into seven levels occurs widely in both East and West. The Myers texts, coincidentally or not, divide the afterlife realm into seven planes as well. They also follow a fairly well-established tradition in describing the first four planes as planes of "form" and the three planes above that as "formless." The fourth plane, and the last of the planes of form, he calls the Plane of Color. In the Myers model, the astral body is left behind here, as the etheric was left behind before, and as the physical body was left behind before that. And just as the discarding of the etheric body is associated with the first life review, the discarding of the astral body is connected with this second one.

That the postmortem soul—usually with one or more supernatural beings present—judges his or her earthly actions in the world beyond is one of the most widespread statements about the afterlife there is. In modern descriptions of the afterlife journey two judgments tend to be described, but more important than the number of judgments or when exactly they happen is the idea, central to all the more sophisticated descriptions of this event both ancient and modern, that the real person doing the judging is our own higher self.

In most modern afterlife literature, the second life review has a more pronounced moral component than the first one does. One doesn't see the whole thing flash past like a movie one is watching, but much more, this time, like a movie one is actually *in*. This review also takes longer than the first one and, because one reexperiences not just one's own actions but their results upon others, it is generally agreed to be quite painful—especially if one's actions on earth have been less than perfect.

On the vibrational level that the Myers texts call the Plane of Color, the fact that the universe is *structurally moral* becomes more apparent than ever. The important idea here is that the higher up on the scale of the transphysical levels we go, the less our actual identity with others becomes an abstraction and the more it becomes a *felt reality*. And it can be a reality that feels either good or awful, depending on how we behaved to others while down in the insulating costume party of earthly existence.

To say that we share our identity with other beings does not mean that we are all exactly the same, but, again, to suggest that we are like different parts of a universal body (like the Adam Kadmon or primal man of Jewish mysticism, or the body of the cosmic Christ in Christianity). The universal wisdom here is that the more aggressive or uncompassionate our actions were on earth, the more we now experience the fruits of those actions upon ourselves. Again, this is not a simple tit-for-tat doctrine of punishment, but rather the inevitable result of our discovery that the people or beings we behaved poorly to are actual parts of the same cosmic body that we are part of.

Imagine an upside-down tree. Then imagine that we are at the tip of one of its lowest branches. In life on earth we are aware of ourselves, in general, in this way. There are the tips of other branches around us, but they don't seem to have much to do with us. But when we die we rise, traveling from the tip of that upside-down branch to the point where it meets up with a thicker one, and then to the point where that one joins a thicker one still . . . until finally the trunk is reached. As we move upward and upward, ever closer to the central point where all the upside-down branches meet the trunk, we don't (according to this model at least) lose our individuality. But we become ever more conscious of the fact that we are part of an organism that encompasses not only our being but that of all the other beings we have ever come into contact with as well. What the Myers texts call the Plane of Color, then, is the place where one's actual connection to the rest of the universe becomes finally and fully apparent—and that restored connection hurts to the precise degree that we have, up to that point, ignored or acted aggressively counter to it.

The Plane of Color is also the level where, according to most of the voices that have provided us with the descriptions that create this modern lens on the afterlife phenomenon, individuals choose whether to go back to earth to reincarnate.

The reincarnation question is responsible for more disagreements than any other among people who take the concept of the afterlife seriously. Do people reincarnate? If so, how many times? Do people reincarnate as humans alone, or can humans become animals or, as in Buddhism, other supernatural beings, from gods to devils?

These questions aren't just complicated and vigorously argued—they're also dispiriting. For the degree of disagreement is such that it can distract one from the considerable effort required to approach the afterlife question energetically, imaginatively, and openly. In terms of the emerging Narrative we've been talking about, in which Eastern and Western afterlife concepts are coming together and, inevitably, merging with the scientific perspective, what is probably most important is isolating a few key statements that can with minimum argument be made about the phenomenon.

The first statement that can be made with real assurance is that regardless of what the intricate mechanics of reincarnation are or are not, *something* very definitely passes from one life to the next, and to deny this at this point, either on religious or scientific grounds, is simply to be bullheaded or cowardly.

In support of this statement are the several thousand cases "suggestive of reincarnation" compiled over more than forty years by the late professor Ian Stevenson, head of the Division of Perceptual Studies at the University of Virginia. The subject of a number of books as well as the author of half a dozen himself, Stevenson was another scientist who refused to be told what were and were not appropriate subjects for scientific study. Early on in his career he became frustrated at the limited nature of current psychological models for accounting for the complexities of individual human character, and in the early sixties started collecting examples of what appeared to be children who remembered previous lifetimes.

A classic example of the kind of case Stevenson devoted himself to tracking down and documenting was that of Jagdish Chandra, a child born in Uttar Pradesh, in northern India, in 1923. At three, Chandra started mentioning his previous, "real" life, which had taken place in the Indian state of Benares. Chandra's father was a lawyer and took to documenting the boy's statements, which included the name of his "real" father (one Babuji Pandey), details on Pandey's wife and other children, and the unusual (for India at the time) detail that he drove a car. Chandra also gave his "new" parents a detailed description of the house he had lived in, even telling them the precise location behind a wall of a safe containing his former father's valuables. Gallingly, he also complained to his "new" parents of the food they gave him to eat. In his previous life, Chandra had been of the Brahmin class, and was not accustomed to eating the food prepared in the less exacting manner that his present, lower-class parents did.

Finally, Chandra's "new" father had enough and embarked on a search for his son's previous father. Through a story published in a Benares paper, he eventually discovered one Babuji Pandey, and took his son to Benares to meet him. When they arrived at the city, Chandra's father told the boy that if he really had lived in Benares before, he should be able to locate his house. Wending his way slowly through the town's labyrinthine streets, Jagdish did just that.

Stevenson, who amassed case after case like this one, was often criticized for the number that he collected from India and other countries where the doctrine of reincarnation is an accepted part of life. But Stevenson, and others after him, have argued that this higher incidence is due not to the details of the stories having been invented, but rather to the fact that in those countries, stories of children who claim to remember past lives tend to be taken more seriously. There have, in any case, been a fair number of documented American examples of children who announce to their parents that their "real" house and their "real" parents are elsewhere, and who then supply bewildering strings of factual details to prove it. The most famous of these is probably still that of the "Watseka Wonder," a thirteen-year-old girl named Lurancy Vennum. In 1877, after suffering a series of trancelike seizures, Lurancy "became" for a time, a girl named Mary Roff, who had died twelve years earlier. Like Jagdish Chandra, Lurancy, while "Mary," recognized friends and family members of Mary, addressed them by name, and told Mary's former Sunday school teacher, whom she also recognized without prompting, that she'd "changed the least of anyone."

Just as it is at this point basically incontrovertible that the experiences undergone in NDEs can't be explained by stress on the brain due to hypoxia, excess buildup of carbon dioxide in the blood, and the long list of other hopelessly reductionist explanations offered by the phenomenon's materialist opponents, so it is also a losing proposition to argue that every last one of the hundreds of compelling cases of past life recall, either in children or in adults, is a simple fantasy. There is, quite simply, more to it than that.

But how *much* more, and how, precisely, does it all work? It may be that cases like the kind Stevenson devoted his life to collecting are, for the moment at least, chiefly valuable not because they give any complete answer to these questions, but because they provide strong evidence to counter that inner, materialistic voice most of us carry around. Beyond the fact that *something* is really going on, however, they don't help us all that much with details. But they do make it easier for us to listen to the details that come to us from other sources, without immediately dismissing them as nonsense. In the end, consciousness is either able to exist beyond the neural workings of the brain, or it isn't. If one can't accept that it does, then all the details discussed in this book are absurd. If, on the other hand, consciousness can and does function beyond the brain, then everything changes, and it's suddenly possible, as we are doing in this book, to talk about all kinds of seemingly crazy things and be open to the possibility that at least some of them might not be so crazy after all. The work of Stevenson and cases like that of Lurancy Vennum are, more than anything else, tools to help break down that initial door of denial and disbelief.

In the sketch of the afterlife we're laying out here, using the reports of the Myers texts, the collected findings of Crookall and Raynor Johnson, along with the insights of David Lorimer, Michael Whiteman, Paul Beard, David Fontana, Christopher Bache, and other recent researchers as further guides, and keeping the ideas of the Romantics, the Transcendentalists, Steiner, and Kardec's spirits in the background at all times as well, the general idea is that if we do reincarnate, we do so not hundreds or thousands of times (as the traditional Buddhist and Hindu views state) but only several or at most a dozen. For if the universe is at bottom an arena for growth rather than a cosmic trap, this doesn't leave much room for the "eternal round" model of reincarnation as a punishment that goes on incessantly and involves the rebirth of human beings in the form of animals, subearthly demons, or—as in Buddhism—insects.

In the Myers-Crookall model, people spend more—much more—time out of the body than in, and however much of the individual takes birth on earth, the larger portion of their personality remains behind—or rather above—in the super-conscious region of ourselves that we have only intermittent contact with through the course of our earthly life. If the after-life realms are envisioned as a hierarchy, with each level being tougher to reach than those below, the general idea is that each life we live brings us a little higher, so that if a soul is incapable of attaining to that region the Myers texts call the Plane of Color in one afterlife interval, it might manage it the next time around, or the next.

A key argument for the idea that we spend more time "out" than "in" comes from the simple and obvious fact that far too much happens far too quickly in life for us to be able to examine it properly while we're down here. The afterlife is, in this view, a realm of exegesis—that is, a place where the textual material of earthly life is sifted and interpreted, where its impossible densi-ties of meaning can be teased out and absorbed. Earthly life, in this view, is, again, a little like one of the DVDs I possess of movies that I first saw with my father as a child and now find myself returning to again and again, watching and rewatching, looking for . . . what I don't always really know, exactly. Watch a movie nineteen or twenty times and most of your attention goes to the things on the periphery. A line of trees at the edge of the screen, moving gently in the wind as the actors up front go about their familiar business: because that line of trees still moves, I know that everything else that ever happened must be moving out there too somewhere, if only I could recover the lost or occult machinery that would enable me to see it.

Life—even a painful life—is like a movie worth watching. On the theory that we're here to learn, and that even painful experiences have stuff to teach us, we can't do that learning unless we have time above, when back in touch with our full personalities, to examine what happened to us. This, to my mind, is the most compelling explanation for why the grinding, eternal-wheel model of reincarnation is incorrect, and why we might genuinely hope that it is in fact true that we spend much more time between earthly lives than in them. If the more contemporary descriptions of the between-life state offered by the writers my father gravitated to in his last days sometimes strike me as excessively sugary, I am nonetheless in complete sympathy with their attempts to formulate our existence as an event *saturated with meaning:* an existence in which even the smallest moment contains significance beyond measure. In this view of things, even when it seems most boring and uneventful, our full personalities, the ones that only can unfold when back in the world above, are taking in what is happening to us while we are down here, making sense of our interactions with others. And it is only when we are once again reunited with those larger aspects of ourselves on the higher levels of being that we can even begin to make sense of the things that happened down here in this highly claustrophobic, confusing, but nonetheless essential realm.

In deciding on the reincarnation issue, there is also the matter of the phenomenon of past life regression therapy, which has become ever more popular since its birth in the seventies and has yielded a trove of provocative if often still confusing and contradictory evidence. One of the more compelling facts about contemporary past life regression material is that most of the more convincing reports from these regressions suggest that people who have vivid and detailed past life memories rarely remember having been people of wealth and importance, as the clichéd image of new age past life explorers usually makes out. Life, typically, was dull more than anything else, it was a relief to finally get out of it, and there was no great desire to return and go through another one. These reports fit well with the old Neoplatonic idea that earthly life is a kind of "cave" into which we descend for a time: a *useful* cave, and one that assists in the forward movement of the soul, but a cave all the same. In this view, souls, in accord with their "astral" nature, return to earth like falling stars, drinking first from the waters of the river Lethe so that they forget, once born, their existence in the world above, and when they leave the body they gradually remember their larger existence once again. In this view also, three or four earthly incarnations are all most souls would be up for. Unless one is what Christianity calls a saint and Buddhism calls a bodhisattva, life on earth is simply too difficult, too reduced an affair, for any but the most intractably wrongheaded soul to desire to return to it for more times than that.

And paradoxically, it's also too rich. For if earthly life is in many ways a reduction from the freedoms of life outside the body, it is also, as I've stressed throughout this book, the domain of a certain kind of experience that can *only* be had here: an experience defined by limitation but at the same time by possibility and mystery. Earth is where, each time we return to it, we lose ourselves, but where in the course of refinding ourselves we experience our selfhood, our true spiritual identity, and our relationship to the universe that gave birth to us, in a way that we can on no other level of existence.

Or, as Rilke put it, in his poem *Duino Elegies:*

Perhaps we are here to say: house,
bridge, spring, gate, jug, fruit-tree, window—
at most: column, tower . . .

To use still another metaphor, earthly life is like taking a scientific journey to an exotic place to collect material for later examination. The stuff of our life down here is supersaturated with meaning, a meaning made up in large part of pain and limitation but that is meaning nonetheless, and it is in the world beyond the confines of this one that we are able, finally, to make sense of it. Too often, I think, the idea that we live more life than one, and that the life we are currently leading is actually a learning experience, is dismissed as two-dimensional: a shallow new age answer to ultimate questions of the meaning of our existence, and one that shortchanges the real mystery, terror, and singularity of human life. But again, in another way this view of things is really the only one that can make any sense of the fact that for most of us, most of the mystery of our lives passes us by before we have a chance to truly take any of it in. A single morning waiting at the bus stop before school when we are, say, thirteen years old, can contain enough to occupy one for an untold amount of time . . . if one were only allowed to return to it and do it justice. When communicators speak of life reviews and of going over the life we have led, this, I think, is the sense in which we should look at those statements. If something like the life review really exists, it's not a matter of simply counting off the bad actions that one has committed and of making amends for them, but something infinitely more complex and multilayered. Viewed this way, the notion that we spend more time "above," processing the life we have lived here below, really makes a considerable amount of sense—both logically and emotionally.

But even when we view it within this general framework—the universe as a realm where human significance matters and where the meaning of individual existences might, as so many of us dream, someday be fully uncovered—dozens of questions still arise about the mechanics of reincarnation: questions that, while valid, tend to lead into endless thickets of discussion and metaphysical nitpicking.

One concept, not exclusive to the Myers texts but discussed in detail there, that can be of tremendous help in rescuing us from such thickets of pointless argument is that of the group soul. This is, in the view of the Myers texts, a group of souls who know each other above the earthly world, who see each other again when they rise out of it, and whose "wisdom and strength," says Crookall, are "more or less available to all the others."

To get an idea of what this means, think of the Plane of Color as the surface of a large, deep lake, and of the group soul as a raft floating on its surface. The earthly world, in this image, is the bottom of the lake, and being born into the physical world is the equivalent of diving down to the bottom from the surface. We stay down there at the bottom for a short time, relatively speaking, moving around and seeing what's going on with difficulty. Dying is the equivalent of our departure back up from the lake bottom, far down in the darkness, toward the surface.

Swimming upward, we pass first through the murk of the Hades realm, and then through the more light-shot waters of the astral realm. Things get lighter and clearer as we go up. Reaching the Plane of Color is like breaking the surface of the lake. Taking air back into our lungs, we look around and see that there are others all around us, diving down and coming back up, and that these are assembled into groups, floating and talking together. These are the group souls that contain the souls we know and have known for ages, and whom we lost contact with when we dove down to the bottom to incarnate, except for brief moments when, all but blind down there, we bumped into each other and vaguely recognized our connection from the world above.

Like every image we're using here, this is to some degree cartoonish and simplistic. The fact is that the further up we go, the harder it is to talk about any of this stuff without drifting either into abstraction or into imagery that oversimplifies processes complex, as we suggested in the introduction, beyond all our imagining. It's all simply too far away from where we are now for us to do otherwise. But if we consider this lake-and-swimmers image while keeping in mind that it is *just* an image, the idea it gives us is one of a heightened form of common interiority: one in which we share what we are and what we think and even what we have lived through in the past with certain other souls in an especially intense way, even while at the same time retaining our own individual identities. With the rediscovery of the group soul to which one belongs, writes Johnson, "the soul discovers the reality and joy of communion with others to an extent which it can never do on earth." There is no arguing that higher communion with others is a longing a great many of us suffer, and it may be that, as we suggested a number of times earlier on, the very intensity of that longing argues for the reality of such a phenomenon, just as thirst argues convincingly for the existence of water.

The fourth plane is often called, by the sources we are using most, the plane of true archetypal reality. What *is* an archetype, though? Plato thought of it as a kind of spiritual original of the things we find on earth that are like copies of it, the example usually used being a horse. Way off somewhere, we learned in high school, Plato imagined a kind of perfect, ultimate horse, of which all the horses we find on earth are models. That's fine, but it's also vague, filmy . . . abstract. What an archetype really is, however—and what a number of his followers, especially in the philosophic school of Neoplatonism, felt Plato really had more in mind—is not some abstract, colorless, hairless horse floating in some zone of "higher" reality that bears no relation to the one we're in now, but something much more interesting and much harder to talk about. We might envision it as the reality that exists behind the televised image of a horse. From that perspective, every horse we see down here in the material world is the equivalent of a horse on a TV screen, and a horse on the archetypal level is the equivalent of the real, flesh-and-blood horse that was photographed to obtain that image.

But archetypes, while being more "real," are also supposed to be more "general." That's really where the trouble starts, because as soon as something becomes "general" it stops being personal, immediate, and particular, the way all the really important things we encounter on earth always are. An archetypal person then becomes, in our imagination, something like a department store mannequin: it looks a little like everyone we know, but at the cost of its essential humanity. It is not a person but a thing.

Though this is inevitably the kind of picture of archetypal reality that a high school reading of Plato tends to leave us with, when the authors we are looking at here bring up the word *archetype,* they appear to be doing it much more in the manner that the metaphysical/esoteric thinkers of mystical Islam were when they spoke of the archetypal world as being not only more real than this one but also more *specific and personal.* Aristotle taught us that we need matter for particularity—that for a thing to be unique it needs to be made of physical stuff. But in a world where brute physical matter is really just the lowest and roughest level of a multitiered universe where higher and higher grades of spiritualized matter (the etheric, the astral, etc.) exist, it becomes easier to understand archetypal reality as being exactly the opposite of that generalized, abstract realm that *archetype* tends to conjure for most people. The true archetypal world is the *real* world: a world of which ours is a kind of echo or shadow. We can't see it now, because it's producing, generating, the world we *do* see. That means that we can never fully know any personality—or any animal, or any object, even—down here on earth, because the source of everything down here lies above, in the world of which this one is a lesser projection.

All this is difficult, but in order to get the real point of it, all we need to do is realize that all the little details that make life matter exist in relationship to a larger, currently hidden world, and that rather than erasing the detailed world we experience down here, that higher world instead renders it *more* detailed, and more personal. It shows the true fathomless depth and meaning of a world that, as we voyage through it now, can appear all too often as mere passing surface.

If the concept of heaven means anything, it means this: a domain where all that is most personal, profound, yet fleeting is recovered, in a dimension where the strictures of linear time and three-dimensional space are removed. This is the heaven hovering behind all the best and most curiously haunting descriptions of the life beyond this one that have been cropping up over the past hundred years or so. It's what Raynor Johnson wanted to suggest when he wrote that in the archetypal world, "the power and sensitivity of mind are now vastly increased, so that the depths and heights of emotional experience are greater. Joy and sorrow are part of the soul's lot in an intensified and rarefied form, and the zest of living is far beyond the pale conceptions of earth."

The Myers texts call the landscape one inhabits on the Plane of Color "the original of earth." This, again, expresses the old Platonic idea that the world we currently inhabit is a kind of shadow of a currently hidden, more real one, which exists in a domain so far removed from us that our current existence is like living in that cave of Plato's my father liked to talk about, staring at the shadows we cast upon the wall and thinking those shadows are reality. "You are doubtless aware," say the Myers texts, sounding extremely Platonic, "that the copyist, when he produces his painting of a masterpiece, usually fails through being unable to convey the soul of the work in question. The measurements may be correct, coloring and line excellent, but the life is not within it; so you are left cold and aloof, you are merely stirred to a petty irritation when you perceive a copy of an old master you loved. The earth, as you know it, is this unreal thing—a copy of a masterpiece. It is a shadow with all the defects of a shadow. It is, at times, distorted and grotesque; at times, a mere dim outline. Animation is absent. The true life is not expressed in it."

This sounds slightly shocking, but it expresses a sentiment that has been voiced not only by certain voices in the Platonic and Neoplatonic traditions, but by Australian Aborigines, Native Americans, and medieval Arabs. It sounds like a "world-denying" idea but in fact is a "world rescuing" idea, for it suggests that basic argument that has surfaced again and again throughout this book: that nothing down here that matters is ever truly lost, for we in fact only see the very edges of the true and multileveled world we genuinely inhabit, as well as only the very edges of every person we encounter down here. The rest of it—the vast trove of meaning and inner personal significance lying beyond the tip of this inverted iceberg—lies in the worlds above this one; worlds that we visit, and revisit, each time we leave this world behind; a world where all that is passing and momentary down here survives, just as it is, outside of time, "forever."

13

The Pulse of Life, Keeping Heaven in Your View, What Lies Beyond the World of Form, and What Waits Beyond the End of Time

As we have seen in the Myers texts and many of the other modern reports like them, the higher worlds are described, just as in visionary descriptions from a number of mystical texts from earlier times, as being more, not less, specific, more detailed than this world. They appear, one might say, in a higher resolution. Again they are, though not physical in the sense that we think of things being physical, worlds of *concrete specifics.* They are not vague and abstract. They have stuff in them. They have people in them. The things and creatures in them glow with life, in the way that the things and the creatures of this world glow with life, at least in their best moments. This is the dreamtime earth of the Aborigines, the "first world" of T. S. Eliot's *Four Quartets,* and what ancient Iranian mysticism called Hurqualya, or the Earth of Visions.

It's the world that countless people search for when they go into the natural world with its pulse and flash of animal and vegetable life. It's why Hemingway liked to go fishing and why Van Gogh liked to paint wheat fields. It is the world where all true vitality lies, and it lies not within but above this one.

It is also the last realm that we can come even remotely close to conceiving from our earthly level.

To enter the Plane of Color is to transcend form as we know it, but we again have to remember that *transcendence is not necessarily denial.* What's going on here is that we are gradually working our way out of matter, but not by denying matter's relative reality and its innate value: a value that we spend our whole time on earth learning to appreciate. This is, again, the sentiment which Rilke voiced when he suggested that "perhaps we are here to say: house, bridge, spring . . ."

It's also the sentiment expressed by a survivor of an NDE quoted by Hampe who struggled to cope with the feelings of loss and disappointment that came along with the return to the body.

"I have just returned from a pleasant, slow, mile-and-a-half jog," this person wrote. "I am sitting in our garden. Overhead a tree moves gently in a mild, southerly breeze. Two small children, holding hands, walk down the street absorbed in their own world. I am glad I am here. But I know that this marvelous place of sun and wind, flowers, children and lovers, this place of evil, pain and ugliness, is only one of the many realities through which I must travel to distant and unknown destinations."

In these words there is a sense both of profound appreciation for the particularities of this world, with its wooden gates

and its fields and its fruit trees and its early September after-
noons, its unarguable joys and its equally unarguable and cruel
disappointments . . . and an equally profound appreciation of
the fact that this world is far from the only one there is. That a
better and more specific and more personal ones lies beyond it,
anchoring it, as it were, from above.

The idea that the levels we are now looking at exist on the
very edge of form is expressed vividly in this outlandish but
also somehow strangely authoritative description from the
Myers texts:

"Within the subtle world of which I speak," suggests the
voice that came down to Geraldine Cummins and called itself "Myers," "you will perceive a variety of forms which are
not known on earth and therefore may not be expressed in
words. Yet there is a certain similarity, a correspondence between the appearances of nature and the appearances on this
luminiferous plane. Flowers are there; but these are in shapes
unknown to you, exquisite in color, radiant with light. Such
colors, such lights are not contained within any earthly octave,
are expressed by us in thoughts and not in words. For, as I
previously remarked, words are for us obsolete. However, the
soul, in this plane of consciousness, must struggle and labor,
know sorrow but not earth sorrow, know ecstasy but not earth
ecstasy. The sorrow is of a spiritual character, the ecstasy is of
a spiritual kind. These two transcend imagination, but they
finally lead the soul to the borders of the Super-terrestrial region."

If all this feels "new agey" in the extreme, one should keep
in mind that all of these descriptions were laid out well before
1950. We are looking at all of this as we would look at "struc-

tures in a mist," to quote the poet Wallace Stevens. The higher up one gets, the greater the danger, in these descriptions, of slipping into generalizations that don't resonate enough for us to get any kind of clear idea of the realities they might describe. They become dead and abstract, or silly and ludicrous, because they are simply too far away for us to do justice to imaginatively.

"If the reports of communicators are correct," writes Fontana, summing up in a few lines everything we are trying to convey here, "the Plane of Color is the world made perfect, the archetypal, ideal world of which the earth is a very imperfect copy. It is in fact the ultimate manifestation of form, the pure expression of what is possible when perfect harmony reigns between all beings."

The Plane of Color is also, it's worth adding again, what most of us would like the Internet to be, whether we realize it or not. It's the place that haunts our entire culture's interest in otherworldly lands of beauty and perfection, and of the new cybernetic dreams of human interactivity that transcend but do not destroy the specificities of the body.

On the Plane of Color, objects glow with their own light (just as the buildings do in the City of Revelation in the New Testament, and just as the trees and rivers do in mystical Iranian descriptions of the heavenly earth of Hurqualya). Colors are more beautiful than those on earth (hence the domain's name in the Myers texts) and there are *more* of them as well. The Plane of Color comes closest to the descriptions of heaven given in Christian sources, but at the same time it is not static, not frozen and abstract: in no way a bloodless, clouds-and-halos one. It is, instead, much closer to that supremely dynamic and forward-moving heaven that Gregory of Nyssa hinted at, and that, in the twentieth century, Teilhard de Chardin may have been alluding to when he said that "when a man has found the secret of collaboration and self-identification with the universe as it advances, then all dark shadows disappear."

We are, here, one more step up on the psychospiritual ladder leading toward the "source of all being," as Fontana likes to call it. Or God. Or nirvana. It doesn't matter. It also doesn't really matter how many or few times we reincarnate, or how many or few of us enjoyed lives of importance in the past. What does matter is learning how to seize the opportunity our modern world offers to really envision the universe as an arena for the individual soul's genuine growth and forward movement. Doing so is the modern equivalent of what I once heard a minister on a recording of an old sermon call "keeping heaven in your view." Getting a completely clear picture of things at the spiritual levels we're now approaching is impossible, and all descriptions from these regions that make it down to us, whether from traditional or modern sources, are constantly in danger of slipping into caricature. They are all too easy to make fun of, all too easy to take less than seriously.

This maddening combination of the mockable and the profound is well illustrated by a story Fontana reports of a gardener who came through via a medium in the 1940s, and who, it appears (following the old afterlife rule that we are drawn to the place in the worlds beyond where we most deserve to be), bypassed the realms below and went directly to the Plane of Color.

"The first thing I was pleased about," this gardener reported, "was that I should have books and be able to enjoy them. Years ago I had a natural liking for books, and if things had been different with me I might have been rather a scholar."

Believe what we want to about this little story, it nonetheless summarizes everything we truly want, if we allow ourselves to admit it to ourselves, from a world beyond this one. We want to transcend this world, to escape from it. But we also, paradoxically, want to bring it with us. We want to bring the thousand small promising moments we encountered down here and allow them to fall into the ground and grow. We miss so much in life—practically everything—the first time around. That what we miss down here now might be available to us later, that we might be allowed to see those old and now gone events and encounter them anew, having all of them before us and bringing all that is best in ourselves to them as well: this is one of the most profoundly optimistic and energizing conceptions imaginable.

But it is also not, according to our model, where things end.

The Plane of Color is the last level on which form as we know it plays a part. Beyond it, we are in the "formless"—the levels that Buddhism is so interested in and the levels that, it insists, are the only ones that are actually *real*.

We may, at this point, be able to nod our assent to this. Sure: only these realms are real. But what, in this context, does the word *real* really signify? In our day, when computers have made us so completely used to the idea of highly complex "generated" environments, it isn't that difficult to imagine that the mind, if it is capable of existing independent of the body, might be capable of generating an image world that is both real yet at the same time a creation of that mind's image-creating capacities. But a world beyond images altogether? That's considerably harder. What's important is that in the new map of life and afterlife sketched by the sources we're relying on, the transition from the worlds of form to the worlds of the formless doesn't imply the complete loss of what we learned and what we became while still within those worlds of form. Those things, this perspective says, are not, perhaps, fully real, but they are *real to a certain degree.* And on this all but inconceivably high level that means quite a lot. As such they matter, for they are part of a universe that is growing and moving forward, *toward a state of unity that embraces the material* and *the spiritual, and that transcends yet doesn't cancel out individuality.*

In other words, a state where—paradoxical as it sounds— we leave both ourselves and the world of form and limitation behind, but at the same time don't leave them behind. It is here, at this close to impossible height, that the real possibility of a meeting of the highest Eastern and Western, the highest modern and the highest traditional thought, shows a promise of occurring.

From the Eastern perspective, all the unlived possibilities of material life—all the infinite suggestions of particular ful- fillment that life holds out—are said, again and again, to be gone and gone forever when we die. But in the paradox-laden pronouncements of the Eastern sages about the truly ultimate levels of reality, we are also confronted constantly with state- ments that seem to contradict this fact. Nirvana, we are told in more than one Eastern text, is in fact samsara. In the final analysis, the two are not different. We also receive hints, in the Buddhist concept of the bodhisattva as a being who will not enter into the bliss of perfect enlightenment until all sentient beings reach it as well, of an end state in which this event *might truly occur.* Even the cyclic religions dream on occasion of a time, immeasurably distant though it may be, when the cycles will come to an end.

> Immortality! Not as some vague and distant possibility! But you—here—now! This is the thing you must recapture. . . .
>
> —postmortem communication, 1940s

> What is not here is nowhere.
>
> —Vishvasara Tantra

Still further worlds, we are told, lie above these last that we have been trying, tentatively, to describe. But again, because they are characterized first and foremost by being "formless," describing them in any meaningful way from our perspective is virtually impossible. "From a full experience of living on the fourth plane," the Myers texts report, "it is very exceptional to find a soul undertaking re-incarnation, for he has already experienced 'the height and the depth and the fullness of life' in form. The soul is beginning to realize that form itself is not essential and that the most advanced souls of its group are 'calling it to the Flame-world, to that level of consciousness whereupon perception, insight, and imagination extend mightily, slowly and surely gathering within them knowledge of the inter-stellar spaces, knowledge of the third disguise, of the starry raiment, and of those (to us) blazing fires that light up the heavens when day has died.'"

Hidden in the flowery language of this passage (to which, it appears, Myers was often as much prone in death as he was in life) is the idea that the transcendence of form is a further step toward a condition in which one retains one's individuality (the great focus of the West) but recovers one's original universality (the great focus of the East). We are moving, at this level, toward the condition that the haunting final image of the film *2001* made so many viewers inexplicably homesick for: a state in which we are reborn as both personal *and* cosmic beings.

Above the levels of form, then, we become entirely those larger beings that, while on earth, we constantly suspect we are potentially, but which we can never fully become in fact. In short: *We grow into ourselves.* This condition of what Henry Corbin called "soaring archetypal individuality" is one that we can only imagine in the vaguest and most shadowy way from where we are, but it is one that, all the same, many people feel an instant spark of kinship for when it is described to them. It is outlandish, it is hopelessly far from anything we currently experience as incarnate humans, but it speaks deeply to us—or at least many of us—all the same.

"You have at last," says Myers, "entered into Reality and cast from you all the illusions of appearances. But some intangible essence has been added to your spirit through its long habitation of matter, of ether the ancestor of matter, of what the scientists call empty space, though, if they but knew it, empty space is peopled with forms of an infinite fineness and variety."

Here is the old familiar idea of the parabolic drop of unity into multiplicity; of the long journey through the illusion of separation, with the final triumphant return to unity, only—as the Myers texts are careful to point out—with a difference. Some "intangible essence" has been added, some victory gained by the long, rhythmic journey in and out of earthly life. The

dip and climb into and out of the material has, in short, produced a result.

"To be of the universe," say the Myers texts, "and to be
apart from it is, possibly, the final achievement, the goal of all
endeavor." To be in the world yet out of it. To be allied with
its joys and its horrors, yet at the same time to be absolutely
and safely removed from and beyond them. Descriptions of
this condition are as old as the Vedas and the gospels, and as
current as Whitman, Emerson, and the writings of Myers both
before and after his demise. It's also the essence of what the
new age should be (and in its best and smartest moments is
already) all about: a vision of the universe as a stage for the
soul's growth that transcends the limitations of the old traditions but retains their deepest insights.

"In a few brief words," say the Myers texts, stretching the
limits of the language, "I have spanned existence within aeons
of time, and I have endeavored to give you a glimpse of that
mystery, timelessness. When you dwell out Yonder, you, as a
part of the Divine Principle in its essence, are wholly aware
of the imagination of God. So you are aware of every second
in time, you are aware of the whole history of the earth from
Alpha to Omega. Equally all planetary existence is yours. Everything created is contained within that imagination, and
you, now by reason of your immortality, know it and hold, as
the earth holds a seed, the whole of life, the past, the future, all
that is, all that shall be for ever and for ever."

This is a handful, and passages like this make it easy to see
why most authors trying to lay out this new series of maps of
the afterlife sometimes use the texts Myers wrote while alive,
but rarely go near these ones he apparently created after his

death. They're too much—too much to believe, to take seriously: both in what they say and in the manner in which they were said.

And yet . . . When I stumbled on them in the course of putting this book together, there was something about them— something hiding behind their flowery, obscure, and occasionally just plain silly prose—that I couldn't shake off. A picture of the universe and the place of the soul within it that, this or that quibble aside, struck me at a deep level as simply . . . right. Something in me recognized what the texts were describing, and that recognition/recollection struck me as worth addressing, and worth taking seriously.

So they are what I am ending this book with. Perhaps the real upshot of these pages is that just as the earthly artist separates him or herself from the world in order to truly comprehend that world, so it is that only when we climb out of the garment of our life will we see that garment hanging clean and perfect—only when we are no longer fully wearing the "suit" of who we are down here right now will we be able to grasp those identities for what they really and truly are. All the traditions, both ancient and modern, that we have looked at insist that it is the heart of us that matters, and if we are, at heart, beings in transit, then our knowledge of this fact is capable of lighting up every leg of our journey, no matter how dark that journey might at times become. This place or endpoint that we are on our way toward is not fully describable with our earthly vocabularies or fully comprehensible by our earthly minds. But it is a place that we can make out in dim but promising outline all the same. It is a place lying, in the words of the poet Paul Celan, "north of the future." And one that, as Eliot suggested in *Four Quartets,* we will recognize when we arrive at it, because it is a place we all have known before.

As I described in the beginning of this book, it was my father who first taught me to appreciate the idea of the afterlife, and who first taught me to doubt all I heard about it as well. His own life was, I found myself thinking in his last days, in many ways a wasted and terribly misused one.

But in the end, whose isn't?

In the poem "Anaphora," Elizabeth Bishop wrote:

The day was meant for what ineffable creature
we must have missed?

That "creature we must have missed" is, of course, ourselves: the person who none of us, no matter how perfect and blameless a life we lead, truly gets a chance to be down here. Yet that larger, better being might nonetheless exist, and if it does, the life we are living now is the seedbed for it. Life, my father always told me, is a journey: the journey through the world of time and space of a being whose true country is above and beyond the limitations of life as we know it. We come, as that sticker in the *Guideposts* offices said, from a larger, better world than this one, and we return to it when our time here is finished.

Is this—*any* of this—really true?

I, of course, don't know. Like the views that came before them, the modern view of what lies beyond will always be flawed to a degree, because, as St. Paul said of all worldly views of what lies above and beyond, we see now through a glass darkly. But flawed or not, we owe it both to ourselves and to those spiritual mapmakers from the countless traditions that came before us to take the possibility of that larger landscape seriously, to assemble a vision of the life beyond the body that is truly our own. Such a map will always be *just* a map, and, to quote one of the most popular, but true, clichés of new age thought, the map is not the territory. But good maps do describe real places, and point to real journeys as well. Journeys taken by real beings, toward a goal that is both impossibly far in the future and yet, paradoxically, present with us, right here and right now.

Acknowledgments

M any thanks to the following:

Robin and Stuart Ray; Jonathan Merkh (who originally suggested a few years ago that, contrary to all evidence, I might still have a book or two left to write); Kate Farrell (for her friendship and her endlessly useful discussions with me about the subject matter over the years); Richard Ryan (tireless promoter of my online presence); Emily Zinnemann (for crucial help in research on some aspects of the Ouija Board); Nicholas Vreeland (who most likely will not like it, but who nonetheless played a hugely important role in its formation); Bokara Legendre (for help both intentional and inadvertent); Richard Smoley, editor of *Quest* magazine (for very kindly holding back on publishing a section of the book at the last minute after I decided it all needed to be different); Mara Lieber; John David Ebert (whose series of talks on the afterlife on his website, cinemadiscourse.com, was a source of innumerable valuable insights); Elise Wiarda; Dave Stang; Rebecca Weiner Tompkins; Mitch Horowitz; Gail Ross; Howard Yoon (without whose tireless work on the proposal the book would never have come together); Jennifer Manguera; Anna Sproul; Gene Gollogly; Godfrey Cheshire; Karl Taro Greenfeld; Jerry Smith; Terry McGovern; Gary Lachman (for providing a generous blurb for this book, not to mention helping me understand the idea of the evolution of consciousness through his own books); Evie Scherman (for making sure I was always working when I needed to be); Lulu Scherman; my editor at Atria Books, Sarah Durand (for helping me make it a whole lot better than it would have been otherwise, not to mention editing the last draft on her honeymoon); Alexandra Arnold; Thomas Pitoniak for his excellent copyediting; and Judith Curr, also at Atria, for being one of those rare, old-fashioned publishers who are still ready to give chances to manuscripts (and authors) who are a little on the quirky side.

This book would not exist in the shape it does had I not stumbled on a little known volume by Robert Crookall called *The Supreme Adventure: An Analysis of Psychic Communications.* Long, dry, and by today's standards completely uninviting, the book proved nonetheless to be one of the most fascinating I've ever read, and gave me my first real hint that there exists a deeply convincing and compelling geography of the afterlife that people by and large don't know about today. It was this book that led me, in turn, to *The Road to Immortality* and *Beyond Human Personality,* the two volumes of channeled material received from the deceased Frederic Myers—or at least someone claiming to be him—via the medium Geraldine Cummins some eighty years ago, that I make such extensive use of in the final pages of this book. Crookall also led me to the writings of another underappreciated pioneer in the modern geography of the afterlife, Raynor Johnson.

The Supreme Adventure is in print but quite expensive, while both the channeled Myers volumes are long out of print and extremely expensive to get online. Johnson's books—most notably *The Imprisoned Splendour* and *Nurslings of Immortality*—are also currently out of print. But for any reader intrigued by the picture of the afterlife sketched out in these pages and curious to delve deeper, all these titles are well worth tracking down.

My understanding of how current science is making it much, much easier to envision the human personality as capable of surviving the death of the body, and specifically of the brain, was immeasurably increased by Edward and Emily Williams Kelly's massive and meticulously documented book *Irreducible Mind: Toward a Psychology for the 21st Century*. The Kellys' book is also an excellent place to find out more about Frederic Myers, though they—like most serious writers on the subject—omit mention of Cummins's channeled material. Mario Beauregard and Denyse O'Leary's *The Spiritual Brain: A Neuroscientist's Case for the Existence of the Soul* also provided much interesting material and many insights.

Of the vast library of material on the near-death experience, two books were especially useful to me: Mark Fox's *Religion, Spirituality, and the Near-Death Experience* and Dr. Pim van Lommel's *Consciousness Beyond Life: The Science of the Near-Death Experience*. David Fontana's *Life Beyond Death* (currently in print) and David Lorimer's *Survival?: Body, Mind and Death in the Light of Psychic Experience* were also enormously helpful.